DUTY AND DELIGHT:

ROUTLEY REMEMBERED

The Revd. Dr. Erik Routley 1917-1982
in Princeton University Chapel at
Westminster Choir College Commencement, May 1976
Photo: John Simpson

DUTY AND DELIGHT: ROUTLEY REMEMBERED

*A Memorial Tribute to
Erik Routley
(1917–1982)*

MINISTRY
•
CHURCH MUSIC
•
HYMNODY

Robin A. Leaver
James H. Litton
Editors

Carlton R. Young
Executive Editor

HOPE PUBLISHING COMPANY
CANTERBURY PRESS NORWICH
1985

CONTENTS

Fascimiles of Erik Routley's handwriting and his hymn tune manuscripts appear on pages 18, 34, 46, 96, etc.

ACKNOWLEDGEMENTS

Acknowledgement is gratefully made to the following publishers for permission to quote from their copyrighted material: Abingdon Press, Nashville, TN, for various quotations from Hoon's *Integrity of Worship* in chapter 3; Concordia Publishing House, St. Louis, MO, p. 52 © 1970 and pp. 59f. © 1978; Eternity Magazine © 1983, Evangelical Ministries, Inc., Philadelphia, PA, p. 196; John Murray (Publishers) Ltd., London, first quotation on p. 101; SCM Press, London, p. 47; The United Reformed Church, London, which now controls the copyright material formerly published by the Independent Press, London, pp. xii, 19, and the second quotation on p. 101; and the other copyrights acknowledged in their respective places throughout the book.

Plate section appears between pp. 50 & 51 and pp. 82 & 83

PREFACE

On the occasion of Erik Routley's memorial service, Westminster Abbey, February 8, 1983, several of his friends from Great Britain and the United States proposed that it would be appropriate to invite a number of persons who had been influenced by Erik's life and work to make evaluations of his varied career in ways other than collecting a series of personal anecdotes or publishing a random assemblage of essays on which authors had already been working. The group made the proposal to the publisher for a new collection of essays which would not only provide for some focus upon the life of Erik Routley but would also commission fresh contributions to the bibliography of church music and hymnody, thus furthering the discussion already begun by Erik. Something of the breadth and stature of the man can be gauged by the fact that it has taken eighteen different contributors in England and America to cover the ground of Erik's activities.

The first section of the book serves as a reminder of the theological roots of Erik's life and work. The late George Caird, who was associated with him at an early stage of his career as a fellow student at Mansfield College, Oxford, expounds the dialectic of duty and delight, perfection and grace, which lies at the heart of Biblical theology and Erik's thinking and writing. Don Saliers, who was associated with Erik in conducting workshops in recent years, picks up his concern for the unitive aspect of corporate worship. Robin Leaver, whose writing career was prompted by some of Erik's writings, develops some of the themes found in *Church Music and the Christian Faith*, Carol Stream 1978.

The second section of the book marks Erik Routley's involvement with church music, both as a performer and historian-commentator. Ruth Micklem, a long-standing friend, reminds us that he was not only able to speak with insight and knowledge to the professional church musician, but was also able to inspire, encourage, and broaden the horizons of people in the pew. Alec Wyton, another Britisher who found a home in the states, charts developments in America which have taken place since Erik's *Twentieth Century Church*

Music, London 1964. Erik Routley was an ordained minister who also taught church music. Paul Wohlgemuth, Erik's last post-graduate student at Westminster Choir College, and Carlton R. Young, who in 1962 began introducing Erik Routley to American audiences, explore the need for ministers to study church music, and for church musicians to study theology.

The third section of the book deals with hymnody. In the first four articles, Erik's work as compiler and editor are celebrated. Alan Luff, who collaborated with Erik in creating responsorial canticles, looks at a particular example of Routley's editorial practice and draws some wider conclusions; John Wilson, to whom *The Music of Christian Hymns*, Chicago 1981, was dedicated, investigates the criteria by which tunes should be judged; Raymond Glover records Routley's contribution to the editorial process of the Episcopal *Hymnal 1982*; and James Litton, a former colleague in Princeton, explores the liturgical functions of hymnody. The concluding contributions in this section reflect Erik's activity as a composer and hymnwriter. Ian Fraser charts, for the first time, the important Dunblane Consultations, in which Erik took a leading part—the spark which set-off the so-called "hymn explosion" in Britain and was so influential in America this past decade; Russell Schulz-Widmar deals with recent American developments in hymnody, including Routley's contribution; and the three British hymn writers, Fred Pratt Green, Fred Kaan, and Brian Wren, review their own hymn writing and look at the future of hymns, hymnals and hymnsinging.

All these contributions are framed by a brief account of the life of Erik Routley and an extensive bibliography of his writings. Erik Routley had much to do with various members of the Micklem family: Nathaniel Micklem, Edward Romilly Micklem, Caryl and Ruth Micklem. In the beginning essay Caryl Micklem writes of his friend of more than forty years. Erik was Professor of Church Music at Westminster Choir College, and it is particularly appropriate that the president of the college, Ray Robinson, has prepared the bibliography—an eloquent testimony to Erik's immense capacity for writing. The extensive bibliography contains all that could presently be found of the Routley output, but we suspect that it is still incomplete.

Erik Routley's far-reaching influence on hymnody in Britain was in a great part through his long editorship of the *Bulletin* of The Hymn Society of Great Britain and Ireland. His infectious enthusiasm displayed in the many issues of the *Bulletin*, as well as his other books and articles, almost single-handedly created an awareness of hymnody, in particular the need for contemporary expressions of congregational song. Many in Britain were encouraged as writers and composers to make a contribution to the "hymn explosion" of the 1960's and '70's. Without Erik Routley, that "explosion" as it was felt and measured in the States would hardly have been more than a dull thud in an avalanche of "pop hymnody."

Erik's first visit to North America was in 1962 as a lecturer in Montreal and Toronto. Later that year he came to the States. Prior to that visit he had become known to church musicians and some pastors through the books *Church Music and Theology*, London and Philadelphia 1959 and *The English Carol*, London 1958 and New York 1959. During the '60's Alec Wyton, Austin C. Lovelace and others championed these two books in lectures and workshops throughout the United States. In time a growing American audience eagerly awaited the publication of his most recent book or article. Erik gave the 1966 Stone Lectures at Princeton Theological Seminary and The Gheens Lectures at Louisville Theological Seminary. These two lectures were published as *Hymns Today and Tomorrow*, Nashville 1964 and *Words Music and the Church*, Nashville 1968. Erik's lectures and teaching at Perkins School of Theology, Southern Methodist University, and his summer visits to the large gatherings of musicians at Green Lake, Wisconsin, and Montreat, North Carolina, increased his popularity and influence throughout the States.

During the early 1970's these frequent visits required several trans-Atlantic crossings each year. As he became more in demand in America as a lecturer, preacher and hymnologist (though he resented being labeled a "professional hymnologist"), it was inevitable that Erik and Margaret should become residents. And there are those who say that they settled in the most "English" of American towns—Princeton!

It was of course difficult for a pastor and his wife to leave their parish and begin a new life in America; but Erik never ceased being a pastor. His "parish" expanded greatly including those weekly, tightly packed 20 to 30 minute chapel services (always including a sermon) at Westminster Choir College to weekends filled with Saturday workshops and Sunday morning sermons in churches of all denominations in every part of the States and Canada. Erik often said that this was not a difficult schedule because the then airline shuttle dropped him off in his back garden, which was adjacent to the Princeton Airport. On the rare occasion when he spent a weekend at home, Sunday would find him preaching at a local church or leading an adult education discussion. There were times when he and Margaret quietly slipped into a pew of a Princeton church, often Trinity Episcopal, creating a moment of terror for the church musicians. Following the service he always had words of encouragement for the choice of hymns and other service music, but characteristically *also* a few words of constructive criticism!

During the Princeton years, many of Erik's finest works were completed, including his editorship of several large and small collections of hymns for churches and schools. These collections, which contained the best of the "hymn explosion," will continue to influence hymn singing and hymnal revisions throughout North America well into the next century.

To fully understand the work of Erik Routley, one must understand that he was primarily a pastor and preacher, and all that he accomplished was conditioned and graced by his calling as an ordained minister in the Church of Jesus Christ. Upon hearing of his death, musicians, students, professors and pastors knew and expressed the loss they had suffered, but no more than those who were members of his parishes in Britain, especially his former congregations in Newcastle and Edinburgh. As one parishioner put it: "Others will recall Erik's achievements in the wider world, but we remember him as a comforter of the bereaved, the sick and the troubled, a dynamo of energy, an encourager of all of us, and a man who taught in praise 'to make one music for the Lord of all' ". Another recalled: "One of the first things he said to me was, 'People think of me as primarily a musician, but my deepest interest is in interpreting the Bible'—". This reflection is confirmed in a passage found in one of Erik's books:

> "A preacher needs to be consumed by a personal passion to communicate, and to be equipped with a faculty of sensitiveness such as will enable him to communicate with *these* people. Preaching at the exalted level which Protestantism has upheld in the past requires a preacher to regard every occasion of preaching as a great occasion, every sermon he delivers as a climax of his life up to that point."
> *Into a Far Country*, London 1962, p. 122

As a pastor, Erik fostered the ministries of others, as many who studied with him during his days on the staff of Mansfield College would testify. Perhaps one of the most telling sentences in this volume is Caryl Micklem's comment about his first pastorate:

> "Speaking for myself, I can say that Wednesbury will for me always be the place where, thanks to Erik, I recovered my faith and vocation."

That is a measure of Erik's ministry and a testimony that could be echoed by many in Britain and the States who are grateful to him for his positive and assured commendation of the Christian faith.

The title of this volume, "Duty and Delight," may puzzle some, but hardly those who through the years heard what Erik Routley spoke or read what he wrote. "Duty and Delight" is a phrase that Erik frequently used. The words, found in Watts' hymn, a version of Psalm 147

> Praise ye the Lord; 'tis good to raise
> our hearts and voices in his praise:
> his nature and his works invite
> to make this duty our delight.

convey the rich understanding that true worship is a paradoxical and joyful combination of God's demands and our responses in Christ. Erik was influential, as the first chairman of the Doctrine and Worship Committee of the newly formed United Reformed Church, in incorporating in their 1980 *Book of Worship*, Edinburgh 1980, that paradoxical phrase in the second eucharistic prayer; a slightly revised version of that which had previously appeared in Caryl Micklem's pioneering *Contemporary Prayers for Public Worship*, London 1967

"It is our duty and delight, Lord God our Father—"

(*Book of Worship*, p. 32)

However it was not only Watts who could use a memorable phrase, and as Cyril Taylor, whose hymn tunes Erik much admired, and to whom *The English Carol*, London 1958, was dedicated, reports, someone wrote to him after Erik's death: "Erik chose epithets so well." Erik had stated that the "epigramatic style—is always the mark of the great hymn writer. The memorable phrase, packing immense amounts into a few simple works, is what makes a hymn live" (*A Panorama of Christian Hymnody*, Collegeville 1979, p. 17). That ideal was modeled in his hymn, FOR MUSICIANS,* written in 1976.

> In praise of God meet duty and delight,
>   angels and creatures, men and spirits bless'd;
> in praise is earth transfigured by the sound
>   and sight of heaven's everlasting feast.

* The text and the tune SHERIDAN were commissioned by Westminster Presbyterian Church, Lincoln, Nebraska, and performed there at a service of dedication of an organ, November 14, 1976.

In praise the artist and the craftsman meet,
    inspired, obedient, patient, practical;
in praise join instrument and voice and sound
    to make one music for the Lord of all.

The desert is refreshed by songs of praise,
    relaxed the frown of pride, the stress of grief;
in praise forgotten all our human spite;
    in praise the burdened heart finds sure relief.

No skill of ours, no music made on earth,
    no mortal song could scale the height of heaven;
yet stands that Cross, through grace ineffable
    an Instrument of praise to sinners given.

So, confident and festive, let us sing
    of wisdom, power and mercy there made known;
the song of Moses and the Lamb is ours,
    through Christ raised up to life in God alone.

The editors would like to thank all the contributors to the volume, as well as those who have helped in other ways. But there are three people whose help and support cannot be unnamed and unthanked: Carlton R. Young, Executive Editor, for seeing the volume from early conversations, through the press and arranging its publication; George H. Shorney, the publisher, for having the vision to proceed with the work and for the unstinting way he has supported and encouraged us; and for Margaret Routley for the way she has quietly watched over the project and kept us on the right track. Finally, we have only to say that for us it has been a delightful duty to bring together this memorial tribute to a man much respected, loved and missed.

Robin A. Leaver
James H. Litton
Editors

ERIK ROUTLEY
1917–1982

ERIK ROUTLEY 1917–1982

Caryl Micklem

It was on 25 July 1942, a week before my seventeenth birthday and some three months before his twenty-fifth, that Erik first signed in to our family visitors' book. My father, Edward Romilly Micklem, was at that time the minister of the Congregational church at Gerrards Cross in Buckinghamshire. Until 1938, however, he had been for sixteen years Chaplain and Tutor at Mansfield College, Oxford, which in those days was a purely theological college mainly concerned with preparing graduates for the ordained ministry in Congregational churches. My father's last six years there had been under the Principalship of his elder brother Nathaniel: and it was the latter who had suggested that Erik, as one of the Mansfield ordinands, should spend some time with us during the Long Vacation in order, to borrow a phrase from the world of James Herriot, to "see practice".

His reputation had preceded him, for he was not the first to come to us. The previous year we had welcomed his fellow-ordinand and close friend Peter Scott—a magnificent pianist of great height and charm who, whenever any of us complimented him on anything, would say, "Ah, you should hear/see/meet Erik Routley". Those who were their contemporaries at Mansfield cherish the recollection of their duo performances at the piano, both "straight" and not-so-straight. I think that from Erik there were also songs, probably scurrilous. I, to my sorrow, never heard him sing except as one of a congregation, and was unaware that others had been more fortunate until, after his death, I was talking to Sir Ronald Johnson of Edinburgh, who told me, as something not widely known, what a beautiful singing voice Erik had. It is possible, though I do not remember it, that I heard him and Peter play the piano together in the early days, though our house in Gerrards Cross was so small that I doubt if we could have entertained them together. Once, much later, the three of us and our wives were together at Erik's house in Newcastle on the occasion of a family wedding. He was giving temporary lodging to his son's grand piano as well as his own. I do not think any of the rest of us in the room is likely to forget Erik and Peter sitting down at the two pianos and playing, from memory kept since their student days, Erik's arrangement of that loveliest of folk-melodies, "Hunsdon House". (It should be explained that Erik married Peter's sister Margaret, and also that my wife Ruth, who writes a later chapter in this book, had come to know them both, by a route other than mine, some time before our own first meeting.)

Let me, however, return to 1942 in order to recapture, if I can, my first meeting with Erik himself. The awe with which I awaited the new visitor's arrival was not at all diminished by the actuality, though Erik was by no means as I had pictured him in my mind's eye. Well, that is not quite true. One or two things I had imagined right. A dogmatic way of expressing himself, a resounding and frequent laugh—these I had correctly imputed to him by inference from the characteristics of his friend. Again, the names and work of C. S. Lewis and Charles Williams were once more topmost among non-musical conversation-subjects. But who could have foreseen the thrust of Erik's chin, the quickness of his movements and repartee, or, above all, the wonderful beaming smile which was never a grin yet which occupied his whole face from the very top of his forehead, so that his entire aspect seemed to become in the same instant both plastic and yet doubly firm, and one could feel a warmth and perceive a shining both of which came, one was sure, from the depths of the man? At first I found myself embarrassed, in talking to him, by the cast in his eye: but as it so obviously did not embarrass him it was soon hardly noticed. Besides, it too was transfigured by the smile.

I do not remember, from his first visit, his actually playing our piano as much as Peter had: but then, Peter was still having lessons—from James Ching—and practising hard. I recall clearly the pieces he was working on, and can never now hear them without thinking of him. Erik was also a fine pianist and perhaps even finer organist, but while he was with us he did not, like Peter, sit down and play for hours. As far as music was concerned what he did most, apart from discussing the analytical theories of Heinrich Schenker in which he was very interested at the time, was to play, and talk, hymn-tunes. I knew a little about these, having lived among them all my life, having also sung many descants in my days as a treble, and having had my mind broadened from the book we used in church (the *Congregational Hymnary*) by *Songs of Praise* and *The Oxford Book of Carols*. My grandmother Curwen composed hymn-tunes, so I knew that they did not just "happen"; but Erik was the first person I had met to whom the writing of hymn-tunes was such a compelling interest, whose knowledge of the whole subject of hymnody was so vast, and who could formulate so cogently and express so vigorously his opinions about what was good and what was bad.

4

I believe that it was during that first stay with us that he composed CHALFONT PARK for Thomas Binney's hymn, "Eternal Light!" The tune was a sort of "thank you" present to my father, and was named after a piece of open country near our home where we often went for long, discursive walks. I had not previously had my attention focussed on Binney's words, since, although they were in our book and my father loved them, he seldom chose them for worship because of his dislike of the tune NEWCASTLE to which they were set. Singing them round the piano to the new tune, and suddenly being caught by words and music together, each because of the other, was for me one of those life-experiences which enabled me, in later years, to understand at once what the theologian Ian Ramsey meant by "disclosure". It also made me want to try and do something of the same sort—to enter, if I could, into the experience of making a new thing which might actually in some way enhance others' lives and open others' eyes. It was the first time I had been motivated to compose rather than merely doodle. Looking back, of course, I am aghast that such immaturity could be possessed, even briefly, of such confidence. Up till then I had been content to improvise melodies at the piano, with little reason (and inadequate technical accomplishment) to attempt the difficult task of trying to write them down. Now it was different. Erik was amazingly tolerant of my pedestrian efforts; went through them with me in such a way as to teach me the rudiments of harmony; and, to crown his generosity, left with me (this must have been a year or two later) two hymn-texts from the forthcoming *Congregational Praise* which needed tunes and which had so far failed to inspire him to produce any himself.

No portrait of Erik at this time would be complete that did not mention his manners, his expletives and his pipe. He was one of the most perfectly courteous people I have known, yet quite without affectation. I believe that his manners sprang directly from his fundamental belief in community as man's highest good, in the respectworthiness of other people, and in one's duty to play a listening as well as a performing rôle in the "chamber music" (a favourite metaphor of his) of human conversation. He was, in the best sense, formal: and this trait was reflected also in his dress. Canon Cyril Taylor has told me how, at about the time of which I have been writing, Erik was invited to visit the committee then preparing the *BBC Hymn Book*, and what an unforgettable impression this young student, black-suited, erudite, authoritative, made upon those present.

Courtesy chooses words fastidiously when addressing someone directly, but does not of necessity entail being mealy-mouthed when speaking of that person to others. Erik's world in those days was fairly thickly populated with

TOADS and OWLS—the first being nasty and more or less wicked, the second being merely (but sometimes culpably) silly. Nothing but capital letters can convey the open-vowelled vehemence with which a member of either class would be categorised. Afterwards the pipe, which was always removed for these sentences so that they could be given their due orotundity, was replaced and relit. One sometimes had the impression with Erik's pipe that the lighting was more important than the smoking. From the moment he felt in his pocket for his tobacco-pouch he seemed to settle into a kind of concavity around his pipe—hunched, almost—as if, even when he was indoors and no wind threatened the operation, he must guard, like Neolithic Man, the precious gift, the central yet vulnerable fire which he carried with him everywhere in its bowl.

In 1943 he was ordained and inducted to his first pastorate, Trinity Congregational Church in Wednesbury, nowadays in the county of West Midlands but then in Staffordshire. The town was at the heart of the Black Country, which had not yet been liberated from its pall by the Clean Air Acts. The church belonged to that tradition of "self-help", "I-know-what-I-like" Congregationalism which the commercial spirit of the Birmingham conurbation had tended to nurture. It was hardly to be expected that the young Erik, full of the ideals of classical Puritanism, and unpersuaded of the musicianly virtues of Dr John Bacchus Dykes, let alone the lesser yet ever-popular Victorian hymn-tune writers (he did later relent somewhat on Dykes), could minister in such a context for long without hackles being raised and fur being rubbed up the wrong way. The most charitable will in the world cannot indefinitely dismiss or deny incompatibility. On the other hand for the members there with whom the style and content of his ministry "rang bells", his two-year stay was God's gift of a lifetime. Speaking for myself, I can say that Wednesbury will for me always be the place where, thanks to Erik, I recovered faith and vocation. Our conversations at this time had an inauspicious start. Erik had been approached by someone who was worried about me, and who asked him to help me with my intellectual and emotional problems. I had discovered this, though not from him. Yet the fact was never mentioned between us, and I am not even sure if he ever knew that I knew. In any case his courtesy, of which I have already written, caused him to make nothing of the therapist-to-patient rôle which had been thrust upon him, and to ignore the age-gap between us which he could so easily have traded upon. When I stayed with him, and our conversation at last turned, as it generally did, to my doubts and difficulties—unique and all-important as I felt them then, boringly commonplace as I now know them to be—he would listen and listen far into

6

the night with unflagging attention, asking questions, offering no superficial answers, and at last, by sheer patient "alongsideness", enabling me to get back on course.

I venture to offer this recollection, unduly personal though it may seem, because I believe that Erik's dealings with me then were typical of him as a pastor all through his life, and because I think it is true to say that of all his gifts—the hymnology, the Church history, the versatile pen, the eloquent preaching, the wise committee-work—the greatest was pastoral. Fewer knew it than knew the others: inevitably so, since the exercise of it is private where the others are public. It is one-to-one, and time-taking, and so it cannot be exercised for great numbers by any one person. Nor would Erik for one moment have countenanced his pastoral commitment to people being likened to a case-load. Enough to say that throughout his ministry there were those, like myself, for whom his counsel and friendship were a gate of heaven.

I do not recall whether he and Margaret ever acquired anywhere proper to live in Wednesbury. Folklore has it that they were asked to leave one set of rented rooms there because they laughed too much: and I partly believe it, since both had laughs of which it was impossible to be unaware, and they laughed often. It is further rumoured that the particular occasion of their eviction was mirth over a game of chess. That is perhaps harder to believe, but if it could be true of anyone it could be true of Erik and Margaret.

The next pastorate, at Dartford in Kent, was also dogged by problems —among them, I suspect, being the fact that this was the home church of Erik's parents. The great advantage was that he was now near London and could thus the better manage the meetings and secretarial work connected with the compilation and publication of *Congregational Praise*. He often came to spend the day talking to my father about this, and they wrote regularly to one another, about hymns and everything else under the sun. This correspondence, begun, I suppose, at the time of Erik's first visit to us, continued until my father's death in 1960 and was important to both of them. I doubt if during that period either of them had a friend quite as like-minded as the other. Certainly their table and after-dinner talk, which was what I could chiefly overhear, memorably exemplified the views they shared on what good con-versation should be like, and why it matters. My father toyed for a time with the idea of writing a book on the art of conversation; but he never found a bone-structure for it. I have often wondered if the talks the two of them had together about it gave Erik some of the ideas so wonderfully deployed and developed in his Congregational Lectures, afterwards published as *Into A Far Country*.

7

In 1948, the year I took my Arts degree at Oxford and began full-time theological study at Mansfield, Erik came to the college as Lecturer (later also Chaplain), and he and Margaret moved into what had been my parents' house at 17, Norham Road. Two memories of that time are both of Erik at the keyboard: at home, filling in an odd moment before lunch playing on the piano a movement from a Brahms string quartet, reading without hesitation straight from the open score; and in the Mansfield organ loft, allowing me to be his page-turner and stop-drawer as he played a Bach fugue after the service or, as on one occasion, his own fantasia "Wrestling Jacob", based on Eric Thiman's tune TRAVELLER. (It is a minor mystery to me that although Erik felt that tune to be a perfect match for Wesley's "Come, O thou Traveller unknown" he was nevertheless impelled, in later years, to write another himself for the same hymn.)

In readiness for the launching of *Congregational Praise* in 1951, Erik conducted a virtually single-handed publicity campaign, arranging and leading "sing-ins" up and down the country. There was no pre-publication brochure, and each of these events needed its own leaflet, complete with copyright clearances on all the items chosen. He put in a vast amount of work on this, and in the course of his travels he both improved his talent for popular presentation and came to know a wider circle of Congregational organists. Perhaps this was one reason why, when the first conference of Congregational organists was convened at Mansfield in the summer of that same year, 1951, ninety came and forty-five more had to be turned away. So began a Guild of which Erik was looked to as the revered founding father and which eventually, at the union of the denominations in 1972, joined with the Presbyterian Guild to form a single and still-flourishing group. Erik was the uncontested choice for President. He tried to relinquish the title when he moved to the United States, but the Guild persuaded him not to do so. Since his death the honorary Presidency has been unfilled: it would be a fitting tribute to him if it were to remain so.

I left Mansfield for a pastorate early in 1949, and completed my training course by correspondence. Erik had no direct part in this, but he and Margaret put me up (in what had been my own childhood bedroom) while I sat the final examination in theology. Just how much I missed by not experiencing Erik's chaplaincy for longer will be clear to readers of my wife's chapter. I must be grateful that at least I had the chance of spending a week in the Lake District as an "old boy" of the University Congregational Society in one of the years when their annual Easter-vacation holiday was under Erik's pastoral care; and I add my voice to the testimony of many others when I say that a day in the courts of the Cumbrian fells in such company is better than a thousand where there is neither a Great Gable nor a Routley to minister to one the truth about that majestic presence.

One receives many requests that are to be endured rather than welcomed. This was for me never true of what Erik asked, for I found that whatever one did for him one always finished by learning more than one had contributed. Was it a review for the Bulletin of the Hymn Society of Great Britain and Ireland, which he edited for half his working life? His comments on one's comments were invariably an illumination. Was it a series of articles for him as editor (more briefly) of the *Congregational Monthly*? Very likely he would refer to them in an editorial and, in so doing, add greatly to their stature.

It was a blow to many in England besides myself when, in 1959, Erik left Mansfield to become minister of Augustine-Bristo Congregational Church in Edinburgh. Had it not been for the chance that I had some Scottish connexions also, our meeting for the next eight years might have been confined to the occasion when he arranged for me to be the external examiner for a doctoral thesis on Isaac Watts which he had supervised and for which we conducted the *viva voce* together. (Although I gained much from reading and reflecting on the thesis itself, I gained whole new horizons from Erik's handling of it and of my reactions to it.) Fortunately for our family, this isolated encounter was supplemented by an annual picnic-meeting with some or all of the Routleys at one of several favoured spots in the Southern Uplands more or less half-way between Edinburgh and the village in Galloway where we spent our summer holidays. For the rest of the year we had to be content with Her Majesty's mail.

Not long before Erik's move from Edinburgh to Newcastle-upon-Tyne, a group of us in the London area ("us" being Congregational ministers)—who had all, I think, like Erik, belonged to the Church Order Group, later to merge with Friends of Reunion and the Anglican group "Parish and People" into "One for Renewal"—began work on a projected book of church prayers in modern English. Our aim is taken for granted today but was considered very daring in the mid-Sixties. The publisher felt that our material should be submitted to an assessor with a well-known name whose critique would curb our excesses and whose approval, blazoned on the dust-jacket, would persuade doubters to have a second look. Erik had taken a keen interest in our work from the beginning, and it seemed natural for us to turn to him. As I remember it, the typescript of *Contemporary Prayers for Public Worship* came back with many felicitous suggestions of detail but with only one word which he thought we had really better avoid lest it give offence to some (though it did not to him). It was the word "hangover". His judgment that the rest would be acceptable was proved right when the book appeared. Indeed it is perhaps not too much to say that the currency of this small volume for the past eighteen years in Britain, the Commonwealth and the United States, has instigated and undergirded a complete change of attitude regarding liturgical language in the English-speaking world: and there is a sense therefore in which the whole revolution was begun thanks to the confident breadth of mind of one wise and level-headed man.

Nor, happily, did his reputation suffer by association with our book. I am thinking not so much of his call to St James's, Newcastle, in 1967, the year the book appeared, as of his election two years later to serve as President of the Congregational Church in England and Wales for twelve months in 1970–71 —the highest honour the denomination could bestow—and of his appointment as the first chairman of the Doctrine and Worship Committee of the new United Reformed Church, formed in 1972 by the union of Congregationalists in England and Wales with the Presbyterian Church of England.

It goes without saying that, all this time, he had been intimately involved with new developments in hymnody. The two trail-blazing books of *Dunblane Praises*, fruits of consultations begun in 1962 at Scottish Churches' House in Dunblane, owe a large debt to him. At the other end of the country there came a day when, at his suggestion, a group which included Sydney Carter met at my manse in Kensington to discuss the monitoring, weeding and distribution of new material so as to get the best of it more widely known and sung by the Christian community in general. For some time after that he was one of a "round-robin" list of eight or ten people who replenished the robin with new material whenever it reached them, and added their comments to the comment-sheet enclosed for each item already included. Erik's remarks often consisted of a single well-chosen word.

This groundwork proved useful when the Doctrine and Worship Committee of the United Reformed Church was called upon to oversee the compilation of a hymn-book supplement which churches could use alongside *Congregational Praise* and the then-forthcoming Third Edition of the *Church Hymnary*. Erik was too busy with other projects to play a central rôle in the preparation of *New Church Praise*, as the supplement was eventually called; but his wisdom and counsel were always available and freely drawn upon. The denomination was fortunate indeed that the work on this book was completed before he left England for America at the end of 1974.

To those of us on the wrong side of the Atlantic his emigration was cause for sore regret, mitigated only by his extraordinary facility and felicity as a letter-writer. As in his books, he wrote as he spoke, so that reading him was as nearly like having him there in the room as it could possibly be. His account to me of the journey to the USA will illustrate what I mean.

Well—to give some account of our own doings: we had a wonderful sea-trip leaving on 23 December. The wind was 55–65 mph all the way and the captain said at the end he'd never known such heavy weather so continuously even at that season: this had at least two consequences. One was that added to our pleasure in a life which included nothing except sleep, food and Bloody Marys, was a touch of moral uplift since neither of us felt ill for one moment. It was a lovely ship: Swedish in everything except dollar currency. There were 200 first class passengers who were mostly stoned all the time, and 140 tourists who were great fun and among whom we made a lot of good friends. Thank heaven for segregation! The ship was built to take at least 750, so there was oceans of room to sit and lie and snooze and walk about. This was good, and our quarter-ton of baggage came with us at no extra expense to anybody. We were, however (second consequence), unable to visit Bermuda; we'd been promised 25 hours there, but the ship was slowed down so badly that we had to head straight for New York. However, we entered New York harbour at 6 a.m. on a perfect morning—cold, cloudless, rosy-fingered, and the Manhattan skyline looked its best. We were met by a thoughtful housing manager with a pickup truck, which just nicely held our household gods, and landed us in this apartment by noon.

From that time onwards we corresponded every couple of months or so: and I am intrigued, looking back through the letters, to see that for the most part they would make as little sense to anyone but myself as does overhearing one end of a telephone conversation. Conversation is what they are— vivacious, companionable, taking up bits of one's own news and opinion and reacting, so that hardly a paragraph is free of allusions which are bound to baffle anyone but the addressee. I, of course, was one among a very large number of his correspondents. How he found time for us all I cannot imagine—except that he could type so fast that his typewriters needed to have, figuratively speaking, a specially high melting point so as to continue working when almost incandescent. It was all of a piece with the quickness of the rest of his movements and of his thought. Perhaps he really did pack into his 64 years an amount of work that would take an ordinary mortal a much longer lifetime. Sometimes his friends would say to one another, "How *does* he get through it all? He will burn himself out". But Erik was Erik: you could not slow him down. And if, even for him, time must needs have a stop, and all who loved him here must feel irreparable loss, the knowledge that he is there among the eternities gives us a new notion, much more interesting than we had before, of

11

the meaning of heaven's everlasting rest. Fulfilment, yes: torpor, no; wordless-ness, no—or I will (if blessed with the chance to verify the matter) eat my halo.

This is a personal memoir and does not—could not—set out to be a full biography in however compressed a form. Of Erik's books, for example, I can say no more than that I have read most of them and marvelled at the range of his interests and knowledge no less than at the fecundity of his pen. Some of his very best writing is outside the scope of his two specialisms of Church music and Church history. My own top rating goes to *Into A Far Country*, which I have referred to above. In his self-assessment I believe he would have put at or near the head of the list *The Gift of Conversion*—a book which strangely enough never enjoyed the success of his others.

His connexion with the Royal School of Church Music is hardly less noteworthy than his long service with the Hymn Society, already mentioned. Of the RSCM he was for many years a member of the Council; and when he was made a Fellow, *honoris causa*, it was the first time that a non-Anglican had been accorded the School's supreme accolade. He was tremendously pleased, and had a new book-plate made, saying simply, "Erik Routley, FRSCM". It is to him that I owe my own introduction to the School and to its gracious premises at Addington Palace, Croydon. In 1956, the jubilee year of *The English Hymnal*, he smuggled me into a celebratory meeting there at which we heard Vaughan Williams reminisce about the making of the book. I remember thinking that only on my grandfather had I ever seen such enormous ears. RVW told us how Dearmer would send him texts to be found tunes for, and how he made a point of never questioning the words, until one day he came upon the line, 'Lord Jesus, bring us thistles". He thought that the request for such very specific mortification (and why thistles, anyway, rather than net-tles?) was going a trifle far, especially for singing about, and said so. It turned out to be a misprint for "thither".

That day I was introduced not only to RVW himself but to a large number of distinguished Church musicians, several of whom I am proud to number now among my friends. One whom I would dearly have liked to meet again and get to know better was Kenneth Finlay (1882–1974), some of whose tunes I had known and loved since my childhood. The holy simplicity of his music was, I realized, the expression of a personality of unusual grace and charm.

Erik knew them all, of course. He was after all one of them, though quite unlike any of the rest of them in looks and manner. In fact, the only other person, apart from his children, that I have ever thought might be mistaken for a brother of his is Donald Swann. Donald had been one of Erik's heroes long before they met. I wish I had been there to see those two uplifted chins and hear those ebullient inflexions approaching one another for the first time: and I was not at all surprised to learn from each of them subsequently how much admiration and affection he felt for the other.

Erik was not, as Donald was and is, at home in radio and television, though what he did there was always well done. His extraordinary knack of getting people to sing and enjoy it was seldom, I fancy, more severely tested than on one day in the television studio, when he was preparing a programme of lesser-known carols. I remember that they included "Tomorrow shall be my dancing day" and "Awake, awake ye drowsy souls" (*University Carol Book* 168) with its leaps and syncopations. Erik had arranged for singers to come along from local churches, but the Musicians' Union insisted that the programme was not a service of worship and therefore an amateur choir could not be used; so a scratch assemblage of paid vocalists was quickly rounded up within the building from another programme that had been recorded earlier in the day. It was apparent the moment they arrived in the studio that their professional scene was that of pop music. The copies of the tunes which Erik handed out were of little use to them. When he managed to secure their attention rehearsal began. There they stood, round the grand piano in the middle of the studio floor, most of them smoking as they sang, all of them tapping doggedly with their feet as they tried to master this totally unfamiliar idiom. It says much for their professionalism as well as for Erik's gifts in helping people to see visions that by the time the programme went out they were not only singing the music as he wanted it sung but were also singing the words as if they meant them.

Of Erik as preacher, two of his books give some impressions. *Ascent to the Cross* (London 1962) is a series of Lenten sermons on the Psalms of Ascent given in St Giles's, Edinburgh, in 1961. (His tribute in the preface to the co-operation, there, of Dr Herrick Bunney, the Cathedral organist, is worth mentioning: Dr Bunney's friendship meant a great deal to him, and indeed in the musical life of the whole family.) *Saul among the Prophets* (London 1971) is a collection of sermons preached between 1963 and 1969. The title-sermon was given at the opening of the Edinburgh Festival in 1964. Most of the rest are on Abraham, Jacob and Joseph. I heard him preach a sermon very similar to one of those in the Jacob series: I believe it was at the City Temple on Holborn Viaduct, London, a bland building in which it is not difficult for the cutting edge of the Gospel to become muffled. To convey in that place the awesome "otherness" of God and at the same time his equally awesome "seekingness" was an achievement characteristic of Erik's preaching, and was

13

also in itself a striking vindication of the claim that he was making, namely, that if Luz is not God-forsaken, nowhere is.

As with his great exemplar Bernard Manning, the power of his preaching did not stem from any use of rhetorical tricks but rather from clarity of thought allied to plainness of speech. He had thoroughly assimilated Dorothy Sayers's distinction (in an essay in *Unpopular Opinions*) between art and spell-binding. William Sargant's *Battle for the Mind* and J. A. M. Meerloo's *Mental Seduction and Menticide* both struck responsive chords in his own understanding. The former's analysis of Wesley's methods was a constant reminder that a sacred calling does not deliver the preacher from the perils of the power to persuade. Erik was scrupulous in his avoidance of meretricious effects. At the same time he was a very accomplished word-smith: and whenever he allowed himself enough time to polish his work the result was lapidary in its precision. I think of a phrase he used at the memorial service for my father, who had suffered a stroke while playing the organ at a Sunday worship-service. "In the midst of mortal praise he turned and took his journey." In a less direct sense the words are equally appropriate to Erik's own sudden going.

If I ask myself how it was that he could convey the mystery and the awe as well as the compelling "down-to-earth-ness" of the Biblical message, I find myself convinced that it was because he himself was perpetually awe*struck*. He was speaking of what he knew. This apparently thrusting, self-assertive, know-it-all man was actually devoting all his energy and skill to getting himself out of the light, so that thanks to his testimony we might look past him and see what he had seen.

My last earthly meeting with him was in Oxford in January, 1982, when he was over with a group of students and staff from Westminster Choir College. Based at Addington Palace, they took time to visit my church and sing for us in the course of Sunday worship. The College's President, Dr Ray Robinson, was amongst those present, as he was also at a subsequent gathering at St Columba's Church of Scotland in Pont Street, London; and it was some consolation to us Britons in our keen sense of deprivation through Erik's emigration that we could sense from our American friends that they knew very well the value of the treasure they had borrowed from us.

As for Erik himself, his contentment in his job did not prevent him from looking forward greatly to the sabbatical leave he was due to take in 1983. I feel sure he was using a throwaway phrase and not voicing any premonition when he wrote to me, as long ago as July, 1981, "I know what I should *like* to do: that is, to hole up in some quiet spot in GB and write one decent piece of

14

music before I die . . . Nous verrons. It is quite something to achieve one's first sabbatical in the year *following* one's 65th birthday!" If we are to speak strictly, that achievement was denied him: but *O quanta, qualia sunt illa sabbata/ quae semper celebrat superna curia*! Happily enough, moreover, there did come to him, in time for him to complete them before he died, and even hear some of them performed, one or two commissions for chamber works which one hopes enabled him to feel that his wish for a chance to write a "decent" piece of music had been fulfilled. There is no doubt that the Princeton years gave him welcome scope. He was teaching what he loved; he was travelling widely within the USA; he was still editing hymnals, right to the end (*Rejoice in the Lord*, on which he had just finished work, promises to be not only the last but also the best of the memorials to him in this field); he was still writing. Yet he often told me that the centre of it all for him—what mattered to him most in his job—was the Westminster Choir College Chapel, where he was responsible for most of the worship: and my guess is that for the staff and students on campus it would be there in the Chapel that they too would locate the greatest part of the greatness of this faithful servant of God.

On the cover of his last letter to me appeared a postage stamp carrying a mind-blowingly sentimental picture of a slightly elderly-looking couple (perhaps grandparents?) and a soulful and snuggling child (grand-daughter?) looking down dotingly at the latest Junior. The motto alongside was "Aging Together". This apparition had been smudged into partial and merciful obscurity by the post-mark, and I did not notice it until I happened to take a second look. It was then that I saw that below the stamp Erik had written, in tiny letters, the single word "Wow!" Not a bad last word to receive from such a man.

ERIK ROUTLEY
Chronology

1917	Born 31 October in Brighton, Sussex
1925	Fonthill Preparatory School, Sussex
1931	Lancing College, Sussex
1936	Magdalen College, Oxford
1939	Mansfield College, Oxford
1940	BA, Classics, Oxford University
1943	MA, Oxford University
	Ordained 4 September to the ministry of the Congregational Union of England and Wales
	Minister, Trinity Church, Wednesbury, Staffs.
1944	Married Margaret Scott, 16 May
	Secretary to committee preparing *Congregational Praise*
1945	Minister at Dartford, Kent
1946	BD, Oxford University
1947	Birth of first son, Nicholas
1948	Lecturer in Church History, Librarian, Chaplain and Director of Music, Mansfield College, Oxford
	Chaplain to Oxford University Congregational Society ("Congsoc")
	Editor, *The Bulletin of the Hymn Society of Great Britain and Ireland* (a position he held until 1974)
1949	Birth of second son, Patrick
1950	President, Oxford Organists' Association
1951	Founding President, Congregational Organists' Guild
1952	DPhil, Oxford University
1953	Birth of daughter, Priscilla
1955	Visiting lecturer at Montreal and Toronto
1957	Editor, *Congregational Monthly*
1959	Minister, Augustine-Bristo Congregational Church, Edinburgh
1961	Editor, *World Mission*
1962	Visited USA
	Union Theological Seminary, New York City
	Garrett-Evangelical Theological Seminary, Evanston, Illinois
1964	Preached Inaugural Sermon for Edinburgh International Festival
	Editor of the Series *Studies in Church Music*

1965	Fellow of the Royal School of Church Music

1965   Fellow of the Royal School of Church Music
1966   Visited USA
         Stone Lectures, Princeton Theological Seminary
         Gheens Lectures, Louisville Theological Seminary
1967   Minister, St James's Congregational Church, Newcastle upon Tyne
1968   Council, RSCM. First non-Anglican member
         Visited USA
         American Baptist Musicians, Green Lake, Wisconsin
         Chairman, editorial committee, *Cantate Domino*
1969   Visited USA
         Perkins School of Theology, Southern Methodist University, Dallas,
            Texas
         Fellowship of Methodist Musicians, Sioux City, Iowa
1970   President, Congregational Church in England and Wales
         Visited USA
         Perkins Lectures, Perkins School of Theology, Southern Methodist
            University, Dallas, Texas
1971   Visited USA
         Fellow, Westminster Choir College, Princeton
1972   Committee, *New Church Praise*
         Chairman, Doctrine and Worship Committee, United Reformed
            Church
1973   Visited USA
         Mo Ranch, Texas
1974   Visited USA
         Maple Grove United Methodist Church, Columbus, Ohio
1975   January: Visiting Professor of Music, Princeton Theological Seminary
         August: Professor of Church Music, Westminster Choir College,
            Princeton
1976   Editor, *Westminster Praise*
1977   Editorial Committee, *Ecumenical Praise*
1978   Director of Chapel, Westminster Choir College
1979   Chairman, RSCM in America
1980   Editor, Reformed Church in America Hymnal, *Rejoice in the Lord*
            (1985)
1982   Died 8 October in Nashville, Tennessee
         (12 October, Memorial Service, Bristol Chapel, Westminster Choir
            College)
(1983) (8 February, Memorial Service, Westminster Abbey, London)

God of Glory, around whose eternal throne
all the heavenly powers offer their ceaseless
songs of praise: grant that we may
overhear these songs, and with our own
lips and lives interpret them to all in
whose presence we play or sing: that your
church may behold the beauty of its King,
and see with mortal eyes the land that
is afar off, where all your promises are
celebrated, and where all your love in every
sight and sound is the theme of eternal
rejoicing: through Jesus Christ our Lord.

A prayer composed for use at Westminster Choir College

MINISTRY OF THE WORD

The minister, in preaching, seeks to bring his hearers to a decision which will issue in action. He wants his people to renew their decision for Christ then and there (or to make it for the first time), and then to go home and patch up the quarrel or make the awkward apology or write the difficult letter or do whatever it is the voice of Christ, newly heard that day, demands. But the musician in his own way seeks more than simply the demonstration of his own skill and the amusement of the listener . . . He, like the minister, is dealing with *people*. He cannot do what he wants to do without the listener's help, given in an act of faith comparable to that which must precede the effective hearing of the Word of God . . . Both preacher and musician are artists . . . If the preacher disdains the graces of communication—rhetoric, technique and clear thinking—he should not be preaching. The church musician is more obviously an artist. Both he and the minister are artists under obedience. They seek not merely to add to the honour and beauty realized in the world, but specifically to advance the Kingdom of God; that does not make them the less artists. Both find their inspiration in prayer; that does not make them the less artists . . . Both need the comfort of Christ, whose Gospel is the real pattern of communication, and whose Cross and Resurrection display the heart of the complexity and the secret of the victory . . . The clue to the resolution of all the tension and confusion between Church and music is in the Cross of Christ and in the Promises of God. Those who attend faithfully and humbly to these things will be honoured by God in their ministries. They will attend to the Word of God in Christ, and men will attend to them, and in them, ministers and musicians, shall the families of the earth be blessed.

Erik Routley, *Music, Sacred and Profane:*
Occasional Writings on Music 1950–58,
London 1960, pp. 41–43

1

PERFECTION AND GRACE

George B. Caird

Christians believe (in common with Jews and Muslims) that God is one. Theologians accordingly ply their endless task of showing that the truth of God is coherent and consistent; and their work is necessary because of the universal experience that this truth impinges upon us in a series of conflicts. Underlying all the rest there is the conflict between contemplation and action, between entering God's presence and entering his service. On the one hand religion consists in worship, the heart's response of wonder, joy and love to the revealed goodness of God; and this goes hand in hand with an attitude to the world which sees all things as ends in themselves, to be appreciated and enjoyed, not to be regarded as means to any ulterior end, except that of being pointers to the greater glory of their Creator. On the other hand religion is obedience to a divine purpose: there is work to be done, and all things, even life itself, are means subservient to the one all-controlling end. It is all very well to argue that the two are inseparable, mutually supportive, mutually corrective, mutually indispensible; that worship which does not issue in good works is as sterile as the waters of the Dead Sea which has no outlet, and that good works can be soured by self-regard unless they are kept sweet by worship. The fact is that the balance is notoriously hard to keep.

There are, however, other conflicts, related to this fundamental one, but distinguishable from it. Nobody has better understood or more lucidly expressed than Erik Routley the conflicting claims which the gospel makes on both preacher and musician. To superficial minds, which have failed to grasp the nature of those claims, it has often seemed that the conflict was between the preacher and the musician; and in situations where the musician had no theology and the preacher no taste, this may indeed have been the regrettable fact. But one whose own career and writings have so admirably combined the two roles could not rest comfortably with so shallow a judgement. In public worship preacher and musician share a common task. Both are called to celebrate, the one with words, the other with music, the many-splendoured wisdom and works of God. The conflict, like the task, is one they share; and

21

they do well to face it together, in the hope of understanding it, and so of learning to live fruitfully with it.

On the one hand they are artists, committed, like all others engaged in the performing arts, to the daily quest of perfection. Like David, they will refuse to offer to God a sacrifice that has cost them nothing. In the exercise of their craft no training can be too rigorous, no discipline too exacting, no attention to detail too scrupulous, no standard too exalted. In their own hypercritical judgement performance will always fall short of vision (*O quanta qualia!*), yet the vision never ceases to impose its authority. Nothing but the best is good enough for God. Moreover, what they demand of themselves they will expect also of others. It is the characteristic and proper hope of all who are devoted to the pursuit of excellence that, expecting the best from themselves and others, they may elicit the best from others by the stimulus of their expectation and by the infection of their own enthusiasm.

On the other hand the gospel they celebrate is a gospel of grace. It proclaims through the example and teaching of Jesus a God of love who sympathises with human weakness, forgives human failure, and can use human inadequacy for his own purposes more readily than the strength of the self-sufficient. "I thank you Father, Lord of heaven and earth, for hiding these things from the learned and wise and revealing them to the simple. Yes, Father, such was your good pleasure" (Matt. 11.25–26; Luke 10.21). "Blessed are you poor; the kingdom of God is yours" (Luke 6.20). "Few of you are men of wisdom, by any human standard; few are powerful or highly born. Yet, to shame the wise, God has chosen what the world counts folly, and to shame what is strong, God has chosen what the world counts weakness. He has chosen things low and contemptible, mere nothings, to overthrow the existing order" (1 Cor. 1.26–28).

In public worship the clash between excellence and grace is complicated by two other factors. The first is that worship, whether its structure be prescribed or free, or a mixture of the two, entails a delicate balance between personal performance and corporate participation. Beautiful choral music, exquisitely performed, and a well-prepared address, eloquently delivered, may fail in their true purpose if they do not express a corporate sentiment or conviction and elicit a corporate response. But a service of another kind may equally fail by alienating those who care for standards and cannot regard either enthusiasm or habit as an excuse for banality and slovenliness.

The second factor is that the power of music and words to express and to evoke depends in no small degree on association. They will fall on deaf or resistant ears unless they attach to something in the listener's experience,

22

however limited that may be. All members of a congregation will have had some occasion in their past when they have been deeply moved, and they need that which will set the bells of memory ringing. Yet undue attention to the familiar can preclude the possibility of growth towards maturity; and in the spiritual world, as in the natural, that which has ceased to grow has begun to die.

The purpose of this essay is not, however, to provide a perfunctory sketch-map of territory which Erik Routley has explored in detail, but rather to point out that the tension between excellence and grace, however acutely the artist in words or music may be made aware of it through his professional training and commitment, is not confined to him, but is integral to the Christian life as the writers of the New Testament expound it.

This point is well illustrated by the most puzzling and tantalizing of all the books of the New Testament, the Gospel of Matthew. It announces itself as a gospel, with the promise of a Saviour who will be Immanuel, the embodiment of God's presence with his people. But before long we come to the great sermon, which from first to last strikes the note of inexorable moral demand. God's people are to be perfect, as God himself is perfect (5.48). In striking contrast with the beatitudes of Luke, which pronounce a blessing on the emptiness and need that is open to be filled by the limitless resources of God's kingdom, freely bestowed on all who ask (cf. 12.32), the Matthaean beatitudes give their blessing to spiritual states and attitudes which the followers of Jesus must evince if they are to be the salt of the earth and the light of the world (5.13–16). Jesus has come to ensure that not one jot or tittle shall disappear from the law, and to interpet the law with a rigour far beyond that of the strictest Pharisee (5.17–20). The Decalogue had forbidden murder, adultery and perjury; but the new law of Jesus stretches them to cover areas of which no law court, ancient or modern, could take cognisance, penetrating to the intentions, the motives, even the dispositions of character out of which these offenses arise (5.21–37). The old law placed a limit on retaliation; the new law not merely forbids it, but requires in its place a positive act of benevolence that will rob aggression of its sting (5.38–42). The old law commanded love for one's neighbour; the new law redefines "neighbour" to make it include one's enemies (5.43–47). The Christian is not to look for recognition or for security (6.1–34), nor must he buoy himself up with a sense of superiority to others (7.1–5). He must be content to follow the narrow path that leads to life (7.13–14), knowing that no profession of loyalty, however fervent, can be a substitute for radical obedience (7.21–23). That is the only foundation on which the house of life can stand secure (7.24–27).

23

At one point, to be sure, the whole duty of man is summed up in a single rule: "always treat others as you would like them to treat you; that is the law and the prophets" (7.12). But this rule, so far from easing the legal obligation, so far from simplifying or relaxing the requirements of the sermon, merely epitomizes its stringency. The old law forbad any action to the detriment of others, and provided rules by which a court of law could deal with any case in which injustice had occurred. The Pharisees, in their passionate devotion to the law, attempted to make it applicable to every vicissitude of daily life; and their method was to spell out in detail the exact reference of its terms, so as to define the precise limits of their liability.[1] Their rabbis had encouraged them to go further and "set a hedge about the law", i.e. to leave a margin of safety by always doing a little more than the law ostensibly required. But the righteousness which exceeds that of the Pharisees demands a positive commitment to the well-being of others; it is an ethic of unlimited liability.[2]

This contrast arises in large part out of the Jewish identification of ethics with law. For the Jewish Torah comprised not only the Jewish religion, but also the code of criminal and civil law of the Jewish nation. The procedure of the Pharisees was that followed by lawyers in any culture in order to make the laws of their country enforceable by the courts. In court, though a person may be found guilty of attempt to commit a crime, they cannot be charged with the intention to do so, let alone with being a suspicious and unsatisfactory character. One of the criticisms levelled against the Pharisees is that, through their concern for practicality, they concentrated on minor pieties which were within their competence, even carrying them beyond the bounds of common sense, but neglected "the weightier demands of the law, justice, mercy and good faith",—comprehensive principles which nobody could ever claim to have satisfied (Matt. 23.23). We need not here enter into the long and often heated debate concerning the extent to which this accusation was justified. Jesus was not innovating, but was claiming to remind his fellow-Jews where the heart of their inherited religious faith lay; and there were no doubt many Pharisees who had a profound appreciation of what he was saying. But Matthew includes this verse in his account of the teaching of Jesus, not as a polemic against Jews, but as a warning against a similar scrupulosity within his own Christian community. In his day, as in many later periods of the Church's history, there was a tendency to turn the ethical demands of the gospel into a new legalism; and it was Matthew's concern to point out that the effect of this was to *reduce* their scope.

The severity of these familiar chapters resists all attempts to tone it down.

Yet it is well to recognise that in the history of Christian discipleship it has frequently been exaggerated in ways quite foreign to the evangelist's mind. Many have been led by it into an anxiety which he would have deplored, a neurotic and wholly unchristian preoccupation with the state of their own souls and with their eternal destiny ("Whoever would save his life shall lose it"!); and the reason is that they have mistaken the meaning of the phrase peculiar to Matthew, "the kingdom of heaven", treating it as a synonym for heaven, and so turning the ethical standards of the kingdom into a qualification without which nobody can hope for life after death in the presence of God.[3] This misapprehension has been increased, quite unintentionally, by the title accorded to these chapters, "The Sermon on the Mount", which has caused them to be regarded with special veneration, and so has had the effect of isolating them from the rest of the Gospel, even from the rest of the New Testament, and of constituting them a canon within the canon of Scripture, as though they encapsulated the sum total of Christian teaching. In reaction against this error, there have been theologians who have gone to the other extreme: ignoring Matthew's repeated emphasis on doing what Jesus said, they have argued that the demand for perfection contained in the Sermon goes so far beyond the limits of practicality that it must have been designed for no other purpose than to reduce the sinful soul to despair and so to reliance on the unfathomable mercy of God.

When, avoiding such pitfalls, we proceed to the rest of Matthew's Gospel, we find that Matthew is second to none, not even to Paul, in his forthright exposition of the gospel of grace. He does not, indeed, use the predominantly Pauline term *charis*, but he explores the concept in a variety of ways. Jesus is the promised Servant of the Lord who comes to remove illness and disease (8.17), and to mediate God's forgiveness (9.8). When he sends out his disciples on their mission, he reminds them: "You received without cost; give without charge" (10.8). He calls the heavily burdened to learn from him and find that his yoke is easy to bear (11.30). But for our purpose the important point is that Matthew sees God's grace at work not only in the death of Jesus for the remission of sins and as a ransom for the many (20.28; 26.28), but also in his continued presence with his disciples afterwards (18.20; 28.20). This is shown, for example, in one of his characteristic additions to the narrative of Mark. To Mark's story of Jesus' walking on the water, on which Mark comments that the disciples were dumbfounded and failed to understand what it meant, Matthew adds as a sequel Peter's attempt to do what Jesus was doing; and he clearly regards this as a parable of the Christian life. Peter is the typical disciple, prompted by impetuous faith to attempt the impossible in

25

imitation of the Master, but doomed to sink in the waves unless constantly upheld by the Master's hand (14.22–23).

It must be freely granted that at no point does Matthew discuss how the demand for perfection is to be related to the free and unconditional offer of grace. He is content to set the two side by side, to allow the one to complement and qualify the other. We may regard this as one of the products of his Semitic mind and upbringing,[4] since he follows the same practice on a smaller scale in his arrangement of his traditional material. Christians are to let their light shine in public, so that the good they do may be seen (5.16); but they are to do their acts of piety, including acts of kindness to others, in private so that only God will see them (6.2–6, 16–18). They are to pass no judgement on anyone (7.1), but must avoid throwing their pearls to those whom they judge to be pigs (7.6). On a missionary journey they are to give without charge, but to expect their keep. (10.8–10).[5] It is of course possible to give a long, precise and boring proof that each of these apparently contradictory pairs is complementary and mutually corrective; but that is not Matthew's way, nor was it the way of Jesus before him. However uncomfortable we rationalists may feel with the method of simple juxtaposition, it has one great advantage: it does not conceal the fact that, when all explanations are exhausted, the problem of balance remains.

There is a suggestion, which has gained wide acceptance, that at 13.52 Matthew has put his signature to the portrait of Jesus he has painted: "any scribe who is apprenticed to the kingdom of Heaven is like a householder who can produce from his store both the new and the old." With this we may compare the remark which the grandson of Jesus ben Sira made about the book that his grandfather wrote in Hebrew, which he himself had translated into Greek. Out of his comprehensive knowledge of the Scriptures his grandfather had written a compendium of the wisdom they contained, "so that, with this further help, scholars might make greater progress in their studies by living as the law directs" (Ecclus. Prologue). To him it was self-evident that the study of the Jewish way of life was inseparable from the living of it. Like any other craft, or indeed any practical modern enterprise, such as swimming or riding a bicycle, it could be learned only in the doing of it. So too Matthew thinks of himself not merely as the pupil of Jesus in an exercise of understanding, but as his apprentice in the greatest of all the performing arts. It is this that transforms the impossible ideal into a practical standard for daily life, and enables him out of his storehouse to bring new wisdom for changing circumstance. But it was essential that the trained scribe should also be able to bring out from his store the old, since the old, the accurate memory of the historical Jesus and his teaching, would always remain the test and norm for the validity of the new. There were in Matthew's day charismatics who claimed to have authority to speak to the church in the name of the heavenly Christ, by whose Spirit they were inspired. Matthew gives them short shrift. Unlike Paul, he distrusts prophecy in the church. True prophets there may be (23.34), but they are a good deal harder to find than false ones. So all charismatic claims are to be subjected to the test of conduct: "you will recognise them by the fruits they bear" (7.15–20). The genuine messenger of the heavenly Christ will proclaim his message not only with his lips but in his life; and the genuine message will be consonant with the recorded teaching of the earthly Jesus.

When we turn to the letters of Paul, our first impression, particularly if we are heirs to the Protestant Reformation, may well be that Paul has resolved the dilemma in favour of grace. So strong has this impression been in the past that some commentators have gone the length of identifying Paul as the man to whom Matthew allotted the lowest place in the kingdom of Heaven, on the ground that he set aside the precepts of the law and taught others to do the same (Matt. 5.19). As we shall find, the contrast between these two has been grossly overstated. Yet it remains true that, whereas the first impression made by Matthew is one of rigorous demand, the first impression made by Paul is one of free and unconditional gift. His insistence both on justification by faith and on election had no other purpose than to guarantee the primacy of grace. God's promise to Abraham had to be "made on the ground of faith in order that it might be a matter of sheer grace" (Rom. 4.16). Election could not be based on merit or achievement, "or grace would cease to be grace" (Rom. 11.6). Salvation was God's free gift, unearned and undeserved (Rom. 3.24; cf. 5.15; 2 Cor. 9.15; Eph. 2.8; 2.7), and the evidence for this lay in the cross. "Christ died for us while we were yet sinners, and that is God's own proof of his love toward us" (Rom. 5.8).

Against those who maintained the continuing validity of the law, Paul argued that what had begun in grace must continue in grace. It was God's purpose in Christ "that grace should establish its reign" (Rom. 5.21). Every aspect of Christian life must be controlled by "that grace in which we stand" (Rom. 5.2). To attempt to combine the old life with the new was to be a deserter from the empire of grace and to part company with Christ (Gal. 5.4).

But there is another side to Paul, his unremitting pursuit of excellence. His description of the pious Jew is surely autobiographical. "You rely upon the law and are proud of your God; you know his will; instructed by the law, you know right from wrong; you are confident that you are the one to guide the blind, to enlighten the benighted, to train the stupid, and to teach the

27

immature, because in the law you see the very shape of knowledge and truth" (Rom. 2.17–20). Yet even among his Jewish contemporaries Paul had to excel, outstripping them "in my boundless devotion to the traditions of my ancestors" (Gal. 1.14). No critic was to be given the chance to fault his performance (Phil. 3.6). His conversion changed much, but not this. He remained to the end an athlete, determined to keep himself in peak condition (1 Cor. 9.24–27). Gone was the sense of superiority (Rom. 3.27); for he himself had been exposed as a sinner precisely at the point where he had believed himself to be righteous, since what he had taken to be zeal for God (Rom. 10.3) had blinded him to the glory of God in the person of Jesus Christ (2 Cor. 4.4). Gone is the endless effort to prove himself in the eyes of men and God, and above all in his own sight; for God had accepted him while he was still an enemy, persecuting the church of Christ. But the quest for excellence remains undiminished, transfigured into an inexhaustible gratitude to him "who loved me and gave himself for me" (Gal. 2.20). Paul was a debtor; no effort could be too demanding, no suffering too extreme, no pastoral anxiety too heavy for the discharge of his debt; and since the debt could not be repaid directly, it must be paid to "the brother for whom Christ died" (1 Cor. 8.11), whether he was "Greek or non-Greek, learned or simple" (Rom. 1.14). Even in the passage where Paul most vigorously repudiates his past pride of race, upbringing, religion and achievement, declaring them all to be "so much garbage" in comparison with what he has now gained through Christ (Phil. 3.8), he still shows himself to be every inch a competitor. "I have not yet reached perfection, but I press on, hoping to take hold of that for which Christ once took hold of me . . . forgetting what is behind me, and reaching out for that which lies ahead, I press towards the goal to win the prize which is God's call to the life above, in Christ Jesus" (Phil. 3.12–14).

The standards which Paul demanded of himself he expected of his colleagues and converts. They are to fill their minds with "whatever is excellent and admirable" (Phil. 4.8), to aim at the highest gifts, and particularly that which surpasses all others (1 Cor. 12.31). The Thessalonians have done well and must do better (1 Thess. 4.10). The Corinthians must grow to adulthood in their thinking (1 Cor. 14.20). For the Philippians he prays that "your love may grow ever richer" (Phil. 1.9). He is unstinting in praise for colleagues who are tireless (1 Cor. 16.15–16; cf. 2 Thess. 3.13; Col. 4.13); and, in prison in Rome, he shows a passing shadow of pique because nobody except Timothy is prepared to drop everything else at a moment's notice and make the long journey to Philippi which he cannot himself make (Phil. 2.20).

Thus for Paul, as for Matthew, the demands of excellence lie side by side with the free offer of grace. One reason for this is that Paul believed in the efficacy of grace. Grace had transformed the persecutor of the church into the apostle of the Gentiles, second to none in his devotion to the gospel. "By God's grace I am what I am, nor has his grace been given to me in vain; on the contrary, in my labours I have outdone them all—not I indeed, but the grace of God working with me" (1 Cor. 15.10). Grace had enabled him to triumph over the physical handicap of his thorn in the flesh; "for when I am weak, then I am strong" (2 Cor. 12.10). He can cope with either poverty or plenty, since "I have strength for anything through him who gives me power" (Phil. 4.13). In particular, grace could create that moral goodness which the law prescribed but conspicuously failed to achieve. "What the law could never do, because our sinful nature robbed it of power, God has done by sending his own Son . . . so that what the law decrees may find fulfilment in us, whose conduct is not controlled by the old nature but by the Spirit" (Rom. 8.3–4). At Colossae there were moralists who were worried about the permissiveness of the surrounding culture, and thought to keep it at bay by means of an ascetic regime—"Do not handle this, do not taste that, do not touch the other" (Col. 2.21). Paul dismisses their "philosophy", not only because it contradicts the gospel of grace, but because it does not work. "It has an air of wisdom, with its forced piety, its self-mortification, and its severity to the body; but it is of no use at all in combatting sensuality" (2.23).

By appeal to the example of Christ Paul is able also to hold together also the claims of individual fulfilment and corporate unity. For Christ had achieved a full self-realisation, not in the assertion of rights and privileges, but in the renunciation of them, in order that he might be completely identified with others in their need and humiliation (Phil. 2.5–8). "He was rich, yet for your sake he became poor, so that through his poverty you might become rich" (2 Cor. 8.9). "Those of us who have a robust conscience must accept as our own burden the tender scruples of weaker men, and not consider ourselves. Each of us must consider his neighbour and think what is for his good and will build up the common life. For Christ too did not consider himself" (Rom. 15.1–3).

Nevertheless, the ability to see how two apparently conflicting principles may be reconciled in theory does not eliminate the problem of striking a balance between them in practice; and many of the pastoral problems Paul had to deal with were of this kind. There was, for example, at Corinth a group of tough-minded people who took a thoroughly bracing view of their new religion, deplored the wobbly faith of the less robust, and proposed to put some stiffening into them. They had written Paul a letter (1 Cor. 7.1), not asking his advice, but telling him what line they were taking. One of their complaints is that the weaker members had superstitious scruples about eating meat which they considered to be contaminated because it had come from an animal sacrificed in a pagan rite. We know, they argued, that pagan gods do not actually exist; and that which does not exist cannot contaminate good meat. They expect Paul to agree with them, and for good reason, because he had been the protagonist in the defence of a Christian's liberty to follow his own conscience and the dictates of the Holy Spirit, without being restricted by human regulations. Paul is, indeed, in principle very much inclined to agree. "You may eat anything sold in the meat-market without raising questions of conscience; for the earth is the Lord's and everything in it" (1 Cor. 10.25–26). No doubt these weaklings ought to be encouraged to grow into a stronger grasp of their monotheistic faith and its implications. But a tender plant is not encouraged to grow by being jumped on. It is no doubt outrageous that the wobblers should have the power to restrict the God-given freedom of the strong. But it would be better to turn vegetarian than to put an obstacle in the way of a brother's faith (8.13). In Romans he returns to the theme: "if your brother is outraged by what you eat, then your conduct is no longer guided by love" (15.15). And here we come to the crux, not merely of that discussion, but of the subject of this essay. For the apparent conflict between the unfettered pursuit of perfection and the claims of grace is inherent in the nature of love. Genuine love, whether it is parental, marital or divine, has two sides to it. On the one hand it accepts everything, forgives everything, bears everything. On the other hand it is jealous for the beloved: nothing is too good for them, and nothing must stand in the way of the fullest realisation of their capabilities, not even one's own diffidence, faults, follies or objections.

The problem, then, turns out to be not only ours, but God's. He created mankind to be the image, the reflection of his own character. How could the standard of perfection be maintained without condemning, and so losing, those who fell short of it? How could God forgive without abandoning his own standard and his own purpose? God's answer, according to Paul, an answer which was no afterthought, but had been foreseen from the beginning, was given in the cross. There God "proved himself to be just and the justifier of anyone who has faith in Jesus" (Rom. 3.26), i.e. the upholder of standards and the rescuer of those who fail to meet them. But that is only another way of saying that the cross reveals the two-sidedness of love.

This brings us to the Fourth Gospel, with its profound exploration of the moral imperatives of love. Its theme is the unity of the Father and the Son, into which through the cross believers, and ultimately the world, are to be taken

30

up. This unity is expressed in terms of light, life and truth, of works and mission and mutual indwelling, but above all it is a unity of love. The Father's love for the Son is such that he shares with him his whole purpose: "the Father loves the Son and has entrusted him with all authority" (3.35); "the Father loves the Son and shows him all that he himself is doing" (5.20). The Son's love for the Father is such that he puts his human life unreservedly at the disposal of the divine purpose. "It is meat and drink for me to do the will of him that sent me until I have finished his work" (4.34). "It is the Father who dwells in me doing his own work" (14.10). "I have glorified you on earth by completing the work which you gave me to do" (17.4). It follows, therefore, that when through the cross Jesus offers to his disciples the possibility of dwelling in his love, that promise carries with it the same moral obligation. "If you heed my commands, you will dwell in my love, as I have heeded my Father's commands and dwell in his love" (15.10). They are to be one, and in that unity will lie their perfection (17.23).

It has frequently been observed that, although the Johannine Jesus refers repeatedly to his commands, which the disciples must obey because that is what it means to live in his love, he never gives any commands except the one command to love one another (15.12). The evangelist has therefore laid himself open to the suspicion that he has reduced Christian obligation to this one particular. Even in the community for which the Gospel was first written there were some who drew this erroneous conclusion. For the First Epistle of John was written to repair some of the damage done by such a group, who had already seceded from the church to form a separate movement of their own (2.19). They claimed to be sharing the life of God in a way that put them beyond the possibility of sin, to have an esoteric knowledge of God and a love for God which distinguished them from the common run of Christian, yet without feeling that these claims entailed any serious ethical obligation (1.6, 8; 2.4; 4.20). John insists that those who are to share God's life must "walk in the light as he himself is in the light" (1.7). "In the man who is obedient to his word, the divine love has indeed come to its perfection" (2.5). "Love must not be a matter of words or talk: it must be genuine, and show itself in action" (3.18). John and the opposition movement agreed that God is love. Where he differed from them was in his conviction that the love of God had taken human form in Jesus, revealing itself above all in his death, and that in this way the word "love" had been filled with a new, ethical content. In his theology, then, as with Matthew and Paul, the commandment of love does not negate, but subsumes and enlarges the general quest for perfection. "God dwells in us if we love one another; his love is brought to perfection within us" (4.12).

The theme of perfection is one of the leitmotifs of the letter to the Hebrews. The author cites Psalm 1,10, with its promise of a new order of priesthood, and Jer. 31.31–34, with its promise of a new covenant, to prove the built-in obsolescence of the old covenant, acknowledged by psalmist and prophet alike. Through it perfection was not attainable (7.11): "The earlier rules are cancelled as impotent and useless, since the law brought nothing to perfection." The law, indeed, held only a shadow of the good things that were to come (10.1). Perfection, to be sure, means to this writer the fulfilment of man's destiny in access to God (4.16; 7.19, 25; 10.19–22). But there can be no access to that holy presence apart from consecration (2.11; 10.14), apart from that "holiness without which no one can see the Lord" (12.14). Christ himself had to attain perfection (2.10); "son though he was, he learned obedience in the school of suffering and, once perfected, became the source of eternal salvation for all who obey him" (5.8–9). The Christian life, therefore, must be growth from spiritual infancy to adulthood (5.12–14); "let us advance towards maturity" (6.3).

The rigour of this letter goes beyond anything else of the kind in the New Testament, and it has been mistakenly thought to be unrelieved by any reference to the love of God. Simple reliance on the concordance might seem to confirm this error. But in fact our author makes the point in other terms. It was in keeping with the character and purpose of God that Christ should reach perfection by the road of suffering and temptation because, as high priest and representative of mankind, he had to be able to sympathise with them in their temptations and weakness (2.10, 18; 4.15; 5.2). In that display of sympathy he shows himself to be "the effulgence of God's splendour and the stamp of God's very being" (1.3); for it is the great moving force by which the God of peace can "make of us what he would have us to be" (13.21).

Each of these writers, then expresses in his own terms the common consensus of all, that in the Christian life gift and demand belong inseparably together, because both are inherent in the nature of love. They present this truth with a clarity which makes it seem very simple; but none of them pretends that it is easy. Eternal love is easy to please, but very hard to satisfy.

It may seem that this essay has wandered far from its starting point, since the quest for perfection in the realm of personal relations is a very different thing from the quest of perfection in the professional exercise of an art. My contention has been that it is precisely because they have so much in common that they create the conflict with which this discussion began. Neither the artist nor the Christian can dispense with the impossible ideal. Every performing artist knows that one is never content with any performance; the vision always in the end eludes one's grasp. Yet the vision is kept alive and fed because there are times when, beyond all expectation, something happens which for the moment at least seems utterly right. In the same way the Christian must never attempt to dispense with the impossible vision, either by dismissing it as impractical idealism, or by domesticating it in a code of rules. For the more it is lived with, the more it will teach of grace.

NOTES

1 The question "Who is my neighbour?" is a request for definition; and the answer of Jesus frustrates the lawyer's desire to define his liability (Luke 10.29).
2 Luke (17.7–10) makes the same point in the parable of the Tired Servant: "When you have carried out all your orders, you should say, 'We are servants and deserve no credit; we have only done our duty.'"
3 In fact Matthew uses "Heaven", in a fashion common among Jews of his day, as a proper noun, a reverential substitute for the name of God (Cf. Luke 15.18; Mark 14.62; Heb. 1.3; and for other New Testament instances of this practice, see G. Dalman, *The Words of Jesus*, Edinburgh 1909, pp. 204–232). For Matthew, as for the other evangelists, to enter the kingdom meant, in the first instance at least, enrolling in the service of God the King; and he makes it as clear as do the others that Jesus offered the opportunity freely to all sorts of people, without any qualification except faith. Thus Matthew alone records the words of Jesus to the national leaders in the temple: "Tax-gatherers and prostitutes are entering the kingdom of God ahead of you" (21.31).
4 On this Semitic idiom of speech and thought, see G. B. Caird, *The Language and Imagery of the Bible*, London 1980, pp. 117–121.
5 This particular anomaly was not confined to Matthew. Paul always followed the first rule and worked for his living to make the gospel free of charge (1 Cor. 11.3–18). Yet his critics at Corinth questioned whether he was a genuine apostle, because he did not claim an apostle's right to an expense account (2 Cor. 11.7–21); see G. Theissen, *The Social Setting of Pauline Christianity*, Edinburgh 1982, pp. 26–67.

44

St Blane 8.88.8 1963

1. Lord, look up-on our wor-king days, busied in fac-tory,
3. Thou art the workman, Lord, not we: all worlds were made at

of-fice, store; may word-less work thy name a-dore. The com-mon
thy com-mand: Christ their sus-tai-ner, bared his hand: 5 Give it

round spell out thy praise? them
from fu-ti-li-ty. 5 Give it its
por-tion in thy rule!

Composed at Dunblane workshop 1963   Dunblane Praises I 1
Hymns and Songs (1969) 87
New Songs for the Church I 21.
© Stainer & Bell   Australian H. Bk

G. Schirmer Inc. New York   12 Staves   No. 5 - Printed in the U. S. A.

2

THE NATURE OF WORSHIP:
COMMUNITY LIVED IN PRAISE OF GOD

Don E. Saliers

What life have you if you have not life together?
There is no life that is not in community,
And no community not lived in praise of God.
T. S. Eliot, Choruses from *The Rock*

That question, "what life have you . . . ?" is an increasingly urgent one for many people whom we are called to serve. It is a question pressed upon us by the lacerations and fragmentation of contemporary life. It is a cry welling up in the hearts and lives of human beings, both inside and outside of the churches. It is asked of the churches by people in the streets; but also by persons who, seated comfortably for years in the pews, are quite familiar with the language of Zion. In either case it addresses us directly: we, in our songs, words, actions and gestures, have often been considerably less than a "community lived in praise of God."

In his famous book, *The Shape of the Liturgy*, Dom Gregory Dix reminds us that "the study of liturgy is above all a study of *life*. . . . Christian worship has always been something done by real men and women, whose contemporary circumstances have all the time a profound effect upon the ideas and aspirations with which they come to worship."[1] The Scriptures themselves grow out of the experience of worshipping people whose lives and songs were double testimony to life before God. In the whole sweep of Holy Scripture, the mixture of awe and human terror, of divine compassion and human hope, is sounded in the songs and worship of those called out by God. Scripture is a record of God's mighty acts; but it also records the on-going life-journey and experience of people called out in response. It witnesses to God's self-disclosure to a creation lovingly fashioned yet so far fallen from God's creative intent that it cries for redemption and restoration. The song of earth and the song of heaven seek one another on the lips and in the lives of real men and women from generation to generation.

35

Christian spirituality in the context of worship and life must always take these matters with seriousness. The divine initiative calls forth a communal response which finds its own best being in praise of its creator and redeemer. Yet the shape of that praise lives and unfolds over time. Thus, the forms, patterns and theological content which we call "tradition" are understood and freshly received amidst the ever-changing historical, cultural and social features of existence which characterize real human beings in every generation. *Merely* to sing the songs of Zion is not enough. "The grace of God," Erik Routley once remarked to a workshop we were doing together, "marks the beginning of our responsibility, not the beginning of false consolation."

In the remarks which follow, I will address three main points: first, the contemporary situation in which we struggle to illuminate and understand the nature of worship; second, some theological fundamentals; and finally, some basic experiential features of worship and their implication for authentic Christian spirituality grounded in liturgical action.

1. The Nature of Worship in Our Contemporary Situation

There can be little doubt that we are now living through a period of great turmoil and often great confusion concerning Christian worship. Congregations have become visibly polarized or split into several grudging factions over what constitutes "true worship." Many wish to do away with the old forms and language in the name of relevance and creativity; others regard any such change as tampering with "hallowed and sacred" tradition, in some cases scarcely a hundred years or less old. Those of us given pastoral responsibilities —both clergy and laity, often find ourselves caught in the cross-fire, struggling for integrity and understanding. We live in a time of immense liturgical change resulting from both cultural and theological pressures. Not since the Reformation and Counter-Reformation has there been so much wide-spread concern for the reform and renewal of inherited rites and assumed patterns, in both "liturgical" and "free church" traditions.

Recently I visited a local church which had undergone no less than four major changes in its style of Sunday worship within the past eight years. When a group of the lay leadership took me to dinner, they unloaded: split by charismatics and non-charismatics, subject to the wildly differing styles of four pastors (each of whom stayed for less than three years), subject to wrangling between the choir, the organist and the choir director, and unable to agree over whether they were an "evangelical church" or a "liturgical church," these folks were exhausted. The matter of *how* they were to worship and *who* they were when they worshipped and *what* the connection between their worship and their ordinary lives was supposed to be—all these were matters of personal anguish for concerned people who cared deeply for their church and for the integrity of their fatih. Whatever else was going on among them, I sensed a crisis of faith and spiritual life tied directly to these various tensions and disputes about common worship. They simply wanted to be nourished and opened up to the deeper stream of Christian worship and spirituality.

When we in the American churches attempt to think about the meaning and point of worship in our context today, our primary instinct is to speak of the problems of cultural pluralism and relevancy. Of course, we tend to make an industry out of the problems as well. We "shop around" for the church and the style of worship and life which fits *our* needs. These are very American things to do. Nevertheless, the shocks of cultural change do impinge directly upon the worshipping life of Christians since the activity of worship is an inescapably human and cultural activity, whatever claims we wish to make about the activity of God in Word and Sacrament. Then, too, the last ten to fifteen years have been unprecedented ecumenically. Every major denomination has undertaken the task of reforming its rites in light of an ecumenically shared knowledge of the history of worship. No one could have anticipated the remarkable convergence in both theology and structural shape of the eucharistic liturgy or Holy Communion. This period of turmoil is not generated solely by the onslaughts of secular culture against the holy peace and order of the churches. Cultural pluralism also generates ecclesial sharing.

As will become clear, I regard this time of uncertainty and mutual exploration as part of a significant struggle for clarity and understanding with respect to the nature of faith and religious life in our age. Thus the current confusions, problems and "cultural" demands in worship are signs of a period of religious vitality and reformulation as important as the century of the Reformation seems in retrospect. In the name of renewal, some persons have spoken of the credibility problem of worship; of the way in which believers hide behind old words and customs, saying one thing but meaning something else. Others have spoken of the "noise of solemn assemblies" as part of their prophetic critique of church life. So far as these complaints are connected with the inability of people to be "at home" in the songs and the other forms of worship, the problems we now face are simultaneously cultural and theological. The clarification of meaning and point of worship in the contemporary world is crucial to the work of Christian theology. More to the point, understanding how to live the Christian life together in a culture of forgetfulness is at stake.

All this leads to an important word of caution. The reform of liturgy may not necessarily signal a genuine "renewal" of worship. *Reform* and *renewal* are different, though related, matters. All of us know that we can have a beautiful text, beautiful musical settings, the most theologically well-informed prayers, and the best of liturgical furnishings, and yet still not have *faithful liturgy*. Some "new songs"—whether of classical origin or Christian "pop" culture—still do not take us further than the narthex or the fellowship hall. Reformed rites do not automatically transform individual and communal lives, as many have already discovered. This cautionary note is addressed to all who compose texts for prayer and praise.

At the same time, continuing to pray and sing biblically impoverished texts which may also lack aesthetic power, no matter how seriously done, cannot guarantee a deepening of spiritual growth and discernment of what it is to be the church today. Petrification, religious self-indulgence, and sanctification are not compatible. Hence, our concern for reform must be related directly to the deeper and more difficult matter of renewing the face of worship. In faithful worship we find our lives remembered and given fundamental orientation to God and neighbor.

Nothing has symbolized more dramatically this "age of liturgical reform" than the Second Vatican Council. That its first item of concern was worship took many by surprise some twenty years ago. As it turns out, concern for reform of the liturgy in Roman Catholicism touched deeply upon all of the important theological and cultural issues confronting the church. The intent was not simply a piece-meal change but an "aggiornamento"—a re-spiriting —of the whole liturgy and the worshipping life of the church. As one commentator observed, the church was in transition to a renewed common life where rites will no longer be mechanically enacted, Scripture blindly recited but not understood, and the like. Rather, the church was in "transition to a liturgy of authentic acts," worshipping in spirit and in truth. Of course the history of that "transition," particularly within Roman Catholicism but across the liturgical spectrum as well, has been anything but smooth and easy.

The crisis in worship, then, is part of a larger cultural crisis which has thrown Christians back upon their own roots. We have been forced to raise fundamental questions again, but now in a new ecumenical context of dialogue and hope. Raising questions about the adequacy of our patterns and forms of worship has forced us to reexamine the relationship between church and world, between God and humankind, and between worship and spirituality. The fact that more and more of human life is established and understood without any reference to God forces the question of "why worship?" The prophetic rejection of "human religiousness" in the name of the Gospel forces the question from another angle. Yet all the while the "crisis of meaning" is related directly to the *absence* of living memory, story and ritual patterns in our lives; more specifically, to the absence of belonging to a community lived in praise of God. This situation demands that we regard Christian liturgy as *both* the expression of religious needs *and* the manifestation of a transcendent mystery of God in order to face the "crisis" squarely and honestly.

It is necessary to question the nature and significance of worship when it becomes disconnected from the realities of human existence. It is also appropriate to question whether certain ritual practices are Christian liturgy at all when they seem only to celebrate and to reinforce the cultural values of the time. In either case, we encounter a failure of faithfulness to the source and summit of Christian worship. Worship is something done in the world, but it is linked to the teachings and practices of the Christian life which are given their articulation and formative power to shape and redirect human beings in the world. The forms and the language must be faithful to the nature of God and provide fitting modes of communication for encounter and communion with the divine life. Determining the faithfulness and adequacy of Christian worship in a time of cultural shifts is not, of course, a simple matter. Learning to remember, acknowledge, praise and petition the God of all creation in a culture of romantic self-indulgence or cynical detachment and loneliness is indeed "counter-cultural." Worship without mystery and a sense of suffering is neither biblical nor redemptive.

One of the most helpful signs in the contemporary discussion of the meaning and point of worship is the recovery of the "roots" of Christian liturgy pointing back to the period of the early church "Fathers" known as the patristic period. The early church itself did not regard liturgy simply as an other-worldly "cult." Worship was a way of realizing and participating in the Kingdom of God, already come and yet to be fulfilled. So the "liturgy" (work of the people) was already something of the Kingdom of God manifest in the gathered community. My point is not to appeal to the early church's understanding of liturgy as an exhaustive norm for judging contemporary patterns and forms. Rather, it serves as a reminder that Christian worship was from the beginning something done in the world, and that prayer was "action" which involved the interaction of God and humanity.

In this sense the contemporary situation makes it easier for us to focus upon the essentials, though the problems of reform and renewal are delicate and complex. Worship is something Christians do together because it is our way of remembering, enacting and expressing our life unto God. But worship is also a characterizing activity requiring time, space, forms and people. Worship gives persons their life and their fundamental location and orientation in the world by virtue of language and gesture addressed to God. Worship gives expression to a story about the nature and destiny of all things. The story itself teaches us to regard all creatures in the world as God's.

The present situation calls for a rediscovery of the essentials. Reflection upon the continuities and the changes of worship and their consequences is therefore something foundational rather than peripheral. In thinking about the nature of worship in light of the foregoing, then, we do not simply "apply" an already systematized theology; rather, we are engaged in theological inquiry of the first order. For the language about God found in our theologies will have meaning and point only if the activities in which it is used to address God have meaning and point. The texts we sing and the musical forms we employ will flourish only so far as they faithfully serve the point of the singing.

2. Some Theological Fundamentals

Let us turn to some theological fundamentals concerning the nature of worship. Worship is corporate dialogue and communion with God. It is a corporate enactment by word, silence, rite and song of the community's memories of God so as to invite the presence and power of God to come to awareness. Born as response to the divine initiative, worship lifts up what is human to the transforming and sanctifying power and presence of God. It ascribes to God the honor due God's holiness, and brings human life to a new intensification before God. The worthiness of the Holy One calls forth praise, and confers a dignity and honor to those whom God has created. Such dependence and interrelationship are not external features of worship but are rooted and grounded in the very nature of the divine life itself. True worship acknowledges the One who creates freely, covenants and reaches to redeem with justice and compassion all creatures in the particularity.

Worship is always two-fold: it is the action of glorifying God and the sanctification of all that is human before God. Glorifying God and giving praise is itself a way of knowing the divine life. But this is precisely how human life itself comes to fullest truth and realization of what its own existence is: to discover and welcome the gift of creatureliness, and to sanctify time and place and every relationship. The cry of pain and the remembrance of suffering co-mingle with praise and are offered together.

The bewildering variety of historical types, both "liturgical" and "free," makes it obvious that human beings worship in and through a variety of historical and cultural forms. Worship is God-centered, yet thoroughly grounded in human life—it is theocentric and anthropological at the same time. Because it is directed toward God and its native idiom is the language of address, worship involves a certain shift of consciousness away from the mundane. To address our lives in wholeness to God demands a discontinuity with ordinary life as well as a continuity. This is one reason why every period of reform and renewal has stressed the need to recover in *fullness* the corporate memories of the church. In focusing upon and re-presenting the story of who God has been and has promised to be, we encounter anew what it means to be present in God now. This is not ordinary wisdom.

In Christian worship, joyful praise and thanksgiving are part of recalling what God has done in Christ. Worship is the communal action of presenting ourselves, in union with the universal work of Christ and all the gifts God bestows upon the human family, before the face of God. The very forms we employ in our prayers and songs of thanksgiving express this theological understanding. They are patterned after the Hebrew concept of *berakah*, the act of blessing God. Life is consecrated and brought to holiness by giving thanks to God for it. This understanding lies at the root of our contemporary ecumenical recovery of the theological character of all prayer.

The corporate memories of the people of God are contained in the Scriptures and in the living tradition of the church's teachings. Thus, the reading, singing and proclamation of the Word in the midst of the gathered community is essential. Neglect of the Word in its fullness has impoverished worship, even among those traditions who claim the Bible exclusively! The crucial element in the acts of remembering is the fresh reappropriation of God-with-us. It is theologically inadequate to merely "remember things past." Rather, as we claimed in the first section, the pattern of the texts and actions are to take us into the continuing and future-oriented redemptive history. In this sense, the celebration of the holy meal can never be mere remembrance, but must be a foretaste of the very Kingdom of God which is and is yet to come. But this remembering stands also as a prophetic rebuke of our self-serving local memory and forgetfulness.

Worship is something Christians do communally in response to God. It is done not just from religious duty or obligation (though this may be the "sociological" fact), but because it is the primary mode of remembering and expressing the Chrsitian faith and the whole story of God in human history. In the actions of re-presenting and entering into the reality proclaimed in the story of the Scriptures, worshippers articulate their fundamental relations to one another and to the world. This is, of course, an ideal view. We are all painfully aware that not everyone who comes to worship is shaped by this language and action. Not all who say the words and participate are fully formed. "Not everyone who says to me, Lord, Lord will enter the kingdom." This will always be a tension we must face.

But to speak of God and to address God in prayer means that we undertake a certain way of existing; it means we are to be disposed in light of the claims expressed in the symbols and stories of biblical faith. We shall turn to this point again in the next section.

A further word is in order about "givenness" of certain essential elements in Christian worship. Put most simply these "givens" are: the observance of time itself as a means of memory and sanctity, the rites of initiation (baptism –confirmation–first eucharist), the eucharist or Lord's Supper and the "divine office" or daily services of prayer. All other forms of worship are dependent upon the defining structures of worship for the main stream of Christianity through the centuries. In every age of reform and renewal, this basic "canon" helps to define the essentials once again. The church ignores their interrelation at its own peril. When they are neglected or obscured in their central significance, as has occurred so frequently in the history of Christian worship, Christian theology and spirituality suffer.

3. Some Basic Features of Worship for Spirituality

We have seen, in short compass, what some of the theological foundations of Christian worship are. But there is another way of looking at worship which has been implied all along in these remarks. Let us turn to the phenomena of the human actions involved in corporate prayer to see how certain patterns of human experience are both shaped and expressed there. These modes of prayer-action should also speak to some of the deepest needs in our humanity, as well as convey the very substance of faith.

Corporate worship is first and last "praising," "giving thanks" and "blessing God." This activity is, in the eyes of the world, utterly naive. It is speaking God's name in gratitude and thankfulness for God's very being, and for the world given to humankind. If someone gives another person a totally unexpected gift—fitted well to that person's delight and life—the primordial response is an unconditioned gesture of gratitude. Unless the world has made us fear that everything has a string attached, this form of thanking is absolutely fitting to the idea of God. It is also essential to our humanity. Insofar as worship is first and last speaking God's name in thanks and praise, it speaks to a deep human need. A life devoid of gratitude becomes incapable of receiving gifts, and eventually of giving gifts. Worship continually shapes us in naming God, thereby keeping an essential aspect of the concept of God in place: Source and Giver of life and world.

But worship is also recalling and retelling. Reading, singing and proclaiming the Word recalls who God is and what our story is. Huub Oosterhuis, author of *Your Word is Near*, has put this point well:

> When the bible prays, the whole of creation is listed and the whole of God's history with man is brought up again. When we pray, with the bible, we appeal to creation and to the covenant. We call God to mind and remind him who he is and what he has done. What God used to mean for . . . in the past includes a promise of the future, the promise that he will mean something for us as well, that he will be someone for us.[2]

Thus, recalling and re-presenting the story of God in relation to human aspirations, hopes and yearnings, becomes the occasion for discovery of true human identity.

Thirdly, worship is the acknowledgement of who we are in the sight of God. To address God, and *mean* what we say, is to encounter the truth about ourselves not known otherwise. Praying explores and continually reveals the difference between who God is and what we are. "My thoughts are not your thoughts, says the Lord." We are to be continually formed in the language of Isaiah in the temple: "Woe is me, for I am a man of unclean lips." Yet confessing and acknowleding our rebelliousness and forgetfulness before God also fits the human features of our life. Truth in the inward parts is also part of our song. This is a connection between the attributes of God's holiness and righteousness and our own status. Worship gives us time and space to discover and express who and what we are when we are in God's presence: saint and sinner, creatures of immense worth yet alienated from our source of life. If thanksgiving, gratitude and living memory are essential to our humanity, so too is confession and truth in the inward parts.

Finally, though by no means exhaustively, corporate prayer and worship is intercession. We are to pray for the world and its suffering. This requires looking clearly and honestly at the world as it is. In interceding for the hurt and darkness of the world, we identify with others and express solidarity with them. This aspect of communal prayer disposes us in compassion toward others. We are to hold the world in all its actuality, up to God. In this respect worship can never be an escape into "another world." Worship and ethics belong together, even though our lives characteristically tell a different story.

In these four ways, and in others not mentioned here, Christian worship gives us capacities and dispositions essential to true humanity. Glorification of God is its primary response, but in doing this faithfully, humanity is brought to truth and sanctity. Worship is the "work and service" of the people of God, responding in the language of praise, thanksgiving, remembrance, confession and intercession through time. We may think of it as a kind of rule keeping activity of the language and central symbols of the faith. In recalling who God is and who we are, we identify the world to itself as what it yet shall be under the reign of God. It is truly a song for the beloved sounded back to its Source in the life of God by the creatures who have ears to hear.

Do we not long for times and places of such freedom and mutuality? Does not the world cry out for times of rejoicing and weeping, of laughter, sobriety and hope? This is what living which is faithful to its divine and human vocation can be. It can never be reduced to what C. S. Lewis calls "detestable good fellowship," nor is it only an instrument of therapy and human enrichment. Yet surely the One we are called upon to seek and to praise desires to give such gifts to the children of earth.

Worship must so focus upon God as to shape and form persons in holiness and true humanity. Our reform and renewal of liturgies in various traditions are beginning to open this out for us. Worship that does not provide the worshippers with the language, action and song for expressing concrete human life unto God fails to be in "spirit and truth." Because this is so, an absolute *uniformity* in text and style is no longer desirable, just as it was not in the early church. But *unity* of praise and love is our earnest hope and prayer.

This point cannot be said casually. It is not an ordinary piece of information, nor is it a clever piece of theology. It speaks a mystery hidden from the eyes of the world, even in a "world come of age." It links the activity of worship with the mystery of God's hiddenness from the plain view, from the indifferent and passionless attitude toward existence. Worship is a time and space where through symbolic action God shapes and expresses us in such a mystery. It is a way of understanding. So we turn again and again to the ideal of that community lived in praise of God.

It was precisely to this community lived in praise of God and service to neighbor that Erik Routley's life and work kept calling us. The integrity of music in our worship, his writings will continue to remind us, depends upon our having understood the nature and function of worship and the living traditions of sung praise.[3]

NOTES

1 G. Dix, *The Shape of the Liturgy*, London 1945, *passim*.
2 H. Oosterhuis, *Your Word is Near: Contemporary Christian Prayers*, trans. N. D. Smith, New York 1968, p. 8.
3 A slightly different version of this essay appeared as a chapter in the author's *Worship and Spirituality*, Philadelphia 1984.

67

ALTHORP 9.10.10.9   1975

Thank you, Lord, for Twa-ter, Tsoil and 'air—

large gifts sup-T-por-Ving ev'-ry-thing that lives.   omit in v 5
                                                              For-

give our spoi-ling and a-buse of them: help us re-Tnew the

face of the earth!

Composed for Ecumenical Praise (# 78)

(c) Agapé

G. Schirmer Inc. New York   12 Staves   No. 5 - Printed in the U. S. A.

3

THE THEOLOGICAL CHARACTER OF MUSIC IN WORSHIP

Robin A. Leaver

One of Erik Routley's earlier books was *Church Music & Theology*, issued in 1959. In the final chapter he summarized his argument in four propositions:

(1) That the relation of service in which music stands to the church should be one of free and cheerful service, such is agreeable to the Kingdom, not of servitude.

(2) That the makers and performers of music in church must especially beware of the sins of pride and greed and the derived error of doing and thinking what is not conformable with good doctrine.

(3) That this "good doctrine" teaches us of the intimate relation between the Church and Christ, through his Incarnation, Passion and Resurrection, and is waiting daily expression in all forms of church behaviour, of which music is one form.

(4) That the criticism of church music in practice should proceed from the ground of doctrine, should avoid facile legalism, and should be constructive enough to encourage the good, before being repressive enough to ensure the avoidance of error.[1]

As in other matters, Erik Routley was shrewd enough to understand that church music is essentially functional and is therefore intimately connected to the theological framework within which Christian worship, work and witness operate. It is a theme that is touched on in one way or another in most of his books. Apart from his own book, *Church Music & Theology*, which he modestly described as "theological footnotes to musical criticism"[2] very little of substance has appeared in English on the subject. There are a number of articles and studies which have been published over the years,[3] but the most significant contributions to a theological understanding of music in worship remain the German studies by Brunner,[4] Kurtschenkel,[5] Schlink,[6] and especially Söhngen.[7]

The intertwining duet of music and theology form the substance of

Biblical theology. Although there is no specific chapter and verse in which is to be found a clear theological statement concerning the nature and function of music, there is nevertheless hardly a page of the Bible from which some musical inference cannot be drawn. Music is the accompanying counterpoint to the Divine message and in all the mighty acts of God music is never very far away. From eternity to eternity, from creation to judgement, from Genesis to Revelation, the sound of music is to be heard. At creation the "morning stars sang together." The people of God in the Old Testament were the singing church of the old covenant, whose responsorial art was begun with the Song of Moses after the birth of the nation in the exodus from Egypt. The birth of Jesus was accompanied by the song of the angels. And in the world to come all the redeemed will join together in singing the "Song of Moses and the Lamb". James Montgomery expresses it well in his familiar hymn:

> Songs of praise the angels sang,
> Heaven and earth with Hallelujahs rang,
> When Jehovah's work begun,
> When He spake, and it was done.
>
> Songs of praise awoke the morn,
> When the Prince of Peace was born;
> Songs of praise arose, when He
> Captive led captivity.
>
> Heaven and earth must pass away,
> Songs of praise shall crown that day:
> God will make new heavens and earth,
> Songs of praise shall hail their birth.[8]

As the Bible unfolds the records of the acts of God the continuous sound of music is heard. That continuity is broken only once in the silence of Calvary. However, even here it has to be recognised that silence is not mere nothingness but rather an active constituent in the structure of music and its performance.[9] "Someone has said that all history is point and counterpoint—two melodies running side by side—God's and man's. Alone one of them is always incomplete, even God's. He preferred to die rather than be without us. Taken together there is meaning and beauty in their rise and fall, their temporal dissonance which is resolved into final harmony."[10]

Music is therefore bound up with theology and theology with music. Thus, on the one hand, the theologian Karl Barth can frequently refer to the music of "the incomparable Mozart" in his *Church Dogmatics*. He asks,

"Why is it possible to hold that Mozart has a place in theology?", and answers, because "he did not produce merely his own music but that of creation, its two fold and yet harmonious praise of God."[11] On the other hand, Johann Walter, composer and first Lutheran cantor, could write that music is "wrapped up and locked up in theology, so that he who desires, pursues, and studies theology at the same time lays hold of the art of music, even though he may fail to see, feel, or understand this."[12]

The ideas of "pure" music, music for its own sake, music—whether classical or pop—with its own cultic following, are modern concepts which are totally alien to Biblical thinking.[13] For the Bible the art is essentially *Gebrauchsmusik*, music with a practical purpose.[14] Music and theology are interrelated and interdependent. The Bible is concerned with practical theology, the understanding and explanation of the interaction between God and man, and also with practical music, the accompaniment to that interaction. Theology prevents music from becoming an end in itself by pointing man to its origins—in the doxology of creation. Music prevents theology from becoming a purely intellectual matter by moving the heart of man to consider its ultimate purpose—the doxology of the new creation.

Thus when one considers the theological character of music in worship the approach must be through a theological understanding of worship and liturgy. But one must do so remembering that, in the metaphor of the Dutch theologian Gerardus van der Leeuw, the theology of worship is but one finger on the total hand of theology.[15] Church Music does not have an autonomous existence: it is music for worship and its theological dimensions and characteristics are therefore derived from a theological understanding of worship which takes into account the major *loci* of dogmatic theology.

There are a number of major theological studies of the content and context of worship one could take as a guide. There is Peter Brunner's profound study written from a Lutheran perpsective,[16] or Geoffrey Wainwright's more recent intriguing book which reflects the author's Methodism.[17] But we shall take the basically Reformed statement by Paul Waitman Hoon[18] as a basis four our investigation here—although he, like Wainwright, writes from within the experience of Methodism. There are two basic reasons for doing so: first, Erik Routley appreciated "the balance and richness of this quite remarkable work";[19] and second, it has one chapter, entitled "The Theological Character of Worship",[20] which is particularly appropriate for a consideration of the theology of music in worship. Much of what follows is written against the background of Hoon's chapter, but with variations and developments which draw out the significance for a theological understanding of music in worship.[21] The sections of Hoon's chapter can be conveniently divided into two main parts: the first has to do with ministry and the second with theology as such.

Music and Ministry

Hoon begins with three sections which consider the theological context of worship: "The Minister as Liturgical Theologian", "The Relation of Theology to Liturgy", and "The Theological Critique of the Category of 'Worship'." As we look at the ministry of music within worship we can usefully take those three sections, modify them, and draw out what is implicit in them.

The Minister of Music as Liturgical Theologian

The conduct of liturgical worship requires an overall leader, the minister, who is responsible for drawing together all the elements of worship to form a theological unity of praise, prayer, proclamation, and response. Similarly, music within the liturgy requires an overall leader, the minister of music, who is responsible for drawing together all the musical elements of worship to form a harmony of voices, congregational, choral and instrumental—a theological unison—in that unity of praise, prayer, proclamation and response. What Hoon has to say about the minister applies equally well to the minister of music. The musician who leads the music of the church at worship functions as a liturgical theologian. By his office "in a very real sense he is already a liturgical theologian whether he accepts the title or not, and the true question is how well he is discharging his task. One cannot even begin to inquire into worship·nor make a single decision about its planning or conduct without having to talk theology from the very first syllable . . . in dealing with worship the question is not the presence or absence of theology; rather, it is a question of how adequate one's theology is going to be."[22] The minister of music is not merely a good technician who produces nice noises at various points in the progress of worship. He is first and foremost a man of grace whose ministry arises out of his own commitment, faith and sense of calling to this particular ministry. His thinking and action in this calling will be fed by his own liturgical life and prayer within the gathered people of God.[23] The well-prepared church musician will not simply be a good performer who has studied composition,

50

Erik with Margaret and the children in Oxford, on the day of Priscilla's baptism, 1953

Singing from *Ecumenical Praise*, Bristol Chapel, 1978

On vacation, Lairig Gru, 1961

Nicholas, Patrick and Priscilla with Margaret, London, 1979

harmony and counterpoint, music history, and has a good grasp of choral leadership and knowledge of the repertory: he will also be a liturgical theologian, that is, someone who is aware of the theological functions of music within the worship of the people of God.

The Relation of Music to Theology

Hoon speaks about "the reciprocal relation between theology and liturgy"[24] and we need to speak about the reciprocal relation between theology and music. It is when the two are divorced that the problems arise. Cut off from its theological roots music in worship takes on the nature of music to entertain the congregation, mood music to create the right atmosphere, or, as someone has said, an "aural lubricant" to smooth the transition from one part to the next. But the opposite is also true. Theology without the music of faith becomes dry, soulless and brittle. "Melanchthon once said, parenthetically, that when the Church's music ceases to sound, doctrine will disintegrate; Bucer held that the Church is built around the hymn; and a Jesuit complained that Luther's hymns had damned more souls than all Luther's sermons put together! In fact, a study of the Church's liturgical music often provides a truer understanding of the Church's mind than a study of the formal writings of her theologians. If one would understand the Methodist doctrine of Holy Communion, for example, or the Puritan doctrine of *sola scriptura*, one can hardly do better than to study the hymns of Charles Wesley or Isaac Watts."[25] The Lutheran tradition has always understood clearly the interrelationship between theology and music whereas the churches of the Reformed tradition have had hesitations and reservations about making a close connection. Luther could say that "Music is an outstanding gift of God and next to theology,"[26] but Calvin was not so sure and gave only a limited function to music in worship.[27] In the seventeenth century this difference of approach gave rise to polemics between the two confessions. For example, an organ was set up in Nordhausen in 1658 with an inscription praising the right use of music but ending in a litany against Calvinist psalm-singing:

> Sound well all your pipes
> To glorify God alone,
> Fill, with your sounds,
> The Church, the house of the Lord,
> And also diligently rouse
> The mouths and tongues of the people,

51

That they with understanding,
And from the bottom of their hearts,
Sing the Psalms of David
And the spiritual songs
Of Dr Luther's composition,
Simply and without ostentation.
From strange melody,
From all false doctrine,
From Calvinistic screaming,
Lord, preserve us evermore.[28]

In more recent times Lutherans have seen that the issue is not one of polemics against other confessions but rather a question of basic theology. For example, Theodore Hoelty-Nickel has written: "Calvin was not entirely wrong when he said that music might be the tool of the devil. All the good orders of God can be misused, all the gifts of God can become a curse to the man who uses them wrongly. But God's intention is that we live our life on this earth within God's orders, and that means also that we live by and with God's gifts to men. Luther, therefore, was more right than Calvin was wrong when he considered music a means to glorify God and to drive Satan away. It all depends on whether we live in the kingdom of grace or are still under the Law and under condemnation. To him who is under the Law, everything is a testimony of death."[29] Music in worship is the language of faith, the response of the redeemed to the grace of God. If, as St Paul says in Romans 10.17, "faith comes from what is heard, and what is heard comes by the preaching of Christ," then music in worship must have a proclamatory function.

The Theological Function of Proclamation.
Here we part company a little with Hoon, but we do not stray that far. His section is entitled "A Theological Critique of the Category of 'Worthship'", that is, worship as the ascription of praise and glory to God which is his due. We prefer to use the term "proclamation", the declaration of God's glory and grace which meet us in the person and work of Jesus Christ. Music in worship thus has a prophetic function of forthtelling, proclaiming the Word of God. This is certainly the emphasis of the New Testament. What is implicit in the songs of Mary and Simeon is made explicit in the song of Zechariah, the *Benedictus*: "Zechariah was filled with the Holy Spirit, and prophesied, saying, 'Blessed be the Lord, the God of Israel, for he has visited and redeemed

his people . . .'" (Luke 1.67–68). The father of John the Baptist was filled with the Holy Spirit and prophesied, proclaimed in his song. St Paul has the same understanding of this prophetic, proclamatory function of music in worship. In Eph. 5.18–19 he writes, "be filled with the Spirit" [as Zechariah was], "addressing one another in psalms and hymns and spiritual songs, singing and making melody to the Lord with all your heart." Again this prophetic note is obvious and the parallel passage in Colossians has a similar thrust: "Let the word of Christ dwell in you richly, as you teach and admonish one another in all wisdom, and as you sing psalms and hymns and spiritual songs with thankfulness in your hearts to God." (Col. 3.16). Here the prophetic role is clear. Christians are to come to terms with the word of Christ and then proclaim it through music. Significantly, Martin Luther translated Romans 10:17 as "So kompt der glaube aus der predigt/Das predigen aber durch das wort Gottes' (which can be translated: "Faith comes from the sermon and preaching through the word of God").[30] Theologically understood, music in worship is akin to the preaching ministry in its liturgical setting. Its function is to proclaim the word of God to the people of God. Sometimes this is done through the single voice of the cantor or minister, sometimes through the combined voice of choir and instruments, and sometimes through instrumental music alone. And then there is that unique proclamation of the whole people of God when they join their voices in one, in psalmody and hymnody, as they proclaim their response of faith to God and give witness of that faith to each other. All the Church's great composers have understood the proclamatory nature of their art, that through it the eternal sound of God's grace focussed in Jesus Christ is made known and shared with his redeemed people. This was certainly true of Johann Sebastian Bach who in his cantatas and passions was concerned to preach the Word of God in Christ.[31] Such objectivity guards against anthropocentric worship which wallows in non-theological sentimentality and a kind of church music which tells us only about what we know already and does not challenge us with the dynamic reality of God's Word. When church music has lost this objective function of proclamation as the handmaid of the Word, then we see the result: Protestant worship becomes "flabby rather than holy, folksy rather than numinous, hortatory rather than adoring, feminine more than masculine, and one is not surprised that it often appeals to infantile elements in human personality."[32] But it is exactly at this point that the interrelationship between music and theology preserves the character of Christian worship: theology prevents music from assuming an independent role in the worship of the church. "If Christian theology is regarded by Christian theologians as a

53

theologia crucis, then church musicians ought to join the ranks of Christian theologians and regard church music not only as *ars musica* but more specifically as *musica crucis*. . . . The life and work of Jesus Christ is the great theme not only for the theologians, the preachers and teachers, but also for the musicians of the church."[33] It is just here that we need therefore to turn to the fundamental beliefs of the Christian faith.

Music and Theology

Hoon's chapter is concluded with four substantial sections: "Liturgical Integrity and Tradition," "Liturgical Integrity and the Doctrine of the Church," "Liturgical Integrity and the Doctrine of the Trinity," and "Liturgical Integrity Determined by Christology." Again, we can use them as a guide for our consideration of the theological character of music in worship, but we shall do so by reversing their order and adding another. It is a change of methodology rather than of theological substance since at the beginning of his chapter Hoon makes the following statement: "The primary category for defining the meaning of integrity therefore must be 'theological,' a term we construe to mean not merely 'the science of God' in the manner of classical theology, but rather, in the manner of the Bible, as referring supremely to the self-disclosure and self-communication of *Theos*, God, in the *Logos*, the Word, Jesus Christ."[34] The focus of theology is Christology. "Christian theology does not begin with God, but with Christ; not with creation, but with redemption. Only soteriology has entrance into theology."[35]

Music and Christology

It is significant indeed that the hymns detected within the text of the New Testament are Christocentric and Christological.[36] At the centre of the Christian faith there is Jesus Christ and at the centre of his life is the cross. In his mediatorial action of death and resurrection is the life of the church, the body of believers in him. And the Church of Jesus Christ ceases to be the Church if it looks for a way to God other than through him. It is just here that music, regarded as autonomous in its own right, can undermine the doctrine of redemption without which Christian worship becomes meaningless. There is a tendency to ascribe to music the ability to mediate between man and God, that somehow through the sound of music the soul of man is attuned to the heart and mind of God. For example, Alfred Pike states, "I maintain . . . that a transcendental conception elevates art to an exalted position of an intermedium between man and his God."[37] But "there is one mediator between God and men, the man Christ Jesus, who gave himself as a ransom for all" (1 Tim. 2.5–6), therefore, "for the Christian there is no redemption in art. There is redemption in Jesus Christ alone."[38] If church music claims the centre of the sanctuary it has displaced the centrality of Christ and has lost its distinctive mission within the life of the church. Historically that happened when the religious oratorio assumed its own importance and was performed for its own sake entirely free from the constraints of Christian worship. But, in the words of Joseph Gelineau, "in Christian worship the art of music is distinguished by the function it fulfils; its primary task is to be the handmaid of the words of the rite."[39] It therefore willingly accepts the role of servant to the Saviour, a function which is liberating rather than restrictive as it witnesses to the grace of God in Christ, who is both the glory of God and the glory of mankind. It is not without significance that many composers have accepted the daunting task of setting the passion of Jesus to music—quite literally the most *crucial* liturgical words in the life of the Church. There are many musical settings of the passion as it is recorded in all four gospels, from plainsong to the passions of Schütz, from Buxtehude's cycle of seven cantatas *Jesu membra nostri* to Haydn's *Seven Last Words*, from Bach's great passions to the St Luke Passion of Krzysztof Penderecki. This is quite literally *musica crucis*, music under the cross. The cross stands at the centre of the life of Christ but it also stands at the centre of the liturgical life of the Christian. The setting of the passion is performed on Good Friday as a prelude to the great Resurrection symphony of Easter Day. These three days between Good Friday and Easter Day stand at the heart of the liturgical church year. The seasons of Advent, Christmas, Epiphany and Lent work towards them and the great season of Pentecost works away from them. The church year is itself Christological in that the pre-Easter seasons, Sunday by Sunday, point directly to the important events of the life and work of Christ, from its beginning to its end and new beginning, and the post-Easter season displays in detail what it means to live in Christ. The whole of Christian dogmatics is to be found in the church year[40] and needs to be explored not only by theologians and preachers but also by church musicians and choir directors. This annual cycle gives us the opportunity to sing and play in psalms, anthems and hymns, Christological music which simultaneously proclaims the gospel of grace to the assembled congregation and also encourages from each member of the congregation the response of faith. "To sing well through the church year is to encounter new aspects of

Christ, for the church year is itself a profound Biblical and Christ-centred treasury."[41] And what is learned within the context of worship is carried over into all aspects of life which take on a Christocentric character. This is to be seen, for example, in the manuscripts of Haydn and Bach. At the head of his compositions Haydn invariably wrote "In nomine Domine" (In the Name of the Lord); Bach's practice was to write two letters at the top left-hand corner of his scores: J.J. = Jesu Juva (Jesus help me). Being centred in Christ opens up all the avenues of a theological understanding of faith and life—including music.

Music and the Doctrine of the Trinity

Through Christ we are brought into the family God and come to know God the Father; also through Christ we are given the Holy Spirit of God. "The doctrine of the Trinity is thus an inescapable frame within which all thought about worship must move ... The Trinity constitutes a basic morphology which cannot be violated if liturgical theology is to be Christian ... here, as elsewhere, the integrating reality is Jesus Christ ... For originally the Trinity was not a dogma of theology but a datum of experience, and the key to the meaning of the datum was Jesus Christ."[42] In many traditions worship begins with the words "In the Name of the Father, Son and Holy Spirit. Amen." It is no empty formula but a statement about the context of worship, as, indeed, it is a statement about the context of life. It is another, more defined way of saying "in him we live and move and have our being" (Acts 17.28). Significantly, in Bach's *Clavierüburg*, Part 3, in which the catechism chorale preludes are set in a context which implies a service of worship, the whole collection is introduced by the Trinitarian prelude, BWV 552/1, and followed by a group of nine chorale preludes, in three groups of three, in honour of the Trinity. The centre of this group of nine pieces is specifically Christocentric: "Christe alle Welt Trost" (BWV 673), underlining the important truth that Christ is the focus, key, and datum of the Trinity of God.[44] Two other clavier collections by Bach begin with pieces with Trinitarian associations. The first part of the *Wohltemperirte Clavier* begins with a simple prelude (BWV 846) which is a kind of musical meditation on the C major triad. According to music theorists of the seventeenth century the basic triad was a symbol of the mystery of the Trinity.[45] Bach appears to have known this and begins his systematic collection of preludes and fugues with a musical ascription to the Trinity. At the beginning of his collection of two- and three-part inventions the first piece begins with a series of nine notes, three groups of three:[46]

56

Similarly, Bach's pupil, Johann Ludwig Krebs, has at the beginning of his *Clavierübung* three settings of the Trinitarian hymn "Allein Gott in der Höh sei Ehr" and the first begins with a group of nine notes, three groups of three:[47]

The doctrine of the Trinity is the frame-work of Christian theology. It forms the substance and structure of the three basic creeds: Apostolic, Nicene and Athanasian. It is also the framework of Christian life as the believer lives his life created by the Father, redeemed by the Son, and empowered by the Spirit. It is therefore the framework for worship and music in worship, as the people of God assemble together to rejoice at salvation in Christ by using the natural gifts endowed by the Father and the sanctified gifts bestowed by the Spirit. Thus man, forgiven in Christ and renewed by the Spirit, uses the Father's created gift of music to proclaim, praise and pray. It is not surprising to find that most attempts to explain the relationship between music and theology are exercises in Trinitarian theology. Jay W. Wilkey uses the Apostles' Creed as a model for his Trinitarian approach to what he calls Theo-musicology.[48] Oskar Söhngen is perhaps more genuinely theological in his evaluation of music within the framework of the Trinity. At the risk of oversimplification, his view is that music is a gift of God in creation, and is therefore not the invention of man. Such an understanding should lead to theocentric rather than anthropocentric music. With Jesus Christ a new epoch of music has begun, the new song of redemption. Music is thus not merely theocentric: it is now Christocentric. The Holy Spirit, who calls the redeemed together, inspires the gathered congregation to respond and answer the Word of God with such words as "Lord, have mercy", 'Holy, Holy, Holy, Lord God of Hosts", "Glory to God in the Highest." Church music, which enables the redeemed to articulate their worship, is therefore both the work and instrument of the Holy Spirit.[49] Van der Leeuw is similar, except that he sees the doctrine of the Trinity as the framework for a theological understanding of the arts as a whole. For him dance and drama are to be found in the rhythm, movement and countermovement of God the Father's creation; word, picture and structure in the speaking, forming and new creation of God the Son's redemption; and music in the intangible, unseen work towards the end of all things in God the Holy Spirit's eschaton.[50]

Music and the Doctrine of the Church

The doctrine of the Trinity, however expressed, implies a people created by the Father, redeemed by the Son, and called together by the Spirit. Hoon writes: "worship is the Church's action before it is the individual's action. Because Christ is the true Celebrant, the Word can only be encountered by the individual through the Body of believers whom the Word has already encountered. Christ's service to his people precedes our service to him . . . Corporateness . . . is to be understood as the mutual priesthood of all believers, a concept vital for liturgical theology . . . It means . . . that every worshipper has the duty to act as priest for his fellow worshippers . . . and our Protestant task is not so much the abolition of the priesthood—as we are wont to say—as the abolition of the laity."[51] In principle we accept the doctrine of the priesthood of all believers but in practice we deny it. A phenomenological study of patterns of Protestant worship would undoubtedly have to conclude that we believe in the priesthood of the ministry, the levitical orders of choirs and musicians, and the largely passive role of the people who are nevertheless permitted from time to time to sing a few hymns and make a few responses. We use the term "congregation", which should mean the whole people of God assembled for worship, for those who have no specific function to perform, as opposed to the minister, organist, choir, etc. But theologically the congregation is comprised of *all* the people of God, whatever the individual functions may be. The priesthood of all believers means that all the elements of worship should serve the needs of the whole corporate body, and this includes music. As Hoon says later in his book, "music especially belongs to the people, and theologically the burden of proof rests on those who support the case for a choir separate from the congregation. *The congregation is the true choir*, and all music should be conceived within this principle."[52] The choir is not separate from the congregation, although for musical reasons it is desirable that its members should be grouped together.[53] But it is not its special place but rather its functional role that is of paramount importance. The choir, and instrumentalists too for that matter, should encourage, lead and develop the music of the total congregation. In practice this will mean restoring or developing the old *alternatims praxis* in which congregation, choir and instrumentalists alternate in singing and playing the stanzas of a hymn or verses of a psalm. It will mean extending the antiphonal style of responsorial psalmody where cantor/choir and congregation proclaim the Word of God to each other. It will also mean contemporary composers learning from the example of J. S. Bach who used the familiar chorale melodies, which were firmly fixed in the people's mind, without necessarily using an associated text, the most obvious example being the *Suscepit Israel* from the *Magnificat* (BWV 243). Rooted in the people's song church music functions in drawing the whole congregation together to voice its response to God's Word. But although rooted in the people's song our church music is not focussed on the gathered congregation: music is but the vehicle of the people of God at worship which is centred on Jesus Christ. He calls the church together: it is his Body. Where church music is performed in a way in which the voice of the total congregation is ignored and in a manner which denies the centrality of Christ it has ceased to be "Church" music. As Hoon says epigrammatically, "insensitivity to function makes worship stammer when it ought to articulate clearly."[54]

Music and Tradition
The doctrine of the church includes more than just the contemporary generation. It includes all the previous generations of the redeemed people of God. Again to quote Hoon, "present-tense or future-tense theologies cannot be permitted to stake out a monopoly on the doctrine of the Spirit."[55] We belong to an ongoing tradition and therefore the music of our worship should reflect this continuity. We thus sing the Old Testament psalms, New Testament canticles, ancient plainsong, old Greek and Latin hymns, as well as the great church music of earlier generations. Like those names listed in Hebrews 11, these composers of earlier generations, some known but others completely unknown, witness to us of their faith and commitment to Christ as we use their music in our worship today. But an understanding of the doctrine of the church informs us that our worship cannot be exclusively in the past-tense. The past needs to be actualized in the present and heard alongside the contemporary. The composer Richard Hillert expresses it thus: "For the parish musician tradition means more than simply an antiquarian preoccupation with the past. The basic concern is to make tradition, any musical tradition, meaningful in the context of worship. . . . A preoccupation with any one style . . . can inflict a passiveness into worship, relegating the art to the level of wall-to-wall music that no one listens to. Tradition is most meaningful when it is allowed to manifest itself in ever-renewing creative expression

59

—when it is carefully balanced with innovation. ... But like tradition, innovation can be used to excess. When a congregation is ... constantly assaulted with strange new idioms, the virtue of newness wears thin and is reduced to the level of meaningless novelty."[56] But whether the tradition is old or new it stands under the authority of God's Word for "tradition is a penultimate, not the ultimate, reality for worship, and it cannot take the place of the Word."[57]

Music and Eschatology

The music of the worship of the Church of Jesus Christ has its roots in the past, its blossom in the present, and its fruits in the future. Revelation 4–5 give us a preview of the music of worship in the new creation that is yet to be.[58] The *Sanctus* heard by the prophet Isaiah (Isa. 6.3), continues in our worship today and will still form part of the worship of the new creation (Rev. 4.8). The *Agnus Dei* of John the Baptist (John 1.29), which re-echoes in contemporary worship, will form the substance of the new song taken up by all the heavenly voices and the redeemed together (Rev. 5.12). This is the theological perspective of our contemporary worship. Therefore the church music of today proclaims the Word of God to the people of God and enables them to respond to that proclamation in faith and witness. This making of a joyful noise in the present is a further stanza of the hymn which the people of God have been singing through all the previous generations. At the same time it is also a doxological anticipation of the future. Thus the connection between music and theology is never solely theoretical and intellectual but always experiential and practical.

In the light of all this, some twenty years after he had offered an "interim conclusion" in the four propositions quoted at the beginning of this essay, Erik Routley withdrew the whole chapter when revising the book *Church Music and Theology* and wrote a completely new one. The revised study was given a new title, *Church Music and the Christian Faith* and the summary of the theological role of music in Christian life and worship was more simply and concisely expressed: "In conclusion," he wrote, "the theological judgements on musical decision I am pleading for are secondary to the greater concern of service to the church whose existence is in and through Jesus Christ. It is true, I trust, no pietistic platitude to claim that our music and our music making should aim at being conformable to a gospel which tells of a crucified and risen Redeemer, and which lays on us all the duty and delight of losing our lives that we may save them."[59]

NOTES

1 E. Routley, *Church Music and Theology*, London 1965[2], p. 108.

2 *Ibid.*, p. 8.

3 See, for example, O. Söhngen, "Fundamental Considerations for a Theology of Music", *The Musical Heritage of the Church*, Vol. 6, 1963, pp. 7–16; J. W. Wilkey, "Prolegomena to a Theology of Music", *Review and Expositor*, Vol. 69, 1972, pp. 507–517; C. Volz, V. Gebauer and M. Bangert, "Theology of Church Music", *Key Words in Church Music*, edited by C. Schalk, St Louis 1978, pp. 334–351. A. Pike's doctoral dissertation, *A Theology of Music*, Toledo 1953, is rather more philosophical and deals with the theological nature of music in the widest sense and not with the particular function of music within the theological setting of music in worship.

4 A. Brunner, *Musik in Gottesdienst. Wesen, Funktion und Ort der Musik in Gottesdienst*, Zürich 1968[2].

5 W. Kurzschenkel, *Die theologische Bestimmung der Musik*, Trier 1971. The weakness of this encyclopedic study is that it is too discursive and lacks a coherent structure.

6 E. Schlink, *Zum Theologische Problem der Musik*, Tübingen 1950[2]. Although quite brief Schlink's study deserves not to be overshadowed by the larger German volumes.

7 O. Söhngen, *Theologie der Musik*, Kassel 1967[2], which first appeared as "Theologische Grundlagen der Kirchenmusik", *Leiturgia. Handbuch das evangelischen Gottesdienstes*, edited by K. F. Müller and W. Blankenburg, Vol. 4: *Die Musik des evangelischen Gottesdienstes*, Kassel 1961, pp. 1–267.

8 J. Montgomery, *The Christian Psalmist; or, Hymns, Selected and Original*, Glasgow 1825[5], p. 455f. The hymn was first published in 1819; see J. Julian, *Dictionary of Hymnology*, London 1907[2], p. 1068.

9 See T. Clifton, "The poetics of Musical Silence", *The Musical Quarterly*, Vol. 62, 1976, pp. 163–181. There were, of course, occasions when man's answering counterpoint ceased (see M. Harvey, *Worship and Silence*, Bramcote 1975, p. 6f.), but these were mere pauses compared with the general silence of Calvary.

10 O. P. Kretzmann, in *Festschrift Theodore Hoelty-Nickel. A Collection of Essays on Church Music*, edited by N. W. Powell, Valparaiso, Indiana 1967, p. v.

11 K. Barth, *Church Dogmatics*, trans. and edited by G. W. Bromiley and T. F. Torrance, Edinburgh, Vol. III/3, 1961, p. 298; see also Vol. III/1, 1958, p. 404.

12 Quoted by O. Söhngen, *Festschrift Theodore Hoelty-Nickel*, p. 26; see also W. Blankenburg, "Johann Walters Gedanken über die Zusammengehörigkeit von Musik und Theologie und ihre Bedeutung für die Gegenwart", *Kirche und Musik. Gesammelte Aufsätze zur Geschichte der gottesdienstlichen Musik*, edited by E. Hübner and R. Steiger, Göttingen 1979, pp. 31–39.

13 E. Werner, *The Sacred Bridge*, Columbia 1959, p. 313: "To Biblical literature the idea that music is beautiful is evidently alien; music had its place in the ritual of the Temple, or it served as a spontaneous expression of an individual or a group, but it did not have any direct connexion with the 'aesthetically beautiful.' "

14 "Music is not so much a thing of beauty but an ethical force . . . In the Near East a special mood is attributed to each melody-type; conversely, each of these modes is capable of evoking in the listeners its specific ethos", ibid., p. 315.

15 G. van der Leeuw, *Liturgiek*, Nijkerk [1940], p. 9. The image is also used by Hoon (see note 18 below), p. 80.

16 P. Brunner, *Worship in the Name of Jesus*, translated by M. H. Bertram, St Louis 1968. It first appeared as "Zur Lehre vom Gottesdienst der im Namen Jesu versammelten Gemeinde", *Leiturgia*, Vol. 1: *Geschichte und Lehre des evangelischen Gottesdienst*, Kassel 1954, pp. 83–364.

17 C. Wainwright, *Doxology. The Praise of God in Worship, Doctrine and Life*, London 1980.

18 P. W. Hoon, *The Integrity of Worship: Ecumenical and Pastoral Studies in Liturgical Theology*, Nashville 1971.

19 *The Expository Times*, Vol. 83, 1972, p. 317.

20 Hoon, *op. cit.*, pp. 79–148.

21 Where my argument relies heavily on Toon the respective passages in his book are carefully noted below.

22 Hoon, *op. cit.* p. 80–81.

23 cp. *ibid.* pp. 84, 85.

24 *Ibid.*, p. 86.

25 *Ibid.*, p. 88.

26 WA Tischreden No. 3815.

27 Calvin was not as negative with regard to music as some of those who followed him; see C. Garside "The Origins of Calvin's Theology of Music: 1536–1543", *Transactions of the American Philosophical Society*, Vol. 69, Pt. 4, 1979, pp. 1–36. For discussions of the different approaches the sixteenth century Reformers made to the relationship of music and theology, see, for example, Söhngen, *Theologie der Musik*, pp. 17–112; R. A. Leaver, *The Work of John Marbeck*, Appleford 1978, pp. 47–65.

28 J. Schäfer, *Nordhäuser Orgelchronik. Geschichte der Orgelwerke in der tausendjahrigen Stadt Nordhausen am Harz*, Halle 1939, p. 33. On the Lutheran/Calvanist debate about the place of music in worship, see J. Irwin, "Music and the Doctrine of Adiaphora in Orthodox Lutheran Theology", *Sixteenth Century Journal*, Vol. 14, 1983, pp. 157–172.

29 T. Hoelty-Nickel, "Church Music and Theology", *The Musical Heritage of the Church*, edited by T. Hoelty-Nickel, Vol. 7, St Louis, 1970, p. 10.

30 *Biblia: Das ist: Die gantze Heilige Schrift/ Deudsch/ Auffs new zugericht. D. Mart. Luth.*, Wittenberg 1545, (facsimile, Stuttgart 1967), fol. cccxl recto.

31 See R. A. Leaver, *Music as Preaching: Bach, Passions & Music in Worship*, Oxford 1982 [in the United States: *J. S. Bach as Preacher: His Passions and Music in Worship*, St. Louis 1984].

32 Hoon, *op. cit.* p. 94.

33 W. E. Buszin, "Theology and Music as Bearers and Interpreters of the Verbum Dei", *The Musical Heritage of the Church*, Vol. 6, pp. 22, 23.

34 Hoon, *op. cit.* p. 79; see also pp. 119–120.

35 G. van der Leeuw, *Sacred and Profane Beauty. The Holy in Art*, translated by D. E. Green, London 1963, p. 328.

36 M. Hengel, "Hymn and Christology", *Studia Biblica 1978. III: Papers on Paul and other New Testament Authors*, ed. E. A. Livingstone, Sheffield 1980, pp. 173–197.

37 Pike, *op. cit.*, p. x; see also p. 9.

38 R. G. Pirner, "Instruments in Christian Worship", *Church Music 70:1*, St Louis 1970, p. 7; see also J. Uhde, *Der Dienst der Musik*, Zurich 1950, p. 25.

39 J. Gelineau, *Voices and Instruments in Christian Worship: Principles, Laws, Applications*, trans. by C. Howell, London 1964, p. 66.

40 See L. Steiger, *Erschienen in der Zeit. Dogmatik im Kirchenjahr: Epiphanias und Vorpassion nach den Evangelien*, Kassel 1983.

41 D. E. Saliers, "A Crucial Catechesis: Hymns and the Church Year", *The Hymn*, Vol. 34, 1983, p. 84.

42 Hoon, *op. cit.*, pp. 114–115.

43 See R. A. Leaver, "Bach's 'Clavierübung III': Some Historical and Theological Consideration", *The Organ Yearbook*, Vol. 6, 1975, p. 20.

44 At the heart of the *Credo* of the *B Minor Mass*, which both musically and theologically a statement of Trinitarian faith, is the *Crucifixus*, again emphasising the centrality of Christ and *musica crucis*; see R. A. Leaver, "Number Associations in the Structure of Bach's *Credo*, BWV 232", *Bach. The Quarterly Journal of the Riemenschneider Bach Institute*, Vol. 7, No. 3, 1976, pp. 17–24.

45 See, for example, B. V. Rivera, *German Music Theory in the Early 17th Century. The Treatises of Johannes Lippius*, Ann Arbor 1980, pp. 120ff.

46 See the facsimile edited by E. Simon, *Johann Sebastian Bach Two- and Three-Part Inventions*, New York 1968, p. 2.

47 See the Peters edition, No. 4178, edited by Kurt Soldan, p. 4.

48 Wilkey, *op. cit.* pp. 512–516.

49 Söhngen, *Theologie der Musik*, pp. 262–340.

50 Van der Leeuw, *Sacred and Profane*, pp. 328–340. See also the various essays under the title "Die Musik und die Trinität" by A. D. Müller in *Die Liebhaftigkeit des Wortes. Festschrift für A. Köberle*, Hamburg 1958, pp. 463–475; *Kirchenmusik heute. Festschrift für R. Mauersberger*, Berlin 1959, pp. 97–106; *Gestalt und Glaube. Festschrift für O. Söhngen*, Berlin 1960, pp. 172–180; etc.

51 Hoon, *op. cit.* pp. 103–106.

52 *Ibid.* p. 339.
53 Just where the choir should be grouped within the place of worship is a matter for debate, but suffice it to say that in practice the decision is largely based on aesthetic grounds rather than purely musical ones, and that the doctrine of the priesthood of all believers is rarely employed as a controlling principle.
54 Hoon, *op. cit.*, p. 225.
55 *Ibid.* p. 97.
56 R. Hillert, "Music in the Church Today: An Appraisal", *A Handbook of Church Music*, edited by C. Halter and C. Schalk, St Louis 1978, pp. 251–252.
57 Hoon, *op. cit.*, p. 102.
58 See L. Mowry, "Revelation 4–5 and Early Christian Liturgical Usage", *Journal of Biblical Literature*, Vol. 71, 1952, pp. 75–84; K-P. Jörns, *Das hymnische Evangelium. Untersuchung zu Aufbau, Funktion und Herkunft der hymnischen Stücke in der Johannesoffenbarung*, Gütesloh 1971; D. R. Carnegie, "Worthy is the Lamb: The Hymns in Revelation", *Christ the Lord* (details in note 36 above), pp. 243–256.
59 E. Routley, *Church Music and the Christian Faith*, Carol Stream 1978, p. 137.

MINISTRY OF MUSIC

Our Lord communicates his teaching by giving pictures of the kind of thing that happens in the Kingdom. These are illustrations of that to which his whole life was dedicated, since he was himself a picture of the Kingdom. On the one hand we have dozens of earthy yet profound parables which describe the ways of God with his people and the perverse ways of the people of God; on the other we have the "signs" in which God's personal presence and spiritual powers disperse devils, heal diseases, and paint a clear picture of what it is like when God's will is his people's delight . . . Three things emerge from this which artists have to ponder. First, the communication achieved by any work of art always has a content of transfiguration or thrill; we gasp, sigh, or exclaim, "How beautiful that is!" If that is all we do, the artist's purpose is not necessarily fulfilled; and conversely, if that is all the artist hopes to get from us, he is not doing his duty as an artist. Just as our Lord firmly resisted people's attempts to offer him empty admiration . . . so it is a meretricious artist whose chief thought is the admiration or reward he or she will receive . . . This is especially obvious in church music, for its purpose is to assist the believer in his journey towards God, not to attach him to the sensations of this world . . . A second consequence of our Lord's teaching is that when making a judgement one is not looking for avoidance of error but for creative energy. It is fair to say that we should look for what is best in the best music and celebrate that, rather than spend much time looking for errors in bad music and warning against that. Error must be identified, but that takes little time and can be disposed of briefly. Distinction must be celebrated, and that is mysterious and unanalyzable . . . Third, perhaps the most obvious point in the recorded teaching of Jesus is that in the Kingdom duty and delight meet. The first Adam destroyed and Christ, the Second Adam, came to restore a condition where what God wills and what delights his creatures is the same . . . A composer understands better than most the proposition that duty and delight can be the same thing.

Erik Routley, *Church Music and the Christian Faith*, Carol Stream, 1978, pp. 85–87

4

MUSIC AND THE PASTORAL MINISTRY: A PERSONAL VIEW

Ruth Micklem

How does one begin to try to write about Erik Routley? Each aspect of him was memorable: his music, his mind, his energy, his personality, his faith: each on its own would have made him unique, together they produced something almost impossible to convey to anyone who did not know him. Contributors of eminence in their own fields have written other chapters in this book. My role is different; not a musician, I write about music; not a pastor, I write about the pastoral ministry. I write for all the ordinary people whose lives were altered by Erik entirely beyond their awareness of what was possible.

In order to show what Erik did for me I must give some brief account of the material he had to work on. Musically, there was not much there. My sense of pitch was grossly defective. At first I did not, as a child, realize that I could not sing in tune. Then I began piano lessons in the mistaken belief that these would cause me to play as my mother did. I discovered that if I sang a tune I knew, without simultaneously playing it on the piano, I finished a long way from the right note. I worked on this quite hard and things improved. No-one, though, could say that I was well endowed by nature.

As a pastoral problem I was perhaps more promising. My parents were brought up with stern prejudice in different denominations. They decided not to influence their children towards either or indeed any denomination, so that when our evacuees in the war, who came from Glasgow, asked us whether we were Catholic or Protestant we did not know. We had been encouraged instead to approach all questions with open minds and assess situations as we went along, and these attitudes led towards independence. I chose in the end to be a Congregationalist because I had been taught to believe that personal responsibility was very important in Christian discipleship; and it seemed to me that one could not carry this out properly without the power to share in the making and executing of churchly decisions.

I was born in Scotland, where I went first to the local school and then to boarding school. While I was there the family moved to London. This meant that I had almost no London friends and all the others were remote. The church I went to in London was my chief contact with my new environment and meant much more to me as a company of people I could trust and respect than previous churches had done. I felt very happy to be part of it. I was beginning to realize that I was ignorant about denominations and their histories and distinctive beliefs but I had also learned something about the value of belonging to a group of Christians.

In this state I arrived at Oxford as an undergraduate fairly early in Erik's time as chaplain to the Congregational Society there, which called itself Congsoc. I was efficiently fielded by my college religious societies group, and became a member of Congsoc. I was naturally perfectly sure that I was unique in every part of my history, character and mental activity. I had to spend the next few weeks, even perhaps months, learning that almost every aspect of my experience or nature or peculiar abilities was duplicated by at least one other person. In some cases one person shared several of my peculiarities. It took me a little while to decide that I was delighted rather than resentful about this. Looking back now, I can see how privileged we were in that society; arriving eager, raw, full of ourselves, we found what amounted to a ready-made company of friends most of whom we would have selected for ourselves, given the time and the detachment, which were exactly the things we did not have. Time burns up with a fierce ardour for the undergraduate; life seems full of opportunity and choice, there are far more things to do than one can possibly fit in. Happy are they who find friends, the occasion for following their favourite pursuits and a sense of personal fulfilment all arriving together; not to mention just about enough time left over to do the work demanded by the course. And happy indeed are they who also find a counsellor in the background who invariably has time to listen if they want to ask questions. I deliberately don't say, to answer their questions; very often, I discovered, by the time the question has been honestly and carefully put the answer will present itself. I hardly need to say that the person through whom I discovered this was the chaplain of our society.

I don't remember at all the first time I met Erik. To some who met him in different circumstances and in later years this may seem surprising. To them I must present the nature of his role among us and how he filled it. He remained, as I think most of the best chaplains do, in the background. Now and then he preached, and this was normally electrifying even in those days when the idea of the celebrated preacher was not dead. I expect he appeared at the tea meetings on Sunday afternoons when speakers were heard and serious things propounded, but I did not, at least for the first year or so. I had a profound distrust of being told things about how I should behave, which was what I thought these meetings might be about. Sermons were different. Fortunately, for myself as for my acquaintances, some of this sense of my own superiority did gradually wear off. I think it had grown too large during the years when my parents were, quite rightly, insisting that we make up our own minds about life and its problems, having made sure that we had as much information as possible to go on first. Being the eldest in the family I invariably knew best. It can be difficult to draw the line between self-confidence and pride. This background may well have had a good deal to do with my distrust of Kirk Session, let alone the Pope ... Instead of learning wisdom on Sunday afternoons I attended the services at Mansfield College Chapel on Sunday mornings during term, and also turned up for the Sunday evening meetings in the tower room at Mansfield where anything between thirty and sixty students, almost all undergraduates, were regaled with readings from the works of Damon Runyon and the possibility that the Cona coffee machine might implode—we were reliably informed that it had done so at least once in the past, with amazingly interesting results. At these meetings Erik was usually to be seen. He was not usually to be heard. He would sit, smoking his pipe (in those days all the best people smoked, especially forward-looking nonconformists) and watching. He was always inscrutable, and this impression was formidably supported by the great difficulty of telling whom he was looking at. Every now and then one might hear the non-committal exclamation, "Hum". Then the pipe would take over again. It did not take long to become aware that a keen intelligence and vigilance, borne up by an alarming memory and a prophetic understanding of our natures, were at work on our behalf.

I am still not quite sure how it was that we so quickly came to know this. My case was slightly different from that of some of the others, because I became a Routley baby-sitter, on the strength of living nearby and also of claiming to like small boys, having one or two brothers who were still young enough to be "small boys" themselves. The gap between my youngest brother and the elder Routley son must have been five years or so, but my credentials were accepted, with dreadful consequences to the Routley curtains, which were distorted by merry infant games to do with hiding and witchcraft, and to the Routley easy-chairs, which I chose to reveal to the Routley offspring as potential substitutes for sophisticated gymnasium equipment. It is astonishing what varieties of somersault can be performed first from the seat, then over the arm, and finally, for the pre-Olympic gymnast only, over the back. (How did Margaret ever forgive me?) Through these not very creditable occasions I became, undeservedly, a friend of the family. Other people took different

69

routes to this friendship; none were excluded. Margaret told me not long ago that 70 students came to the farewell At Home in 1959.

Through his unquestioning acceptance of the good faith of all the members of Congsoc, which nonetheless went with a healthy doubt about the good works of some of us, Erik earned our trust; and in return he gave us the attention which an eager musician would give to the authentic original script of a new work by a great master. Indeed, to him we were precisely that; at the time it seemed to me that he treated us with a respect we did not deserve. This curious reverence was typical of the whole of Erik's approach to life. It was possible to lose it, if one could convince him that one had rejected one's own true potential. In such a case he would discard his own claim to dignity and do everything in his power to restore the imprint of the composer. As a rule the results were dramatically successful, as far as the outsider could tell; but sometimes it was impossible; and sometimes he simply got it wrong. We are all enjoined to be prepared to be fools for Christ's sake. For any conductor there are some musical works better left alone; the task of making the most of them should go to someone else, whose instincts and understanding are different. It is not always possible to tell in advance whether one can make sense of a new work, and in any case the minister does not have the same options as the conductor. The pain and the distress of trying and failing have to be suffered, sometimes over and over again. And yet he was never intrusive, publicly or privately; he did not plunge into other people's affairs unless they had become unbearably idiotic. He simply enjoyed life. Once, not long ago, I told him of a dinner we had given. 'Oh, *how* I should have liked to be a fly on the wall!" he exclaimed, almost capering with mingled glee and frustration. Until that moment I had underestimated the intensity of his interest in people, situations and relationships.

It must have been this interest which sustained him in circumstances which might well have destroyed lesser men. Each year, in those days, Congsoc took a week's holiday in the Lake District, staying in or near Seatoller House, which during the rest of the year catered for "Reading Parties", solemn, august, learned and quiet groups of serious persons. Mrs Cockbain, the chatelaine of the establishment, enlisted the aid of friends and neighbours and Almighty God when we came; thirty or so of us, most of whom disappeared for long walks during the day but came back, alack, early in the evening, with dozens of muddy boots, hundredweights of wet clothes, agonisingly high spirits, demands for baths (there were two bathrooms) and terrifying appetites. And after supper we sang. Erik was not invariably subjected to the rigours of this holiday; I dare say he would have survived even if he had been, but it must have been rather a trial in the evenings. Some of those present sang quite well, almost all sang quite loudly, and our repertoire was extensive enough to keep us going for two or three hours while also being sufficiently limited for one evening's diversions to resemble the next very closely. I remember, as who does not, the vision of Erik lighting his pipe by inverting it over the chimney of the paraffin lamp; it took quite a while, the odours were incomparable, and sparks flew. It was not easy to sing while this was happening. I do not seem to remember Erik himself joining in the singing much, but then the pipe perhaps provided enough entertainment, and he did have a cold on the holiday I particularly remember. The cold did not prevent him from enjoying the outdoor part of our activities. After a day or two I had the temerity to say I had been worried about whether he would be able to see well enough to cope with boulder-hopping, and now perceived I need not have had a moment's doubt. "I think it helps," said Erik. "One doesn't expect something that isn't there". The other day I was listening to a lesson from Romans. "Now to see is no longer to hope," I heard. Immediately Erik was before me. A great many things are possible if approached with perfect faith and hope, no doubt, no inhibitions, no resentments.

On another day, nearing the top of Lord's Rake in ice and snow, I was feeling sorry for myself, exhausted, practically crawling up in spite of the tricounis which I had long saved up for, triumphantly acquired and finally attached to the soles of my boots, and which gave a most excellent grip in those conditions. I paused for breath. Erik, gently swinging his stick, wandered peacfully up, like a man going upstairs. "What a place! What a place!" he said, looking round. I caught myself muttering, "It's not fair". Well, of course life isn't fair; but for Erik this was not a problem. He did with cheerful zeal everything that was put before him. The natural athleticism inherited by his somersaulting sons stood him in good stead in the Lakes. All these things about him fell into place in the attitudes we in Congsoc had towards him and in what he was able to do for us. One couldn't help respecting someone who was so obviously ready to take things and people as they were, and who yet was instantly on the alert if they put a foot wrong, either to their own danger or to someone else's. I remember him saying once, "He should have married her". It sounds like a line from a corny play, but what "he" had done was only to allow "her" to care too much. The remark was made years after things had changed, and all of us knew all that was to be known. I think it was almost the only time I heard Erik deliver what amounted to a condemnation of someone's behaviour; at the time he had been, as far as any outsider knew, completely silent.

His other role for Congsoc students was at first glance absolutely opposite. Instead of being visible but silent, he was invisible in the organ loft but causing a considerable, if not a tremendous, volume of sound. Where in other circumstances he waited to see what we might do, as musical director he decreed our doings, and what is more told us exactly how the thing was to be done; not indeed without reference to our capabilities, though often with very little to what we previously imagined our capabilities to be. It must have been only the least thoughtful of us all who did not soon come to see that what was really going on was more than this. We were being taken on by him in a joint enterprise in which we were all the instruments by which God was making known his joy, his praise, his promises. "Ye servants of God, your master proclaim"; not by saying, "The Lord will provide," and making sure that he does by giving him a helping hand towards yourself, but by putting yourself entirely at his disposal, with all your senses awake, all your will ready, and waiting and working in as much obedience as you can possibly muster.

For me, this particular experience began when Erik unexpectedly arose one Sunday evening through the clouds of smoke and steam in the tower room at Mansfield and made this announcement: "I should be interested to see in the chapel at a suitable time all the following persons; excellent soprano singers; superb basses who have been assured by their choirmasters that they are indispensable; altos, either experienced or willing to have a try; and anyone who has ever dreamt that he might conceivably one day be able to sing tenor". This elegantly calculated invitation produced a choir of about eight sopranos, six altos, four tenors and six basses. I, having once or twice had the good fortune to find myself in chapel sitting next to someone who sang alto really well, asked her whether she would mind if I came and sat beside her. I also asked her whether she thought Erik would be sorry if I did come. "He will let you know if you aren't needed," said she. Later on she even managed to discover a note she said she could not hit and which by some strange chance I found easy, so even my dignity was saved. I thus embarked upon a course which took me through unknown country and taught me things I had not known were there to be learnt. I found in the end that I was singing not because of pride in my own ability, but because in our hands lay the opportunity to do something for other people which would tell them something not about us but about God; there, at that moment, we were putting our whole humanity into proclaiming the Creator who had made us what we were. We were proclaiming him through music written by others in other times and in alien circumstances; we were accompanied by an organ made by a number of other people, and tuned and maintained by yet others; we had practised together, listening

72

to each other, thinking about how we had been told to make this music carry its message most effectively. We were at the same time less ourselves, because we were not thinking about ourselves as separate individuals, and also more ourselves, because together we were achieving more than we could separately.

It was after this first carol service that a friend of mine said, "That was the most beautiful thing I have ever heard". That this should have been said about something in which I had had a part, however small (humming the alto line as quietly as possible, I seem to recall) filled me with a very great awe. It had not occurred to me that doing a thing for other people, with other people, and under the instruction and training of someone else, made one more, not less, important. Looking back I feel I must have been almost incredibly naive. When I consider the thought again, I realise that it is one which can very easily be lost. Which of us really considers himself *more* important, valuable, significant, because he is a member of such and such a church (let us assume, a small and unheard of church) than because he is a graduate, gives away large sums of money, swims for his county, is financial adviser to a powerful company?

I also learned that religion is essentially about joy. Heaven is sound and silence, hell is noise; making music to God on earth is joy; religion, the ritual practice of worship embodying one's belief, is nothing if no part of it captures in time what it looks for in eternity. One can look at something beautiful, a sunset, a building, a painting, and know joy; but visual arts are timeless and therefore cannot be bound into time at one's bidding. Dance, drama and music make time their servant; they use time, and by harmony and balance and design can make time into part of eternity not only for their witnesses but also, and perhaps even more, for those who are necessary for their very existence, the finite creatures who commit themselves to the presentation of the composer's vision. The musician, however humble, is a slave of the infinite. Milton, who knew that "The mind is its own place, and in it self/Can make a Heav'n of Hell, a Hell of Heav'n", also transferred from his own experience to that of the earliest musician in the Bible his understanding of the organ player

who with volant touch
Fled and pursued transverse the resonant fugue.

Here is the power whose slave pants with the desire of the pursuit, and also flees the hound of heaven. Music can impose heavenly order, justice and perfection on all who seek; it can overcome the senseless cruelties, the

73

barbarities, the meaningless discrepancies, interruptions and follies which forever seem to be trying to make a nonsense of our lives. Danger! *Music* does this? Is music then equal to God? Is this the joy the Puritans so greatly feared? If we feel like this about music is it going to get between us and God, or worse, take the place God should occupy in our lives?

Of course we began to ask Erik these questions. I expect we went on doing it, generation after generation of us; and he went on and on patiently answering; yes, music can be wrong; lascivious pleasing of a lute, yes, well, anything, any art form, can do what you want it to. People will always go on being led astray by what seems to them good in the fashion of their time; look out, said Erik—some of it *is* good; nearly all of it has something to say, too, if you'll just listen. Now: listen to *this*: "O Saviour of the world" (Goss). Awful, but it's doing what it sets out to do well, and you are going to sing it, and make it sound good, and enjoy it. Somewhere in this is what this sort of music *ought* to be about, and *that's* what you are going to sing.—And we did.

We sang for several other special services. None was better than that very first one. While we were practising for the Christmas carol service in 1951 Erik spent more time than usual walking up and down between the sopranos and altos, over whose shoulders the tenors and basses could, I imagine, also be heard. My thought was not chiefly for them; I believed that the moment of truth had come, and I was about to be thrown out, possibly with one or two others whose faults I had naturally not discerned. The case was otherwise. After the practice Erik asked eight of us, two from each discipline, to remain with him to hear something to their advantage—"Well, perhaps not". It turned out that he was to provide an octet of singers to perform selections from the new hymn book, *Congregational Praise*, which was to have a publication luncheon a week or two later. "But," I protested to him, "I can only do it because I stand next to X and sing what she does." "Quite," said Erik.

I spent a long time thinking about this response. The implication must have been that with the exception of X we were all much of a muchness; my sole advantage lay in having had to learn about pitch almost from tone-deafness and never having lost awareness of my shortcomings, so that, knowing I was still bad, I never ceased to try to do better. I should also add that I did again ask the other altos whether they would like my place; they all said they would prefer to remain where they were.

I had always been bad at games at school, and had tried something of the same recipe. It did not have quite the same effect. I listened carefully to what I was told to do, I watched others doing it; I did not become able to do it myself. I did become rather a good coach, and was given responsibility for training others to move from the third to the second house team, a promotion I myself never achieved.

In due course I worked out the difference between games and singing; in games it doesn't really do to be following someone else's example precisely at the moment of action, in singing it does. Both can provide patterns for our behaviour in the rest of life. It sounds like a children's address. At the time it was a kind of revelation. Joining in making music had for some curious reason enabled me to re-evaluate my role in games. I realised that what one learnt from other people was not how to be like them but how to assess one's own capacities and not reject any possible means of contributing.

By the time I came down from Oxford my musical understanding had advanced considerably. I knew that there was a difference between music as an expression of sheer high spirits and music intended to glorify God. Our singing in the Lake District may have been to God's glory, but that was not because it was good music; it was because it was our means of expressing our rejoicing in our fellowship, our health and happiness and all we had gained from the majesty and challenge of the hills and the elements. In Mansfield our singing, and all the music, particularly Erik's voluntaries, were another matter. In those, we were trying to use what powers we had to express something about God; we were making an attempt, however feeble and less than perfect we knew it would be, to do something in God's own terms; to pay back to him, as it were, at least a shadow of an acknowledgment of our awareness of what he is like. It had to be, musically, the very best we could do. Nothing casual or spontaneous would suffice. God is not, in his dealings with us, casual and spontaneous; he is eternal, unchanging, perfect. To try to make a fraction of our small span of time correspond for a moment to his unchanging perfection was a project daunting enough to quell the stoutest spirit; but to do nothing at all would have been worse.

Trying to make sense out of these thoughts, I moved out into the bleaker post-Oxford world. I had friends with whom I sang for fun. I pursued one or two ideas about religious music. I became more closely involved with my local church. I did not have very much contact with Oxford, but my minister was a musician and heard some of the things I thought, and added some fortifying ideas of his own. A certain amount of drama, non-musical for the most part, took place in our church. All the time I remembered, and went on trying to understand, that for some people music makes more difference to life than almost anything else; more than theology, more than nature, even, perhaps, in some ways, more than their relationships with other people. I tried to understand better the Anglican emphasis on the musical parts of their services, and to reconcile the emphasis on self-sufficiency I had grown up with and the needs of the rest of the worshipping community. All in all, I think I was not ill prepared for the possibility of finding myself married to a minister for whom music was half the breath of life.

When Caryl and I became engaged, Erik and Margaret had known Caryl for at least ten years and me for about five. They wrote enthusiastically, "How often we have said to each other, 'If only it had been Caryl and *Ruth*, or, indeed, Ruth and *Caryl*.'" This endorsement of our intentions seemed to add the final touch of rightness to our plans. We knew it was a good idea; if such previous winners in the game also thought so, then there was no room for doubt at all.

We kept in touch with Erik and Margaret after we were married. The minister of a church needs a minister himself; if he has none, it is a very lonely business. Erik was in London from time to time, and often spent a night or two with us. Music came into the conversation. Our family must have grown used to the idea that when ministers met music was discussed; it could not be separated from their way of life. There was seldom time to listen to it while he was there; it could be referred to, and later investigated. When people actually met face to face there were other things to be gone over, details and histories and plans, sorrows and complications. Allusions and assumptions came into it and shortened the time necessary to make things clear; not everything had to be spelled out. We sometimes worried that our children might feel left out in these exchanges; we need not have. Either we had related the background so often that they knew it all, or what was said made what was implicit quite clear if one knew anything about music or the people who were talking. When it came to the proof and we were on holiday in the north, and so in a position to arrange a day's meeting with whatever Routleys were about, there was no problem; our children were highly offended by the idea that they might want to stay at home for the day. "They are our friends too, you know," they said. And we realised with great delight that they too experienced through Erik and Margaret something of indefinable value which was by no means to be neglected.

All this had far-reaching effects. Music laid its hand upon the church we were in, and with the thought of Erik in mind we encouraged it as far as we could. All sorts of things happened; once we had an evening including J. S. Bach's "Wachet Auf" cantata with oboe obbligato, and once we had most of the student strength of Trinity College, London, in the gallery, blowing trumpets, banging drums, singing, playing violins, and generally giving more glory to God than they knew, in the works of Monteverdi and others. Such

76

moments, I feel sure, are as good for the performers as for the audience, whom indeed on this occasion they outnumbered.

Perhaps music and communion have a profound affinity. In the very notion of bringing things into harmony there is the implication that everything is bound together in some sort of fundamental unity. Perhaps, if we all paid enough attention to music, our perception of reality would be simpler and more acute. There is so much noise in our lives that we may be tempted to overlook the importance of sound. If we listen carefully and do not allow ourselves to be overwhelmed by the flood, there is truth to be heard. For Erik accuracy of listening, the pinpointing of the value of each sound, was supremely important. When he heard a chord, the tonal quality of each part of it was completely clear to him; and the spacing of sounds in time and the kind of silence that separated them were as significant as the sounds themselves. The tempo of the music continued exact and uninterrupted. As a listener, he gave the speaker his perfect attention; his silence and his concentration were at least as important to those who knew him as his words and his knowledge of music. And yet he could laugh; that inimitable, that irrepressible, that incomparable laugh, must have meant as much to his friends as anything. It was like the moment when the trumpets in *The Messiah* respond to the words "The trumpet shall sound". And the dead shall awake. Like John Peel's "View Halloo", Erik's laughter might well have awakened the dead; the dead of soul, the conventionally suffocated, the bored, the dreary, those who knew it all already. The accuracy of his attention to every possibility of a musical score was matched by his attention to the pastoral needs of his flocks; his silent listening, his galvanic reactions, his unlimited willingness to share his hope and faith. Everything in him seemed tuned to a fundamental consistency which embodied both music and eternity. Certainly this consistency was what we came to turn to in Erik. He was like a perfect bell—incapable of giving a false note. Not everyone will like the sound; it will be too loud for some, too smooth for some, too deep for others; "It gives me wrong vibes," you might say. But in itself it is totally consistent and complete, no room for argument.

Once, when Erik was spending a day or two in Oxford, we were talking about dreams. "If a man's dreams are all right," said Erik, "you can be pretty sure that the man himself is all right too." My goodness, I thought, if that is the test then don't we all fail? So I asked him whether he ever had bad dreams. "No, I think not, no, I don't remember ever having bad dreams," he replied. I ought not to have been astonished. I should have recalled, "If thine eye be single, thy whole body shall be full of light". Erik was the living, walking, breathing evidence of this. And it was this quality we all turned to when we

77

needed help. As it happened, Erik was at hand on both the occasions when our family most needed help. At first we thought, well, what has he said to help? Then we realised that when we really gave our minds to what had been said and not said the answers were all there. The eternal harmony rang out supreme.

Caryl is now to some extent Erik's successor as chaplain to students of the Reformed tradition at Oxford. The whole operation is inescapably shot through with the memory of Erik. What we do is founded on what he did, though it could not be readily compared. There was something about Erik that reminded one of a top spinning so fast that it is said to have "gone to sleep", since it can no longer be seen to be moving at all. Doing so much so fast and with so little shadow of turning, Erik was bound to be consumed early by the zeal of his master's house. We who remained so shocked and deprived had been deceived by the hints of the eternal that hung about him. Could longer days have said more?

I myself feel that I have striven at length to convey something about Erik but have in the end said no more than I did in the first hours after he died, when these lines came to me:

Where he lived, angel trumpets summoned to laughter:
Swift keen intelligence danced and gripped:
Mountains and valleys rang with the joy of their Lord:
Humility and certainty walked hand in hand.
In that world, faith and music and understanding built the archway
Where love, the utterly unexpected bonus, was the keystone.
"This is all so much more than I deserve, and isn't it *good*," he said;
And through that archway he would lead all who could even begin to try
To a land richer and fairer than they had known.
In that country I was usually a bewildered stranger
All too ready to return to my own, my duller, plain.
But somehow this day-to-day world where I am so familiar
Seems strange and empty now
Since he can never return to disturb it again.   © *Copyright 1982 Ruth Micklem.*

Yet the very fact that these lines stand on this page deny what was prompted by the first moments of shock. We shall miss Erik all our lives, but those lives have been irreversibly altered and elevated by our friendship with him. Every time now when we hear music performed by people expressing their longing for God, Erik is with us; he cuts us down to size, he restores our perspectives, he gives us again the sense of the immanence of the eternal verities. He will sing in our hearts for ever.

78

5

TWENTIETH CENTURY AMERICAN CHURCH MUSIC

Alec Wyton

The diversity of style and variety of standards in musical leadership in the churches of the United States poses a challenge in an assessment of the development of liturgical music. Given the size of the country and the diversity of denominational worship, no one composer would have had the influence in America that Ralph Vaughan Williams had in the church in England. But Vaughan Williams had an American contemporary in Charles Ives (1874–1954) who remained largely unrecognized until fairly late in his life. His music is dense in texture, polyrhythmic and sometimes polytonal and he took great delight in incorporating gospel hymns and other folk music into his orchestral music. He wrote four symphonies and a good deal of chamber and piano music and songs and some striking settings of psalms and other choral works. His setting of Psalm 90 is accompanied by organ and bells and makes exacting demands upon the singers. Psalm 67 has the sopranos and altos singing in C while the tenors and basses sing in G-minor. These works are performed with increasing frequency by churches with skilled leadership and they have influenced and continue to influence younger composers. Ives, in his technique, anticipated what composers such as Stravinsky developed so effectively in the twentieth century. Now some thirty years after his death, Ives is regarded as America's first "great" composer and perhaps our greatest composer to have lived to date.

Leo Sowerby (1895–1968), a contemporary of Herbert Howells, like Howells, after early years as a composer of symphonic, chamber and solo instrumental music and the first winner of the American Prix de Rome in 1921, devoted himself almost entirely to the writing and teaching of church music. He was, for some thirty years, the director of music at St James' Cathedral in Chicago and taught at the American Conservatory. In the last years of his life, he moved to Washington and became the first Director of the College of Church Musicians at the Cathedral there. He was active in workshops throughout the country, notably at Evergreen, Colorado where he spent a part

79

of every summer at a church music conference and musicians flocked to study with him. He was for many years a member of the Joint Commission on Church Music of the Episcopal Church. At his death, Sowerby left a large body of splendidly crafted choral and organ music—perhaps not as gracefully conceived vocally as Howells' but with a rich, dramatic color and exciting sense of climax. His cantata, "Forsaken of Man" (1940) is a deeply moving Passion for soloists, choir and organ. It is laid out traditionally with choruses, recitatives and arias and maintains a sustained intensity with rich harmonic color. Of his many anthems, "Now There Lightens Upon Us a Holy Day-break" for Epiphany is especially characteristic with its rich chromaticism and soaring melodic lines. Sowerby wrote scores of anthems and settings of the Prayerbook Canticles and Eucharistic Texts. There are those who feel that his earlier works are more significant than the later ones and certainly his music seemed to become less chromatic in the 50s and 60s. Of his large body of organ music, the Symphony and Suite are landmark works in the 20th century American repertoire of organ music.

In the next generation of mainstream composers, Daniel Pinkham (born 1923) has written steadily for the Church. Pinkham studied at Harvard and his teachers included Putnam Aldrich, Wanda Landowska, E. Power Biggs, Nadia Boulanger, Aaron Copland, Samuel Barber and Arthur Honegger. His output includes many works for orchestra and chamber music ensembles and dozens of cantatas and choral works with sacred texts. Particularly striking are his wedding cantata for soprano and tenor soloists, two horns, celesta and strings and his Christmas cantata for chorus and two brass choirs. In the 1960s he began writing works with prepared electronic tape and his "In the Beginning of Creation" is especially effective as the voices of the singers weave in and out of some unearthly sounds realized on a synthesizer. He has also written effectively for choir with guitar.

Ned Rorem, an exact contemporary of Pinkham was born in Richmond, Indiana. His music has been strongly influenced by his study with Virgil Thompson and Aaron Copland. Early in his career he spent five years in France and his lyrical style is surely influenced by the music of Satie and Poulenc. Many consider Rorem to be America's finest art song composer, but he has written in all forms, and his chamber music is especially appealing. The significant outpouring of choral and organ music, especially during the late 1960's and throughout the decade of the 1970's, has caused his name to appear on an increasing number of church service bulletins and concert programs.

In addition to his music, he has written several books which give us more than a glimpse into his personal life. His music would cause one to regard Rorem as a person with strong feelings and his books more than confirm this assumption.

Rorem's setting of the hymn text, "Sing my soul, his wondrous love," is one of his first choral works to be sung in church. It is a straight forward setting of the text and could be considered a lyrical part song, almost as simple as a hymn tune. This work is now an established part of the American choral repertoire.

His "Three Motets" on texts by Gerard Manley Hopkins was commissioned by the church of St Luke's in the Fields in New York City, and when performed as a choral suite could be regarded as a short but major choral work. Each motet is often sung alone in services as an anthem. Motets one and three have a demanding organ accompaniment; motet two is another example of an unaccompanied lyrical part song.

Many of Rorem's choral works are settings of classic or contemporary poetry, but he has set several liturgical texts in recent years. Two texts from the 1979 *Book of Common Prayer* of the Episcopal Church have been included among his choral works written during the early 1980's. His setting of the canticle, "Surge illuminare" ("Arise, shine for your light has come") and of Psalm 146 "Hallelujah! Praise the Lord, O my Soul!" are exciting works with brilliant and highly rhythmic organ accompaniments.

Rorem considers himself a non-believer and this is clearly documented in an article which he wrote for the January, 1973 issue of *Music* (now *The American Organist*). His music, however, transcends his rational prose, and in many of these choral and organ works we discover music which speaks strongly and eloquently for and to the twentieth century Christian.

Lee Hoiby (born 1925) has written sparingly but brilliantly. He studied at Mills College with Egon Petri and at the Curtis Institute with Gian Carlo Menotti. He has written several operas and a number of orchestral and choral works as well as chamber and piano music. Hoiby's "A Hymn of the Nativity" (1960) is a brilliant short cantata for soprano and bass soloists, mixed chorus and orchestra based on writings of Richard Crashaw. Of his works for choir and organ, "Let This Mind Be In You" and "Inherit the Kingdom" are deeply moving, fairly conservative in harmony but with strong melodic line and good climaxes.

Of composers nurtured in the Church, Richard Dirksen (born 1921), Lloyd Pfautsch (born 1921), Daniel Moe (born 1926), Ronald Arnatt (born 1930), Calvin Hampton (born 1938) have made significant contributions to liturgical repertoire. In each case, the composer has been associated with a

81

large church, cathedral or college choral program where his works have been adapted to the needs and skills of the community. Richard Dirksen has been associated with the Washington Cathedral for many years and is now the Organist, Master of Choristers and Precentor. Many of his works are on a large scale for voices, organ and other instruments such as "Hilariter", an exuberant piece for Easter, "Christ Our Passover" and the Three Canticles he wrote for the American Guild of Organists' convention in Washington in 1982. On a smaller scale, "A Child My Choice" is a provocative Christmas piece and his hymn tune, VINEYARD HAVEN, written for the installation of the Most Reverend John Allin as Presiding Bishop of the Episcopal Church in 1974, was described by Erik Routley as one of the greatest hymn tunes to have been written in the second part of the twentieth century.

Lloyd Pfautsch has, for many years, been the head of the choral program at Southern Methodist University in Dallas, Texas. His very moving "Invocation" is a setting of a well known text of Reinhold Niebuhr whose vocal lines match the flow of the text and whose accompaniment is reminiscent of Bach. Another characteristic work is "The Temptation of Christ", which is a setting for soloists and choir unaccompanied of the first eleven verses of the fourth chapter of St Matthew.

Daniel Moe has been head of the choral program in a number of prominent schools of music and has written extensively for choirs and instruments. Particularly significant is his "Worship for Today", an Ecumenical Service which was commissioned by the American Guild of Organists for its convention in Colorado in 1968 with a text by Don and Nancy MacNeil. This service involves the whole congregation as well as the choir and organ and in a very real sense is a reflection of the post Vatican II emphasis on the involvement of all people in public worship. The work is divided into The Gathering, The Acknowledgement, Hymn of Praise, Confession, Absolution and Thanksgiving, Hymn, Offering, Hymn, Intercession, The Word, Commentary, Motet, and Dismissal. Erik Routley said of this setting, "I feel that nobody that is present at it can fail to be inspired by its combination of seriousness and joy."

Ronald Arnatt was born in England and came to Washington at the age of sixteen where he studied with Paul Callaway. While still in his teens, he won the annual anthem contest sponsored by the Church of the Ascension in New York. He has composed steadily throughout his career and his output includes anthems, settings of canticles and of the Eucharistic texts, hymn tunes and organ music. A fine example of his work is his setting of the text, "Blessed City, Heavenly Salem" for choir with trumpet obligato. The fine contrapuntal

Conducting hymn-singing, Bristol Chapel, 1978

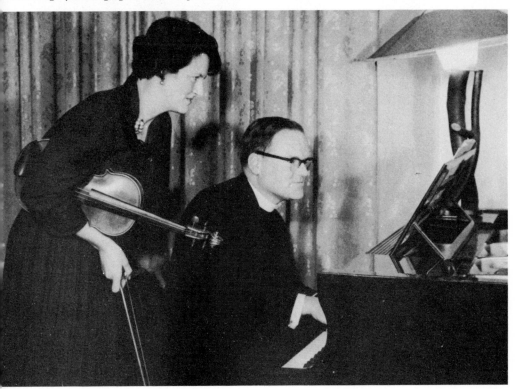

Sonata session with Margaret, Edinburgh, 1962

Tuesday morning service, Bristol Chapel, 1978

With Arlo Duba, former chaplain of Westminster Choir College, 1978

writing for the voices and the splendidly spaced chords at climaxes combined with a judicious use of the trumpet reflect the text in a highly significant way.

Calvin Hampton has worked in many styles as a performer and a composer. For twenty years he was the organist of Calvary Church, New York City where he gave recitals at midnight on Fridays which attracted large crowds of people and where, in addition to the normal organ repertoire, he would play such works as Mussorgsky's "Pictures at an Exhibition" or the Symphony of César Franck. He has written anthems, canticle settings and settings of the Eucharistic texts in a highly personal way and many of his works bridge the gap between mainstream music and "popular" or "folk" music. His hymn tune, DeTAR, has attained wide currency in new hymnals and one piece of his has been played by the New York Philharmonic Orchestra.*

The output of England's Twentieth Century Church Light Music Group did indeed cross the Atlantic and *Time* magazine reviewed Father Beaumont's "Twentieth Century Folk Mass" calling it a "Jazz Mass." This publicity prompted a number of churches to institute "folk masses" for their young people and the quality of these happenings varied with the skill and taste of the leadership. At this time (late 1950s), the music of Malcolm Williamson began to appear in many parts of the country and the composer's visits, particularly his year as a Visiting Professor at Westminster Choir College, stimulated interest in his hymn tunes, cantatas and "participation operas" of which "The Winter Star" has become particularly popular. In fact, the music of Benjamin Britten and Malcolm Williamson is widely used in the United States and their influence has been wholesome and healthy. The influence of renowned jazz musicians has been quite marked in the last twenty years. Duke Ellington was invited in the early 60s to give a Sacred Music Concert in Grace Cathedral, San Francisco and he then gave similar performances in New York at the Fifth Avenue Presbyterian Church and the Cathedral of St John the Divine and in other parts of the country. In his autobiography, *Music is My Mistress*, he said of his concert in the New York Cathedral which was based upon Psalm 150, "I regard this concert as the most important thing I have ever done."

In 1972, Galt McDermott, the composer of the Broadway hit, "Hair", wrote a setting of the Prayerbook Communion Service for his parish church on Staten Island. This was later performed at a huge service at the Cathedral of St John the Divine in which rock musicians sat side by side with the cathedral choir during a very moving celebration of the Holy Eucharist. During the Communion of the People, Olivier Messiaen's "Les Corps Glorieux" was

---

* Calvin Hampton died in August 1984. A.W.

played on the cathedral organ and the coexistence of styles of the conventional hymnody, the rock settings and Messiaen seemed quite appropriate. The play, "Godspell", has been produced in churches and the occasional dramatization of the Gospel during the Eucharist has often proved effective. At St Peter's Lutheran Church in New York, a "Jazz Vespers" is held every Sunday at 5 p.m.

In his book *Twentieth Century Church Music*, Erik Routley lamented the avalanche of hymn anthems and other somewhat meritricious pieces which continue to pour from publishers. He was right, of course, and the only antidote to this is the constant education of those responsible for the leadership of public worship in the integrity of the materials. To aim at the integrity and technique of Britten and Williamson and the American composers mentioned above should be the goal of anybody who aspires to write music for liturgy.

The education of musicians in the liturgical and theoretical appropriateness of music used in churches has been addressed in many places notably at the Union theological Seminary in New York where, in 1930, a School of Sacred Music was founded by Clarence Dickinson. He was also the organist at the Brick Presbyterian Church in New York where his tenure spanned more than 50 years.

This School of Sacred Music was founded with the requirement that all of its music students take courses in Hymnody, Theology and the History of Worship alongside the theological students. There was no requirement, unfortunately, that theological students take courses in Hymnody and other musical areas which might affect their ministry but the daily services in the chapel undoubtedly had a profound influence on the theological students. Graduates of the School of Sacred Music (which granted Master of Sacred Music and Doctor of Sacred Music degrees) took positions in all parts of the world and the influence of the institution was enormous until, in 1973, for financial reasons, it was forced to close and a nucleus of its faculty moved to Yale. Located as it was in Manhattan, the school was able to call upon some of the most distinguished musicians in the country for its part time faculty and churches in the New York, New Jersey and Connecticut area were able to employ some of the gifted students in field work positions. Due in large part to the work of this school, an increasing number of liturgical music programs exists in many parts of the country.

A few years before the founding of the School of Sacred Music at Union Seminary, the excellence of the music program at the Westminster Presbyterian Church in Dayton, Ohio, created a demand for "ministers of music" who could develop similar music programs in other churches. John Finley Williamson, the director of music at Westminster Church responded by organizing a school for the training of musicians to serve the Church, located originally at the Dayton Church.

This church music school developed into Westminster Choir College, and since the early 1930's the college has been located in Princeton, N.J. It has educated several thousand undergraduate and graduate students who direct creative music programs in hundreds of churches, schools, and colleges. In 1975 the college appointed Dr Erik Routley as Professor of Church Music and Director of the Chapel. During his seven year tenure at Westminster Erik Routley made Westminster a center for the study of hymnology. Through his teaching during the regular academic year and during many summer session seminars and workshops, he led the Westminster Church Music Department in new and creative directions.

Another school for the training of musicians for the Church was founded in England during the 1920's. The Royal School of Church Music was conceived as an institution to raise musical standards in parish churches through a resident study curriculum as well as a carefully developed system of affiliated parishes and choirs. During the early 1970's the educational thrust of the RSCM was revamped, and the one or two year resident course was terminated. The Addington Palace RSCM headquarters in England then became an ecumenical center for short length workshops, seminars and courses for church musicians and choristers of all ages. At this time a highly successful six week summer Overseas Course has attracted students from all parts of the world. At the same time RSCM affiliated parishes and choirs have increased and the work of the RSCM has expanded throughout the world.

This new thrust has been guided by the creative vision of the current Director of the RSCM, Dr Lionel Dakers, and Dr Erik Routley, long an active member of the RSCM Council, was very influential in designing the new direction for the school. This is especially true for the work of the RSCM in the United States.

Beginning in the summer of 1967 the RSCM co-sponsored a Boychoir training course at Westminster Choir College in Princeton: thus began a relationship of two institutions whose goals are very similar but who accomplish those goals through different but equally important educational programs. The American summer training courses have grown over the years, and by the early 1980's there are such courses for girls, boys, men, and women singers in all parts of the nation.

Under the leadership of Erik Routley, The Royal School of Church Music in America was established with its own office in Connecticut. Dr Routley was President of the Board of RSCM in America until his death, and in that office and in his position on the faculty of Westminster Choir College, he built a transatlantic bridge which had begun to coordinate the thrust and educational philosophies of two fifty-plus-year-old institutions committed to the raising of standards and creating an integrity in the practice of the music of the Church in the late twentieth century.

A new and exciting development in American liturgical music occurred in 1967 when Richard Felciano wrote "Glossalalia" for the dedication of the organ in St John Fisher Church in Churchill, Pennsylvania. This work for singer, organ, percussion and electronic tape was, as far as is known, the first time in this country that pre-recorded tape has been used in a liturgical setting. Richard Felciano (born 1931) is a professor of composition at the Univesity of California in Berkeley. In setting out to write a piece for the organ's dedication, he felt that everything about the instrument should be dedicated including the means of producing the wind to activate the pipes. His prepared tape, therefore, included the sound of the switch of the motor being turned on and the acceleration of the fan and the filling of the bellows with wind. He then decided that the "sound" rather than the "meaning" of the 150th psalm should be celebrated, so that the singer enunciates with great exaggeration all of the syllables of the Latin text while the organist introduces the several ranks of the organ individually and the whole is reinforced by the tape on which voices and other sounds are heard and responded to by a percussionist. The impact of this work upon some musicians in the church was such that Richard Felciano was commissioned to write other works and he wrote a series of liturgical pieces for Advent, Easter, Ascension, Pentecost and Trinity often using voices in a quite unconventional way, the prepared tape matching the singing with appropriate response. In the Easter tape, the voices of Martin Luther King and John F. Kennedy are heard from some of their significant public speeches, they representing people who were martyred in our own day for their beliefs. At Pentecost the sound of the rushing, mighty wind and the confusion of the choir casting around among the syllables of Alleluia brings a tremendous sense of reality. Among Felciano's organ pieces, "I Make My Own Soul from All the Elements of the Earth" brings the sounds that mankind has created in "civilizing" this earth (car horns, jackhammers, jet planes, etc.) into sharp interjection with organ clusters and finally emerges into the sound of surf breaking on the ocean floor with a fragment of Bach playing through it. Since 1967, other composers have written significant music involving prepared tape and "pure sound techniques" notably Daniel Pinkham, Ronald Perera and William Albright.

Among the many hymnals produced in the United States in the past twenty years, mention must be made of *Ecumenical Praise* which was published in 1977 "as a supplemental hymnal designed to serve the growing points of the Church." Its editorial committee included Austin Lovelace, Erik Routley, Alec Wyton and Carlton Young who was Executive Editor. The book draws heavily upon Erik Routley's experience as musical editor of *Cantate Domino*, the hymn book of the World Council of Churches, Austin Lovelace's broad experience with hymn texts and tunes, Carlton Young's experience as editor of the Methodist hymnal and in the areas of jazz and popular music and Alec Wyton's experience in electronic music and new sound. *Ecumenical Praise* contains texts by W. H. Auden, Dietrich Bonhoeffer, Robert Bridges, Elizabeth Barrett Browning, Teilhard de Chardin, Fred Pratt Green, Fred Kaan, Christopher Smart, Charles and Samuel Wesley and tunes by William Albright, Ronald Arnatt, Leonard Bernstein, Benjamin Britten, Aaron Copland, Richard Dirksen, Hugo Distler, Duke Ellington, Richard Felciano, John Gardner, Iain Hamilton, Calvin Hampton, Gustav Holst, Herbert Howells, Charles Ives, Daniel Moe, Herbert Murrill, Ned Rorem, Carl Shalk, Leo Sowerby, Ralph Vaughan Williams, Malcolm Williamson, and Charles Wuorinen. There are folk songs and carols, two pieces with prepared electronic tape and "An Alleluia Super Round" by William Albright which is an aleatoric study on the word "alleluia" and a twelve tone hymn tune by Charles Wuorinen. That *Ecumenical Praise* has had some influence already in the few years that it has been available is seen in the almost completed forthcoming Episcopal Hymnal which was authorized by General Convention in 1982 and will be published in December of 1985. This book contains music by William Albright, Richard Felciano, Ned Rorem, and Daniel Pinkham to name only four composers who have not been primarily associated with liturgical music to any great extent.

Liturgical renewal has had a strong influence on many American Churches, especially since Vatican II. New liturgical texts, many of which are ICET texts and used in many churches, have inspired new musical settings. The *Lutheran Book of Worship, Worship II*, The *Episcopal Hymnal 1982*, and other recent hymnals have included a representative selection of much new liturgical music.

These extensive collections of liturgical music, mostly with congregational participation in mind, is but a beginning. The creative approach to additional musical settings of these liturgical texts could be an exciting challenge for today's and future American composers.

The Renewal Movement in the churches of the United States has brought with it a spate of songs and hymns of an informal "folk-life" nature, much of which has won no adherents among those who care deeply about the integrity of music. The pioneering work of the Parish of the Redeemer in Houston, Texas, over a number of years, has brought a raising of standards in this type of music and an important emphasis upon a "coexistence" of many styles in the carrying out of liturgical worship. If God is the author of all that we are and have, then all of the styles in the creation of art by human beings has the right to praise God. This could mean chaos and confusion but with skilled and imaginative leadership, the process of including the entire community in the worship of God means that sometimes people should be able to sing with the minimum of intellectual effort and at other times, their experience may be enriched by a sublime performance of a great masterpiece by superbly trained musicians. It is the welding together of somewhat disparate elements which presents the challenge to the leaders in the Church. Where this challenge is being met in all of the denominations, significant things are happening. In the influence which religious institutions have in their communities, music and musicians are growing in a way which transcends mere performance. The education of congregations in the nature and variety of liturgy and the people's role in it must be a prime responsibility of all liturgical musicians. The key to all of this is the *integrity* of what is done. Church music in the United States toward the end of the twentieth century is growing, alive and well.

6

CHURCH-MUSIC EDUCATION IN AMERICAN PROTESTANT SEMINARIES

Paul W. Wohlgemuth

Interest and concern for church-music education have become increasingly evident during the past half-century, particularly in the establishment of church-music degrees in seminaries, universities, and colleges. This interest and concern have also been reinforced by the formation and growth of many organizations for church music and musicians that foster higher professional standards. Groups such as the American Guild of Organists, American Choral Directors' Association, Chorister's Guild, Hymn Society of America, and denominational church-music organizations have provided leadership to church musicians on various levels: local, regional, and national. In addition, music publishers have emerged who not only supply choral and organ music, books about church music, and supplies for a broader spectrum of church-music needs, but also sponsor elaborate church-music conferences, with guest performers and performing groups, speakers, clinicians, and theologians.

All of these have stimulated much activity, resulting at times in high performance standards, and most assuredly have fostered the rise of the church-music professional in unprecedented numbers to match the expanded job market: rivaling as a professional career that of public-school music.

At the same time, American church-music styles and worship practices in both liturgical and nonliturgical churches have undergone great changes, producing diversity and pluralism. Some of these trends have yet to make an impact on the academic institutions that have trained this generation of church musicians. The unsettled, yet sustained influences from the rock cultures of the 1960's generally exist at a distance from mainline church-music styles. Also during the same decade there emerged even in mainline Protestant-church worship music the influence of a movement known as the charismatic renewal with its emphasis on "Worship and Praise." For many it brought a fresh understanding of what worship was really meant to be, a type of "worship-worship," not primarily "doing-worship."

Since this movement may develop as one of the most significant ecumenical music and worship influences of the last quarter of the 20th century, it is important to be aware that this style of worship demands a new type of song leader, choir director, keyboard performer, as well as instrumentalist. Their use of orchestras, usually of popular-music instrumentation, is not uncommon. No worship movement in recent years is so dependent upon music for the heart of its expression. Traditional organ service music, song services, choir anthems, and "special music" in charismatic renewal take on a much broader and extensive leadership role along with a greater emphasis upon the activity of the worshiper. While the traditional Protestant church leans upon the pastor for the major leadership role in its worship service, the renewal calls for a dual leadership of pastor and Minister of Music, called the Worship Leader.

These worship services draw expressions and participation not only from the worship leaders, but also from the worshipers. Thus, the action of worship firmly takes place from within the congregation. A type of "guided spontaneity" prevails, in which events in the service are anticipated but not prescribed or predicted. Expressions growing out of the music being used by the people include clapping of hands while singing songs, raising of hands as gestures of worship, improvisatorial singing of praise, and at times, even spontaneous spiritual dance. Worship in this setting encompasses the expression of the whole person.

Currently, no seminary offers training or a graduate-degree program for a music leader that would be preparation for this new, emerging role as a worship leader. Because of this oversight or neglect, independent organizations such as "International Worship Symposium," as well as churches, are sponsoring clinics and workshops worldwide to help develop this new leadership style.

Seminaries need to become more aware of this trend and prepare students to guide their denominations in this and other worship patterns that are meaningful, enlightened, and experientially biblical. Ignoring these influences may lead the church community to miss a powerful and positive contribution to Christian worship as we approach the 21st century. Since this movement has reached into most mainline church groups, e.g., Methodist, Presbyterian, Baptist, Mennonite, Episcopal, Lutheran, and Roman Catholic, it is imperative that persons responsible for church-music training keep abreast of major worship movements and give leadership and direction to it. Much study, research, planning, and training must be undertaken if seminaries expect to give responsible leadership in this significant area.

Even though theological education has facilitated and often pioneered significant changes in religious thought and worship practices, it has at times exhibited an inability to respond to changes that occur within the larger Christian community. In particular, the need is for trained leaders of the church's worship life who are at least informed about significant, new, and even threatening worship music and practices.

The concern for trained and sensitive pastoral leadership was registered more than a century ago by Henry Ward Beecher in assessing the need for church-music training among ministers, stating in his lecture delivered before the theological department of Yale College in 1873:

> The complaint which I hear from conductors of music is that there is no person in the congregation so indifferent to the cultivation of music as the minister. Now and then there is an exception; but generally the minister is glad to have a conductor who will take the whole responsibility from his shoulders; and then, so that there be quiet in the choir and no disturbance in the congregation, he does not trouble himself any more about the matter.[1]

Some 63 years later, Archibald T. Davison in his book, *Protestant Church Music in America*, expressed similar sentiments:

> Three forces stand in virtual control of Protestant music: the minister, the church musician, and the layman. Considering the importance of their charge all three are, from the point of view of musical training, sorely deficient.[2]

Further indication of the lack of interest in seminary training in church music is noted in the sparse research in church-music education, curricula, and graduate-degree programs. Some theses and dissertations have been written by such researchers as Lloyd A. Pfautsch,[3] Donald E. Morrison,[4] E. Robert Irwin,[5] D. George Dunbar,[6] Jack W. Schwarz,[7] and Melva Ruby Wilson Costen.[8] In 1975, a brief but interesting survey was conducted on "Hymnody in United States Seminaries" sponsored by the Student Music Committee, Princeton Theological Seminary, and directed by James D. Shannon.

In 1983, the author, Visiting Fellow at Princeton Theological Seminary, developed a project including a study of 30 American theological institutions entitled "A Survey of Church-Music Degrees and Church-Music Offerings in Selected American Seminaries and Universities." The effort to assess a true picture of church-music education in American Protestant seminaries in the 1980's is quite difficult. A rather cloudy picture emerges in a composite review of the descriptions of church-music courses listed in seminary catalogs. This seems to reflect a lack of uniformity and standards in terms of church-music offerings within seminary programs. For example, courses with similar content are listed with a variety of titles. Furthermore, courses are often taught only in interim sessions or they may be cycled every second or third year with no assurance that they will actually be taught. Description of courses at times is vague.

The dearth of church-music studies in seminaries is noted in Shannon's survey revealing that in 31 of 100 theological institutions no courses whatsoever were devoted to church music. Furthermore, of the 69 institutions that had at least 1 such course, only 36 offered 3 or more church-music classes.

Schwarz's dissertation notes that of the 46 major participants in his study, only 17.3% of the schools required some work in church music for their ministerial students. This figure, representing only 2.4% of the total required curriculum, also includes courses not specifically devoted to church music such as "worship." Some 70% of the schools offered at least some elective courses in church music or courses that in some way related to church music. Obviously, for those students enrolled in the other 30% of the schools, no opportunity for study in church music existed.

This lack of leadership training in church music for ministerial students undoubtedly has resulted in an inadequate understanding of the ministry of music within the local congregation. Schwarz's critical conclusion was:

> With few exceptions it was concluded that church music training—specific courses or otherwise—was of little consequence in the life of the average seminary ministerial student.
> In spite of the fact that the average ministerial student was not involved in the study of church music to an appreciable degree, he possessed a positive attitude toward such study. Almost all of the students reported a strong recognition of the need for some training in this area. The investigator concludes that most Protestant ministerial students desire to receive seminary training in church music as a part of the preparation for their future ministries.[9]

In addition to the consideration of church-music education for ministerial students, has been the emergence of the church-music degree program specifically designed to prepare students for a full-time church-music ministry as a profession. From an earlier development of bachelor and master degrees in church music, the 1950's saw the appearance of the doctor of musical arts degree in church music at such universities as Northwestern University and the University of Southern California as an accredited degree approved by the National Association of the Schools of Music. Other than in a few theological institutions such as Union Theological Seminary and some Southern Baptist and United Methodist seminaries, interest in developing such graduate programs in church music centered primarily in universities and colleges, not in seminaries. Costen's dissertation reveals that in 1978 only 8 of the 103 surveyed seminaries accredited by the Association of Theological Schools offered church music degree programs. Five of the degrees were at the master's level, two were doctoral degrees, and four were dual degrees.

The author's survey of 30 seminaries that offer one or more church-music courses shows that 10 institutions offer some type of church-music degree program. Table 1 shows that in these 10 schools 4 types of graduate church-music degrees are offered. The 2-year degree programs are the most popular. Apparently because of the indecision on whether ministers of music should be ordained, the *Master of Divinity: Church Music* degree has had fewer takers and is offered by only one of the seminaries.

Table 1
Church-music degrees offered in 10 surveyed seminaries

Degrees	Number of Seminaries
Master of Church/Sacred Music*	6
Master of Arts in Church Music*	2
Master of Music: Church Music*	1
Master of Divinity: Church Music†	1

* 2-year program.
† 3-year program.

Table 2 shows the comparison of the average number of semester hours required in the various areas of study within each degree program. The degree requirements by the three 2-year programs are somewhat similar. The 3-year program differs appreciably in the higher requirements in general music and theology.

Those schools giving church-music degrees generally offer a full spectrum of church-music courses, but are usually weak in ethnomusicology studies. The major courses offered in the remaining surveyed schools were usually courses such as Introduction to Church Music, Christian Worship, and performance ensembles. They lacked courses in hymnology, congregational song leading, private lessons in voice and keyboard, in addition to the above-mentioned ethnomusicology studies.

Table 2

Average number of hours required in the various areas of study within each degree program

Degrees	Church Music	General Music	Theology	Minor/ Elective/ Special Required	Total
Master of Church/ Sacred Music	16(8–19*)	17(6–28*)	13(0–20*)	10(0–27*)	56(45–64*)
Master of Arts in Church Music	12(9–14*)	17(16–18*)	15(15–16*)	7(0–14*)	51(42–60*)
Master of Music: Church Music	8	12	10	20	50
Master of Divinity: Church Music	6	34	27	17	84

* Lowest and highest number of hours listed in the various degree programs.

It seems ironic that if church music is regarded as a ministry within the church, as are preaching and Christian Education, seminaries have abdicated their responsibilities in this area and by default let universities with usually less Christian ministry orientation take leadership in church-music ministry education. Now in the mid-1980's seminaries generally still have not assumed major leadership roles in this specialized area.

NOTES

1 H. W. Beecher, *Lectures on Preaching*, second series, New York, 1973, p. 115.
2 A. T. Davison, *Protestant Church Music in America*, 2nd ed., revised, Boston 1936, pp. 12–13.
3 L. A. Pfautsch, *A Curriculum of Church Music for a Theological Seminary: An Historical Justification and a Formulation*, unpublished master's thesis, Union Theological Seminary 1948.
4 D. E. Morrison, *The Sacred Music Degrees (Protestant) in the Colleges, Universities, and Seminaries of the United States (1956–57)*, unpublished master's thesis, Union Theological Seminary 1957.
5 E. R. Irwin, *An Analysis of Church Music Curriculum of Selected Protestant Seminaries*, unpublished PhD dissertation, The University of Rochester, 1967.

6 D. G. Dunbar, *Church Music Curricula in Selected Religiously Oriented Colleges*, unpublished DMA dissertation, University of Southern California 1970.
7 J. W. Schwarz, *The State of Church Music Education for Ministerial Students in Protestant Seminaries in the United States*, unpublished DMA dissertation, University of Southern California 1975.
8 M. R. W. Costen, *A Comparative Description of Curricular Offerings in Church Music Degree Programs at Accredited Protestant Theological Seminaries in the United States*, unpublished PhD dissertation, Georgia State University—College of Education 1978.
9 Schwarz, *op. cit.*, p. 126.

'Let there be light' – W.M. Vories

69

PASSAIC LM   1976

all but last   last

Composed on a journey from 'Watertown Conn. to' Princeton, 17 Sept. 1976
Extended version

70

SHERIDAN 4 × 10   1976

Commissioned September 1976 by Westminster Presbyterian Church, Lincoln, Nebraska
Performed there at organ dedication 14 Nov. '76
Published in extended version by Hinshaw Music HMC 132

©Hinshaw

G. Schirmer Inc. New York   12 Staves   No. 5 - Printed in the U. S. A.

7

AN ALTERNATIVE MODEL FOR THE EDUCATION OF THE CHURCH MUSICIAN

Carlton R. Young

For while church music is not exempt from the requirements music in general must meet, it stands also under the discipline associated with its being used to further the aim of worship. It is always used in a context where the performers are not exclusively, and hearers are not even primarily, concerned with music itself. It seems reasonable to assume that a musically informed church authority and a theologically informed musical authority can between them work out a counter-point of criticism and precept in these matters. I am afraid, however, that this has very rarely happened and does not appear to be happening at all in our time.

Erik Routley[1]

The present "impasse" between "uninformed authorities" in matters of church music so clearly identified by Erik Routley and supported in Professor Wohlgemuth's survey is primarily the result of a lack of vision and commitment on the part of theological education for the training of professionals, other than ordained clergy, and its own preoccupation with current problems[2] of morale, fragmentation and identity as a graduate professional school among other professional schools.

In recent years theological definitions and descriptions of "ministry" have been broadened and enriched to the extent that the seminary is challenged, perhaps for the first time, with the responsibility of the larger task of "education for ministry" including, of course, music. This challenge has been amplified in two places. First, the local church, which in the past forty years has made, in some instances, massive investments in the means of making music; including the purchase of performing instruments, the building of rehearsal and performance space and the hiring of full-time professional leadership. In the latter regard, this professional is usually the product of a private or state music school with attending high regard for performance at all levels, and minimal attention to educational models of music ministry and the

97

basic theological disciplines. Ironically, many local churches have hired and titled this professional, "minister of music" (!) While at the same time engaging the services of seminary faculty, by way of their involvement in workshops and consultations, to assist in the development of a "theology of use" for music in an inclusive[3] ministry of education, evangelism and recreation.

Concurrently, and unrelated, the general church, in its unsuccessful attempt to define and relate (politically) the levels of ministry,[4] has in the ensuing discussion also turned to the seminary requesting assistance in the development of more specialized education models than the MDiv, but models that do not neglect the traditional grounding of theological education in Bible, theology, and history.

For the most part, theological education is ill-equipped for this task since it has for the past century majored in "clerical" education for ministry, with the primary goal that a theologically informed clergy is sufficient to *any* task of church leadership, including the delegation of authority in matters of the so-called specialized ministry, i.e., education, music, finance and administration. The lack of presence in the seminary of faculty or students in these fields and the lack of "specialized" content in the basic curriculum (MDiv) has resulted in the inability of that degree to provide students with even minimum information about disciplines that have in the past decade undergone enormous growth in bibliography and methodology. Meanwhile these disciplines are represented in force at the local level by professionals with highly developed operational skills who remain in conflict with the goals of "general ministry" lacking basic understandings of the common task of ministry. Thus, the "impasse" identified by Routley, as quoted at the beginning of this paper, has extended beyond music into other specializations.

The alternative model of church-music education model presented here does not take on the critical agenda pointed to by Wohlgemuth, i.e. the reconstruction of basic theological education so as to incorporate introductions to specialized ministries within the basic MDiv degree program. However, this alternative model of church-music education does bring together the three components of the "impasse" in music: music education/performance; theological studies; practical ministries. This model is believed to be both a unique and timely contribution to the ongoing conversation as to the future of church-music education, but in no regard is it suggested that it is a definitive solution to those long-standing, now pressing problems in the seminary-based training of the church musician.

AN ALTERNATIVE MODEL FOR GRADUATE LEVEL CHURCH-MUSIC EDUCATION

Admission

Admission to the program of study is open to those applicants holding the Bachelor of Music (with 3.0 GPA) from an accredited school of music, with a strong performance track in voice and/or keyboard (other instrumentalists will be considered if they demonstrate a strong keyboard minor). The applicant must meet both the graduate music as well as the seminary admissions standards.

First Level

Three semesters (30–36sh). Introductions to Bible, church history, theology, liturgy/ congregational song; church music seminar (three semesters) which includes conducting, choral literature and performance practice; applied music and a half recital.

As determined by the faculty, the student at the end of the first level may be terminated with or without receiving the Certificate in Church Music (CCM), or may receive the certificate and be recommended for level two.

Second Level

An internship of fifteen months' duration (summer, fall, winter-spring, summer) in a local church. The internship model will be shaped in consultation with the student and be administered by the seminary, and funded by both the seminary and the local church. Salary and housing will be provided by the local church according to guidelines established by the seminary internship office.

The internship committee will consist of a representative from the seminary music faculty, the director of music in the local church, pastor-in-charge, or other designated leader, other local and area church musicians, as may be appropriate, and the student.

At the completion of the internship the committee may recommend to the seminary faculty that the student be terminated, with or without receiving the *Advanced Certificate in Church Music* (ACCM); or the student may receive the ACCM and be recommended for degree candidacy.

Third Level

When admitted to candidacy the student returns to the seminary to take additional courses, including those recommended by the intern committee, electives in music and theological studies (24–30sh). After passing a comprehensive examination, which may include a reflective paper and an oral defense, the student will receive the appropriate degree: MSM, MCM.

Comments on the Model

   1. By placement of the course of study in both the seminary and the local church,

the student is afforded the opportunity to combine supervised practice in ministry with theological reflection.

2. At two points in the course of study, the student is assessed as to "gifts and graces" for effective ministry.

3. Denominational certification requirements may be combined with the course of study.

4. The model draws upon: a) the traditional strengths of undergraduate music instruction with its emphasis on performance skills and liberal studies; b) the seminary setting with its faculty/student worship setting and proven ability to teach beginning level courses in theology, Bible, church history; c) the local church with its established distance from both of the above.

5. The internship affords the student the opportunity of participating in the complete year's cycle of liturgy and program in a local church, including summer music programs for children and young people.

6. While the model, by definition does not address the problem of the lack of music/hymnody in the MDiv curriculum, nevertheless, the results of that problem are present in the internship, and in time this may prompt some action by the seminary.

7. In some locales, seminary and graduate level schools of music may combine their resources of bibliography, teaching staffs, instruments of instruction and performance rooms.

8. Seminary education is called to assume a vital leadership role in the education of theologically informed musicians, who in the words of Erik

handle mysteries and make them friendly, who can speak the unspeakable in a language that uses no words, in whose art action and thought are joined, in whose hands applied science is the servant of beauty and honor. In every place where the gospel is being preached, this secret is waiting for its revelation.[5]

NOTES

1 E. Routley, *Church Music and the Christian Faith*, Carol Stream 1978, p. 65.
2 For a complete discussion of the problems, see E. Farley, *Theologia, the Fragmentation and Unity of Theological Education*, Philadelphia 1983, pp. 1–18.
3 For an elaboration of the concept of an inclusive music ministry, see T. L. Are, *Faithsong*, Philadelphia 1981, pp. 12–16.
4 The 1984 General Conference of the United Methodist Church defeated a proposal that would have established a diaconate of "work and witness." There is presently a provision for diaconal ministers.
5 E. Routley, *Music Leadership in the Church*, with a Study Guide by Carlton R. Young, Carol Stream 1985, p. 120.

MINISTRY OF HYMNODY

Hymns are the folk-song of the church militant. They are, essentially, the people's music. If a hymn cannot be sung by the congregation present, it has become for that occasion not a hymn but a choir-anthem or even an organ solo ... A hymn ... must be sung by people whose minds are directed not primarily to poetic or musical but to religious values; which means that the poetry and music have to be the kind of poetry and music which do not fight against religious values; they have to fit into the ancient scheme that prevailed in the Middle Ages when there was no difference between goodness and piety in art. This is a discipline, but not a limitation.

Erik Routley, *Hymns and Human Life*, London
1952, p. 3

The hymn-singing congregation is the last arbiter of sacred folk-song, and its arbitration, always weighty and never carefully calculated, is a direct product of its faith and practice. For the consummation of Christian worship in this world neither the worshipper, with his tradition born in his bones, nor the prophet who interprets the Word of the Lord upon the present moment, can do without each other. That same community embraces both the unpractised singer and the cultivated musician. But both are bound, and the work of both is entirely made possible, by that act of faith which accepts and which builds tradition.

Erik Routley, *The Music of Christian Hymnody.*
A study of the development of the hymn tune
since the Reformation, with special reference to
English Protestantism, London 1957, p. 175

8

A WELSH CAROL AND ITS CONSEQUENCES

Alan Luff

Erik, for all his work on *Cantate Domino*,[1] was not one to be greatly involved in anything outside hymns in English, even though he was more than superficially acquainted with the hymns of many other lands. He was not enamoured, to be honest, of the Internationale Arbeitsgemeinschaft für Hymnologie (IAH: The International Fellowship for research in Hymnology) and did not take part in the 1981 Oxford Conference at which the three societies, IAH, The Hymn Society of America (HSA) and The Hymn Society of Great Britain and Ireland (HS),[2] met for the first time. He was pressed to take part in it but refused, thus making it, despite its many virtues, something of a Hamlet without the prince, and depriving the continental Europeans of the opportunity—the last one as it turned out—of catching something of his enthusiasm.

But of the hymnody of one non-English nation he was very enamoured indeed, one that was geographically near but linguistically distant, that is the Welsh. He had great admiration for the strength of its hymn tunes. In *The English Carol*[3] he recognized the distance and strangeness of the Welsh contribution to our singing in his reference to Welsh Carols: under the heading "The British Isles (excluding England)" he writes: "There are [a] few carols, as foreign to modern English protestant culture as anything from farther away, that come from nearer home." He can be excused for missing in the following paragraphs the important point about Welsh carols, and also for missing an important point about the tune OLWEN about which he writes with great enthusiasm. There has been very little written in English about Welsh hymnody. Few Englishmen have learnt Welsh and the Welsh in writing about their own hymnody prefer to do it in Welsh. May I as an exception to the first rule make an exception to the second too and try to fill in a small corner of Erik's work that he would have loved to fill in himself by writing, first, something about Welsh carols, and secondly, by giving what I think is the true history of OLWEN. The whole may, I think, by giving some picture of a singing people at their song help towards the understanding of the whole Welsh singing tradition and raise some questions of how one worshipping culture appropriates material from another.

The Welsh Carol

There are some Welsh Carols that are folk-songs in the sense that the collectors of the early years of this century understood the word. They have been recorded from an oral tradition and are, words and music, attributable to no known author or composer. The familiar NOS GALAN is one such.[4]

But the overwhelming part of the Welsh carol literature is entirely different from this. First of all, it is as we have it now, primarily a literary and not a musical phenomenon, though there is a fascinating musical tradition attached to it. That words come first in importance if not historically, will surprise no one who has any close knowledge of Welsh life. The Welsh are not strictly a musical people but a singing people. Leaving aside living composers whose place in musical history has yet to be decided, Wales has produced no great composers.[5] At a concert at the Bangor Royal National Eisteddfod in the 1970s which set out to be a panorama of Welsh Music the narrator concluded rather lamely that the great contribution of Welsh composers may in the end be their hymn tunes. It is noteworthy that at the National Eisteddfod every year the two greatest events are the Chairing and the Crowning ceremonies, and that both are for winners of poetic competitions. So, in the humbler field of the carol, for generations, from certainly the 17th to the 19th centuries, local poets were writing ballads and carols and publishing them in small pamphlets. At the head of each item stands the name of the meters, e.g. "Mesur: Mentra Gwen" (Measure: Venture Gwen) or "Mesur: Hir oes i Fair" (Measure: Long live Mary). If there is any music the tunes are given all together at the beginning or the end of the pamphlet. Thus the ballad or carol can be sung to the tune or tunes in the metre denoted by the name, and the name, as with the names of hymn tunes, may have nothing to do with the content. Some of the names are Welsh, but many are English: "Greece and Troy", "Charity Mistress": some appear in both languages: "Susan Llygad-ddu" is "Black-eyed Susan": or can be traced back into English: "Billericay" is "Millerykey" is "Miller's Key"; "Jermin Cloi" is "Charmin Cloi" is "Charming Chloe". There is considerable debate on whether these English names denote an English origin. The metres are not the traditional Welsh ones. Indeed the tunes themselves can in a few instances be shown to be of English origin. "Black-eyed Susan" is a favourite ballad by John Gay ("All in the downs the fleet was moored") and the tune usually found in Wales is that by Richard Leveridge (*ca.* 1670–1758): "Yr Hen Ddarbi" (The Old Derby) is usually seen as a variant of "Grim King of the ghosts"[6] a melody used by John Gay in *The Beggar's Opera* (1728) for "Can love be controlled by advice": and "Hir oes i Fair"[7] which sometimes appears with the name of the "Mesur" englished as "Long live Mary" and has given rise to speculation on how the Virgin Mary comes to be honoured in strongly protestant Wales, turns out to be the melody of the broadside ballad "Let Mary live long" of 1692 in honour of King William and Queen Mary.[8] Suggestively, the metre of "Mentra Gwen" is clearly that of the Captain Kidd ballads (and thus the same as that of the American Folk Hymn "Wondrous Love") even though none of the Welsh melodies are like the English or American ones.[9] These are only a handful out of over a hundred "Mesur" names that I have listed, each of which may have several melodies, so that the case for the English origin of all the tunes is not yet made. A good deal more work needs to be done. What one can, however, say is that there existed a mechanism for the transportation of the melodies. At the key period there was a strong trade in cattle from Wales to the London markets and the drovers (porthmyn) were a distinctive group known both for their toughness and their music.

Thus some, perhaps many, of the melodies came to Wales, with their complex metres (no Common Metre ballads these!) and were adapted to Welsh use and may have engendered new tunes in the same metres. At the same time the local poets poured out their ballads, their memorial songs, their poetical letters ("On returning a friend's hat" for instance), and their carols. These were long pieces, usually of small literary value, twenty to thirty stanzas being common, which covered the history of our Fall and Salvation from Adam to the Last Trump, but dwelt almost always on the details of the Christmas story. Few of these are now sung in Wales. (Not many[10] are available in modern arrangements, and these are not usually the long fine tunes so well fitted to the kind of poetry that at its best has been written for them.) There is one exception, and that is the "Plygain" tradition.[11] In its original form groups of singers, in the purest form of the tradition three or four men only and usually related to each other, would meet in secret in the weeks before Christmas to practise a number of traditional carols. These would be from their own manuscript books carefully preserved within the family, and the musical arrangements, crude but often effective, would be the property of that group. On Christmas Eve the group would spend the whole night moving from farm to farm, singing their carols and receiving refreshment. Very early on Christmas morning the different groups would gather at the Parish Church for Matins (Plygain). After the saying of the Office the meeting was declared open and one by one groups and individuals would take the floor and sing their carols. When all the groups wishing to sing had sung once the first sang again, each following the next in the same order as before, and so on over and over again, the sole rule being that no two groups sang the same carol. Hence after each round a number of groups would drop out, their carols having been already sung, albeit in another group's version. When all had sung themselves out the Parish Clerk would announce the Breakfast Carol, often peculiar to that Parish, and all the singers would go to the Vestry for refreshments. The custom survives in certain parts of Wales, but not as an early morning service. It is now held in Chapels as well as in Parish Churches, usually in the evening, before or after Christmas, though it is still known as the "Plygain". There will be opening prayers, and the first carol may well be sung by the church choir or by the Sunday School Children. Thereafter, however, the traditional form prevails until the Supper Carol is called. There are still groups who sing in the traditional manner in their own versions of the melodies. The following, from a famous 19th century collection *Cyff Eos Llechyd* (Eos Llechyd's Treasure Chest)[12] gives an idea of the style though perhaps in a slightly polished form. The melody is a fine one in the "Mesur: Difyrrwch Gwyr y Gogledd" (The delight of the men of the North).[13]

Tenor 2

Tenor 1

Hos - an - na! dym - a'r dydd, Hoff iawn, coff - awn mewn
An - nw - yl Fab Duw nef, Oen di - nam, gan - wyd

Bass

ffydd Am Un a ddaeth er rhodd-i'r caeth yn rhydd:
ef, Ein Meich-iau mawr, ar gron-fawr ddae - ar gref,

O gar - iad mawr di-der - fyn Duw! Ein car-u'r oedd, un cy - wir yw,—
Dat-gudd-iad car - iad Tri yn Un, Pan wis-godd Ie - su na - tur dyn—

A ffrwyth y car - iad hwn-nw Yw cod-i o far - w'n fyw:
I ach - ub dyn tru - en - us, An - hap-us yn-ddo'i hun.

107

Olwen

This then is the tradition to which OLWEN[14] belongs—"the glorious tune OLWEN" as Erik called it.[15] The tune was recorded on a phonograph in 1910 by Mrs Herbert Lewis, a notable folk-song enthusiast, from the singing of Mr Jones of Croeswian, Caerwys, Flintshire, but did not appear in print until after the 1914–18 war.[16] The words are not known from any other source; no Welsh hymnal editor adds any identification ("Anon, adapted" is the usual wording: I myself did not find the words in my work on ballad and carol pamphlets. This does not however mean that they were not, as usual, written by a village poet and printed in a pamphlet which may yet come to light. A version of the words in English was produced by K. E. Roberts[17] and this is the version normally used. *Congregational Praise* adds a second verse by W. T. Pennar Davies.[18] (Kate Roberts' words, though set out as three verses in most books represent a single long verse in the Welsh: this is typical of the genre.)

The tune was recognized in the Journal of the Welsh Folk Song Society as a variant of the minor mode version of the tune to "Roedd yn y wlad honno"[19] (There were in that country). The Welsh immediately in the 1920's made two arrangements of the tune: Caradog Roberts[20] produced for the Caniedydd Committee (Welsh Congregationalist Hymnal) the version that appears as no. 34 in OBC:

2. Through wise men who found him Laid — rich gifts a
round — him, Yet ox - en they gave — him their hay:
And Je - sus in — beau - ty Ac - cep - ted their
du - ty; Con - ten - ted in — man - ger he lay.

3. Then haste we to show him The — prai - ses we
owe — him; Our ser - vice he ne'er — can des - pise:
Whose love still is — a - ble To show us that
sta - ble Where soft - ly in — man - ger he lies.

As Erik commented,[21] Caradog Roberts was a heavily Anglicized composer. No musician with a background in European 19th century music could see a tune thus notated and take it as anything but being strongly syncopated. Caradog Roberts arranged it accordingly. At about the same time J. T. Rees[22]

arranged the tune for *Emynau a Thonau*[23] in a much heavier, chorale-like style
which masks much of the syncopation.

This version has found favour nowhere else, but, I shall argue, shows that J. T. Rees had understood the problem. It is the OBC version that is taken up in *Congregational Praise* and in all subsequent English books.[24] The syncopated version produces a striking effect of sustained vitality over a long tune, quite unique in the repertoire. Erik in the *Companion to Congregational Praise*[25] says "In rhythm and melody nothing could be more essentially Welsh" and compares it with CRUGYBAR. There is however a problem here. This kind of rhythmic vitality is utterly foreign to Welsh singing, though it is to be found in the instrumental folk dances and in the harp tradition. CRUGYBAR when sung by the Welsh left to themselves is a heavy, often doleful tune, entirely without that kind of rhythmic drive that Erik saw in it.[26] It is possible to be misled here. One may think that the best place to hear what Welsh hymns are like is in the "Cymanfa Ganu".[27] These are, however, *conducted*, often by musicians who like to drive the singing along. I once heard a very cultivated Welshman say after one such session "I hate power-mad conductors". He was right: he knew that good traditional Welsh singing while not by any means sluggish within its own terms, has not the same kind of rhythmic vitality that good English singing has. It lives more on the movement of the words than on the drive of the tune.

What then is OLWEN? She is, I fear, a bastard, an illegitimate joining of two traditions, having the well known hybrid vigour of the progeny of such unions. Let me explain.

I did not come to any understanding myself, or indeed realize that there was any problem until I had worked over a large number of Welsh carol melodies as they appear in various manuscript collections in the Library of Bangor University, North Wales. The largest source is a set of manuscripts, small, thick volumes suitable for carrying in a pocket, in the hand of Ellis Williams of Dolgellau (1835–1911), whose bardic name was "Ylltir Eryri". There is a great variety of material in these books, but what I was looking for was the occasional entry marked "Mesur Carol". These tunes appear to have been taken down from local North Wales singers and it is clear that Ellis Williams had great difficulty from time to time in deciding what the rhythmic pattern of the tune should be. He clearly knew nothing about irregular barring and can be seen trying out different places for the regular bar lines, often leaving a nonsense version. In fact only one of the tunes seems to me to be rescued by irregular barring. His problems can usually be resolved by reference to words in the "Mesur". Then the accentuation of the words makes it clear that he is trying to find notation not for a regular measured rhythm but for pauses. Welsh music has a fixed lively rhythm in the dance music and the

111

harp music. In the purely vocal music however the words take control. A consistent feature of the Welsh language is the heavy accent on the penultimate syllable, which is often quantitatively short. This produces a feminine ending to lines and has shaped many Welsh tunes, for example PENLAN:[28]

The final syllable is often quantatively long, giving the pauses at the ends of lines in PENLAN and the common $\textit{d} \; \textbf{o}$ rhythm both within and at the end of lines. This is what is in action in CRUGYBAR:[29]

This too is what has produced the extraordinary effect in CYFAMOD[30] which is usually printed as here in 5/2.

(see next page)

It would be quite wrong to measure this out exactly in performance as in Holst or Stravinsky, for it is in fact a 3/1 melody (in this notation) with the first beat curtailed to half its length by the strong accent on a short syllable at the beginning of the bar. This makes excellent sense when sung to suitable words. In unaccompanied solo singing the same factor tends to make the singer not only shorten the musical value of the first syllable of a short-long pair, but to

pause on the second. When once I had recognized that this could happen I was able to solve Ellis Williams' problems for him and make sense of almost all the strangely barred tunes.

This led me to see what has happened to OLWEN. Such vigorous syncopation as is drawn out by the Caradog Roberts/Routley arrangement is quite foreign to Welsh singing. I have no doubt what Mr Jones sang. He was singing the words that had been handed down to him for "Roedd yn y wlad honno" to a major mode version of the tune. "Roedd yn y wlad honno" as it appears in OBC 59 has a pause in almost every bar.

An English musician would want to take out these pauses in performance so as to sing the tune as a steady 6/4. To produce a thoroughly Welsh effect the number of pauses would be increased so that there is a pause on the second and fifth crotchet of every bar. It then needs only to be transposed into the major to reach the real OLWEN. I again have no doubt that Mr Jones' pauses almost exactly doubled the length of the second note of every three and that the tune was, in that sense, faithfully transcribed from the recording. Unfortunately, however, there is to the musician brought up in modern conventions all the

difference in the world between ♩ ♩ ♩ | and ♩ ♩ ♩ | even if the pause were to have the effect of doubling the note. The first is three in a bar with one very strong pulse—at best declamatory, at worst laboured: the second is a swinging two in a bar, the impulse of the second beat being all the stronger because nothing happens to it—a conductor will often beat the second minim with great vigour in order to lift the rhythm. So the proper notation of what Mr Jones sang should be:

The effect is forced with English words, but it is not so with the Welsh words. The success of "All poor men and humble" (OBC 34) has much to do with the success of Kate Roberts in handling the continual feminine endings. The fact that, as far as I know, OBC 59 is hardly used has something to do with those pauses, but even more with the fact that she was not nearly so successful with the feminine endings in "Awake were they only".

An examination now of the J. T. Rees harmonization will show that he knew very well that something was wrong: looking at the Folk Song Society's version with its implications of syncopation he knew that no Welsh tune moved like that, and so in his arrangement while preserving the note values he ensured that he turned it into the kind of movement that is in CRUGYBAR. He used a great number of notes in the under parts to do it, but he was successful, though it is not what a folk singer would recognize—nor have I ever heard a Welsh congregation sing it.

Some conclusions

So what are we to do with the Roberts/Routley OLWEN in an English context? (The Welsh have a different problem, which they could most easily solve by singing one or other version of "Roedd yn y wlad honno".) Are we to reject OLWEN because it is "unauthentic"? We can certainly no longer quote it as "essentially Welsh":[31] as it stands it is certainly not that. We can surely however use it. It is attractive and unique, and up to a point that is case enough. But one can also say that we are doing no more than accepting a series of typical folk-song variants. The first is the tune in the major mode (as opposed to the more usual minor mode version of "Roedd yn y wlad honno") which Mr Jones presumably inherited: the second is his singing it in the Welsh manner with heavy verbal emphasis and the pauses generated by that: the third is in the mind of the musician trained in European conventions who saw the tune with pauses written out in measured form. This last is the version now encapsulated in the Roberts/Routley arrangement. Folk singers have always made songs their own by varying the words and melody. Here one tradition has made its own a tune in another tradition. The purist in search of the authentic version might be inclined to complain, but I do not think that the complaint should be upheld.

As soon as one has said that other points arise. In the history of congregational song there has continually been a movement across frontiers. Erik traced the origin of the typical English hymn tune in the Genevan psalm tune, as have others. But in the less sophisticated circumstances of English congregational singing the tunes proved too long and the metres too complex. It was even necessary for the eight lines of DCM to become the four lines of CM. Now that we try to re-introduce the great Genevan melodies they are found to be foreign and difficult, and except for a few do not take hold.[32] The same is likely to be true of the later introduction of the Lutheral Chorales. These have settled down in their stately four-in-a-bar form—a form consolidated in our imaginations by the fact that we find J. S. Bach using similar versions. Musicians may applaud the livelier original rhythms being re-introduced in German speaking countries, but those versions are unlike anything English congregations have made their own and will not be introduced easily. It will be interesting to see how the American Folk Hymnody now being so eagerly re-discovered, and proving often to have been based on hymns originally imported from England, will stand up to being re-imported to England, transformed as they have been by being made to serve the needs of a quite different worshipping community. Looking at another export from England we can legitimately regret that English, particularly 19th century, hymns passed unchanged into the use of many African Churches, despite great problems in the new language. Until they have been taken over and naturalized they are freaks, zoo specimens, so to speak, in an alien culture. The same may have to be said about our exports of contemporary hymns to other languages and our imports from them. In so far as our worshipping cultures are alike the passage can be made with some hope of success. In so far as they are different a process of change must take place and the originators of the hymn being thus transformed must be prepared to observe and be thankful that it is raising another people's hearts to God. This is not easy and some cries of pain may be justified. In lecturing to the RSCM Overseas Course in 1981 on current English hymnody I was twice taken to task for the sophisticated versions I played of music of black origin.[33] We do well to listen to such protests, but should claim the right to say that to make those hymns ours, as they must be for us truly to worship through them, this may be the kind of change that must

117

be made. We are not insulting the original tradition, we are paying it the compliment of making part of it our own.

The problem arises in an acute form when we look yet farther afield. We are being urged, and rightly from one point of view, to recognize that we belong to a world-wide church and to use the hymns and worship songs that come from cultures widely different from our own. We may use them in something like their original form for special effect, in a festival, for example, celebrating the world-wide spread of the Gospel. But they will need to be changed before they can be made our own. This does not mean that they need lose their character. This I think is the lesson of my "tale of OLWEN". OLWEN is attractive to English ears because it sounds a little exotic, but not so exotic as to be beyond our understanding: it has true hybrid vigour; two traditions have met and generated something strong and good by their meeting. This must be what Erik was hoping for all the time in his work on *Cantate Domino*. It has been criticized as not being a collection of the best of the traditional hymnody of the countries represented: such a book is in preparation.[34] *Cantate Domino* is already its supplement, since it reaches out into a wider world to ask what there is that each different worshipping folk may make their own. This is an adventure in worship barely yet begun in Europe. It promises to be exhilarating.

NOTES

I refer throughout to *The Oxford Book of Carols*, London 1928, reset 1964, as OBC.

1 *Cantate Domino* An Ecumenical Hymn Book, published on behalf of the World Council of Churches: melody only edition 1974, Bärenreiter; full score 1980 Oxford University Press. In the melody edition the hymns appear in two or more languages, in the full score in the original and in the English translation where this is needed.

2 Cymdeithas Emynau Cymru (The Hymn Society of Wales) was also represented in that I was present. This society publishes an annual *Buletin* in Welsh and normally meets during the week of the Royal Welsh National Eisteddfod for a Lecture and a business meeting.

3 E. Routley, *The English Carol*, London 1958, p. 214.

4 "Nos Galan" (or "Nos Calan", "New Year's Eve") inhabits a debatable ground between the harp airs and the purely vocal folk song. It appears in early collections of harp airs, e.g. *Welsh, English and Scotch Airs* John Parry, London (1752 or 1761); and *British Harmony* John Parry, Ruabon and London 1781. The

harmonic nature of the harp may be reflected in the present form of the melody.

5 It is significant that there is no tradition of successful opera or oratorio composition in Wales, a country that produces many great singers and fine choirs. From time to time the opera "Bronwen" by Joseph Parry (1841–1903, Professor of Music at Aberystwyth and Cardiff) is revived in a concert version; to all but the most patriotic ears it sounds faintly comic, and is definitely in a strange mixture of styles. Many composers in the 19th and 20th century composed cantatas and oratorios but none has proved of lasting value. The Welsh National Eisteddfod bars any language but Welsh from its platform, and thus at its concerts is almost completely dependent on translations.

6 See below on CYFAMOD, another stage of this tune's history. A version of the tune with English words by Fred Pratt Green appears in my *Llyfr Carolau Deiniol* (St Deiniol's Carol Book) Bangor 1974, and in a rhythmically slightly different version of the tune to the same words in *Partners in Praise*, Methodist Church Division of Education and Youth, London 1979. The whole subject is discussed at length by D. Roy Saer in *Ceredigion* Vol. VI, pp. 423–435.

7 See OBC 155, where it is set to quite unusable words. This surely is a tune that needs to be rescued for use in English.

8 See C. M. Simpson *The British Broadside Ballad and Its Music*, New Brunswick 1966, pp. 437–438: "The tune takes its name from the opening line of 'The Loyal English Man's wish For the Preservation of The King and Queen', 1692. . . . The elaborate eleven-line stanza pattern and the highly ornamented tune are not the sort usually marked out for popular success. But 'Let Mary live long' was instantly in vogue, and in less than a decade some twenty-five ballads called for the air". Simpson implies other versions of the tune but does not print them. In the light of the remark about the highly ornamented tune it is significant that the versions circulating in Wales are in much less ornamented form. Indeed the version in OBC 155, from a manuscript collection made by John Owen of Dwyran, is entirely without ornament. This collection is reported in the *Journal of the Welsh Folk Song Society*, Vol. II, and is said to give versions as sung in Anglesey in the late 19th century. It is clearly a treasure-house of carol melodies. I have been unable to trace its present whereabouts, but it seems to have been in the hands of the publisher, the late W. S. Gwynn Williams, Llangollen.

9 See E. J. Porter, *Two American Tunes: Fraternal Twins? (A study of a hymn family)* [The Papers of the Hymn Society of America XXX] Wittenberg, Ohio, 1975, and my footnote to that in "More on Two Early American Tunes" in *The Hymn*, Vol. 29, No. 4 (Oct. 1978), p. 222.

10 *Carolau Hen a Newydd* (Carols Old and New) Tonypandy, undated, probably 1950's, has 31 items, of which eleven are called "Old Welsh Carol" or can be inferred to be such (the book is attractively produced but very poorly edited). *Clychau Nadolig* (Christmas Bells) Llangollen 1942, has six traditional carols out of seven. The hymn books have very few carols. *Mawl yr Ifanc* (Youth Praise) the

Baptist young people's book of 1970 has the largest carol section, thirty three tunes and fifty one texts, Welsh and English (in a book of 183 tunes and 319 texts) but not a single one is a traditional Welsh carol of any kind. The parent book *Y Llawlyfr Moliant Newydd* (The New Handbook of Praise 1956) has seven carols "for adults" and of these two are traditional. A few carols appear in other general collections of folk songs and there are some single carols available in the publications of the University of Wales. In my *Llyfr Carolau Deiniol* (see note 7) I tried to avoid carols that were already generally available. The most comprehensive collection of the melodies is in N. Bennett's *Alawon Fy Ngwlad* (Lays of my Land) two vols, Newtown 1896: no words are given and the carol and ballad measures given cannot easily be fitted to the words.

11 See D. R. Saer "The Carol singing traditions of the Tanat Valley" in *Folk Life*, Vol. VII (1969). The Department of Oral Traditions and Dialects of the Welsh Folk Museum, St Fagan's, Cardiff, has done much work in recording this traditional custom, and tape recordings of these "carol services" may be heard at the Museum. They have issued a recording of three carols sung in the traditional manner under the title "Ar gyfer heddiw'r bore".

12 Eos Llechyd was the bardic name of The Revd Owen Davies (1829–1898). His *Cyff* was published in 1867 and republished in 1948 by the Bangor Diocesan Music Committee.

13 For completeness one should mention the custom of the *Mari Lwyd*. The origin of the name is uncertain (it means "Grey Mary"). In this predominantly South Wales custom a group of carol singers or "mummers" arrive at a house and start to sing. Those inside the house must reply in impromptu verses until one side breaks down. If that side is the one in the house then the doors must be opened and the *Mari Lwyd* given refreshment. To be understood this custom has to be set in a culture where even now poetry in the old strict metres is appreciated and many still write verse and compete in local competitions leading up to the National Eisteddfod competitions mentioned in the text. There has even been a popular Welsh language television programme "Ymryson y Beirdd" (Competition of the poets) in which week by week teams competed against each other in impromptu verse composition.

14 The tune appears in the following books current in the United Kingdom: *Anglican Hymn Book* 94; *The Church Hymnary* (3rd Edition) 185 (The *Handbook* to this hymnary is most unreliable on this hymn); *Congregational Praise* 721; *Christian Praise* 387; *Oxford Book of Carols* 34; *Y Caniedydd* (Welsh Congregational) 468/883; *Llyfr Emynau a Thonau* (Welsh Presbyterian and Methodists) 631/770; *Y Llawlyfr Moliant Newydd* (Welsh Baptists) 464/813. In USA it appears in *The Worship Book* 289.

15 *The English Carol*, p. 214.

16 In the *Journal of the Welsh Folk Song Society* (JWFFS), Vol. II, part 2, 1919, p. 127.

17 Mrs Katherine Emily Roberts (1877–1962).
18 William Thomas Pennar Davies (1911–   ).
19 OBC 59.
20 Caradog Roberts, (1878–1935).
21 E. Routley, *The Music of Christian Hymnody*, London 1957, pp. 163–4.
22 J. T. Rees (1857–1949).
23 *Llyfr Emynau a Thonau* (The Book of Hymns and Tunes) 1929, the book of the
    Calvinistic and the Weslyan Methodists: No. 631.
24 There is a very odd point here. Though the arrangement in *Congregational Praise*
    is almost identical with the Caradog Roberts version—there is a passing note in
    the tune at the beginning of the third line, and there are very slight differences in
    the harmonization at the beginning of "verse 2"—it is ascribed to Erik. It is more
    accurately "Roberts revised Routley", but subsequent English books simply
    ascribe the arrangement to Erik. It was unlike him not to give credit where credit is
    due.
25 *Companion to Congregational Praise*, edited by K. L. Parry, with notes on the
    music by E. Routley, London 1953 (No. 721), p. 301.
26 A distinctive use of CRUGYBAR is to be found in Anglesey where a funeral in Welsh
    is not thought to be complete without the singing at the graveside of a particular
    hymn on the joys of heaven to this tune.
27 "Singing Meeting". These gatherings were originally instituted in the 19th century
    as a means to improve the week by week singing of the congregation and to
    introduce new tunes at a period of considerable reform and revival in hymn
    singing. They may now be a gathering of a single congregation or of a number in a
    particular area; or they may be large, district or even national occasions. No
    national denominational gathering is complete without its "Cymanfa". Festivals
    that are in other respects secular often include one, and the Royal National
    Eisteddfod ends with a huge "Cymanfa". There is an annual "Cymanfa" in the
    Royal Albert Hall, London to which choirs come from many parts of Wales.
       Denominations print annual booklets for these meetings, containing mainly
    old favourites with the occasional new hymn. (There is as yet no modern revival of
    hymn writing in Wales despite attempts to "prime the pump" with translations
    from current English writing.) Quite a number of tunes have clearly been written
    with the large "Cymanfa" sound in mind rather than that of the small congrega-
    tion (for example TYDI A RODDAIST by Arwel Hughes, with a soprano top 'A' in
    the Amen; and, I would suggest, MAELOR by John Hughes: see *Y Llawlyfr Moliant
    Newydd* Nos 418 and 152).
       It is sadly true that the influence of the "Cymanfa" movement on the singing
    of the local congregation is now small: it may even be discouraging. The new
    hymns are largely reworkings of old motifs in both words and tunes and are rarely
    taken up. The style of the occasion is different from that of Sunday worship. The
    "Cymanfa" has largely become an end in itself.

28 By David Jenkins (1849–1915), widely set in English books to "In heavenly love abiding". In the context of the present argument it is significant that I cannot find a single Welsh hymn book where it is printed without the pauses, or a single book in English which includes them.

29 Welsh Hymn Tune, composer unknown. It was printed first in 1883 but appears in a manuscript of 1846. It is widely set in English books to "The light of the morning is breaking" by H. Elvet Lewis (Elfed) who wrote in both English and Welsh.

30 See D. R. Saer, *op. cit.* also the discussion by Erik in *The Music of Christian Hymns*, p. 117. It is fair to add that in the Bangor manuscripts of Ellis Williams there is a version of the tune notated as clearly but more conventionally:

31 See note 25 above.

32 A happy exception is the magnificent RENDEZ A DIEU = GENEVAN PSALM CXVIII, in use for a century for Heber's meditative "Bread of the world in mercy broken" but now serving equally well Erik's vigorous "New songs of celebration render", those words having been written for the tune.

33 One example was SING HOSANNA in the version by G. H. Knight in *More Hymns for Today* (A Second Supplement to *Hymns Ancient and Modern* 1980), No. 126.

34 A committee of the IAH is collecting material for such a hymn book.

9

LOOKING AT HYMN-TUNES: THE OBJECTIVE FACTORS

John Wilson

This chapter has grown from a talk given to The Hymn Society of Great Britain and Ireland at its annual conference in 1979. A recording of the talk was sent to Erik Routley, and it was an honour and a pleasure when he asked for further copies for use in his teaching of Hymnody. Musical illustrations given at the piano or by a singer must here be replaced by printed examples, or simply by reference to the name of a tune. Wherever possible these references are to tunes familiar on both sides of the Atlantic. In several cases where this may not be so the tunes are printed in full.

My first and less formal title was "What makes a hymn-tune successful, and why"; but because this sounded as if it had all the answers it had to be quickly qualified. We reminded ourselves that all our human judgments are either subjective, or objective, or (most probably) a blend of the two. In the case of hymn-tunes we find it easy, and even enjoyable, to make the quick subjective assessment—"I know what I like" or "What's wrong with the *old* tune?" And because, in singing a hymn-tune, we enter into a relationship with it, as we do with a friend or even with a stranger, the judgment will always be partly subjective. But if we are more seriously involved—if we compose, or edit, or choose, or even just study hymn-tunes—we cannot accept this as the whole story. We soon feel the need to be as objective as we can. Though we cannot pin down the mysterious quality of inspiration that a tune may have, we can nevertheless take a more professional look at its other qualities.

The two broad headings under which these qualities may be studied are those of "singability" and "memorability". The need for "singability" is obvious: there are many excellent melodies that are not congregationally singable. The reason for "memorability" is that the greater part of congregational singing is (musically) done from memory. Our best-known hymn-tunes, as Erik Routley pointed out, have acquired the status of folksongs, and are passed on in the same way. A melody (especially a long one) that is hard to memorise will always be at a disadvantage, however attractive it may be in other respects.

With singability and memorability in mind, our plan here will be to look in turn at the four obvious attributes of any hymn-tune:

(1) its *Melodic Outline*
(2) its *Rhythm*
(3) its *Harmony*
(4) and—very important—its overall *Structure*,

and in each case we shall consider what objective features may help or hinder (if only subconsciously) the singer in the pew. To keep the discussion general we shall ignore the special influence of favourite words, important as this can sometimes be.

We must first remember that singing is not just an affair of the voice. It is just as much, if not more, an affair of the mind. A good voice and plenty of breath are fine things to have; but if you cannot imagine in your mind's ear the pitch of the next note in a tune you cannot sing it. And in matters of rhythm, if you cannot visualise the length of a note you will not know when to stop singing it, which may be just as awkward.

This process of "pre-hearing" is fundamental, because the singing of a melody involves a continuous succession of such pre-hearings. In a familiar tune the process is almost automatic, but in learning a new tune it has at first to be conscious, and any difficulty in pre-hearing will mean a difficulty in singing. So the question of what musical intervals, upwards or downwards, can most readily be visualised brings us to the first of our main topics—Melodic Outline—the actual shape of the melody, apart from other features.

1. Melodic Outline

The intervals in a melody are either *leaps* or *steps*, as Darwall's well-known tune announces:

DARWALL'S 148th

The leaps are not indiscriminate ones. They are all nice-sounding, concordant ones, whose size (as the Ancient Greeks already knew) is governed by Nature and is expressible as simple ratios of vibrations. And if you use such leaps in your tune:

you are not being typically 19th century or typically 18th; you are saying "yes" to facts of Nature that cannot ever change or go out of date.

But in every age and every country people have felt the need of smaller intervals too, and have filled up some or all of the gaps to make a scale. And though there have been many ways of doing this, we in what may be called the Western tradition have for at least 400 years grown accustomed to what we call our "major" and "minor" scales, over which our minds can range easily up or down:

These two examples favour the stepwise. Our general conclusion will be that, whether in major or minor keys, the most successful tunes will have a judicious mixture of leaps and steps. To see how good the balance can be, dwell slowly on the opening paragraph of Nicolai's melody of 1599, WIE SCHÖN LEUCHTET DER MORGENSTERN, in its familiar chorale form:

We may here remember some of the other forms of scale. You can play the early American melody WONDROUS LOVE on the white keys of the piano, staring on *D* as a "keynote", but never using the note *F*. That scale is said to be "gapped". You can play the modal plainsong melody VENI, CREATOR on the white keys treating *G* as a "keynote", but using *F*♮ and not *F*♯. And there is the important class of melodies using the Pentatonic Scale, such as is provided by the black keys of the piano alone. The use of this in folk music is worldwide, and it seems that the human mind can range over a group of notes in this relationship with particular smoothness and ease, taking them in almost any order. Examples, both secular and sacred, are legion—Scottish tunes like AULD LANG SYNE and YE BANKS AND BRAES, Spirituals like STEAL AWAY, DEEP RIVER, and LITTLE DAVID, and old hymn melodies such as AMAZING GRACE and LAND OF REST.

What is not so generally noticed is the pentatonic influence (probably unconscious) in parts of other tunes. We do not think of the Victorians as being "folky", but what about the following openings?

All are pentatonic thus far; and in the early 20th century we find Vaughan Williams walking up the pentatonic scale as if to demonstrate it:

and also using it in a commanding way:

126

So if a composer today finds that he has been similarly influenced, he is in good company.

We pass on now to identify some desirable features in the melody-line as a whole. I suggest, first, that a successful melody will usually exhibit *a sense of purpose* from the start, very often beginning with a rising movement. Examples are too numerous to need quoting (see LUX BENIGNA and DOWN AMPNEY above). But if a tune starts by going downhill we must watch for its balancing recovery (as in GALILEE, GERONTIUS and SINE NOMINE). An exceptional example is the little tune SAVANNAH:

SAVANNAH

which goes downhill twice, then hovers round, and has a burst of life just before it ends. Certain English books have surprisingly matched its downward scales with triumphant Easter lines like "Love's redeeming work is done" and "Lives again our glorious King". John Wesley, who brought us the tune from the Moravians, used it more suitably for a penitential text.

Then secondly—having started purposefully, a successful tune will maintain its *poise* as it moves, balancing rise and fall without spending too long on the heights or in the depths. In the serene style of the 16th century it was almost a rule that if your melody took a leap in either direction the next note returned within it, so restoring the balance; and there is something to be learnt from that. Consider the way this 17th century psalm-tune moves:

LONDON NEW

leaping with great dignity and freedom, yet never losing its equilibrium. For a modern example of exceptional poise we can look at the tune SAN ROCCO written by Derek Williams of Cambridge for Isaac Watts's text "Give me the wings of faith to rise":

SAN ROCCO   C.M.   Derek Williams (*b.* 1945)

This melody, now increasingly familiar in England, has a most satisfying and confident sweep, and is also in use with two or three modern texts.

The poise of any tune is partly reflected in the choice of final notes for its various phrases—the moments of rest, or "ports of call". These should be well varied, as for example in that outstanding psalm-tune ST MARY from a Welsh psalter of 1621:

ST MARY

—and in many other tunes. A slight reservation must be felt in a case like that of Stanford's robust ENGELBERG, where the second "port-of-call" is melodically the same as the first, suggesting some lack of progress.

Thirdly, a good melody will respect congregational limits in matters of pitch and vocal climax, and here the concern must be as much with average pitch-level as with the highest notes reached. NUN DANKET in the key of *F* is a strain for unison singers even though it does not rise above *D*. The great range of WIR PFLÜGEN means that a proportion of unison singers will be uncomfortable at one end of it or the other—a price worth paying, however, for such a favourite. Victorian tune-writers were sometimes thinking of four-part harmony with only sopranos on the melody, which accounts for the original top *F* in Henry Smart's well-known winner REGENT SQUARE. He contributed it to a book used by the English Presbyterians at Regent Square Church in London, where the whole congregation, led by a precentor, was accustomed to singing in harmony without an organ. The tune-writer of today will be wise to allow for unison singing, even if he chooses to present his harmony in four parts.

The pitch of the highest acceptable note depends on so many factors, both psychological and vocal, that generalisation is difficult. For unison singing in a mixed congregation a top *E* is only just acceptable if all the conditions are good. What is important to singers, if they are to make the extra effort, is the appropriate placing of the high note and the way it is approached. But there is room for considerable variety: the summit may be touched more than once, and there may be secondary summits not far below it. Each case must be considered separately.

One of the best examples of successful "summitry" is in the tune CARLISLE by the blind 18th century musician Charles Lockhart:

CARLISLE

The first line reaches the 5th degree of the scale, the second the 6th, and then we go all out for the summit, taking ridge after ridge until the top is reached, after which we take a short cut home. The tune RICHMOND has a similar build-up in its third line, and in REGENT SQUARE the exalted mood leads irresistibly to that (original) top F.

There are also cases where the placing of the high note may seem less happy. In ST PETER (a favourite which the present writer finds somewhat enervating) it comes as early as the second note; the rest of the tune lies below, with very limited ports of call, and each stanza seems to start with a sigh. Various well-known tunes actually start with their highest note, which is not a good idea unless you return to it later. If you can reach the first note of EIN' FESTE BURG you have nothing higher to worry about. The same applies in Britain to the tune MOSCOW; in America, where it is often called ITALIAN HYMN, the sixth phrase follows the original outline and lightly touches one step higher still. We may note in passing that a high note is likely to be sung best if it occurs on a strong pulse rather than a weak one.

In considering the approach to a climax we can take a lesson from Haydn himself, who in composing his famous AUSTRIAN HYMN had second thoughts on this very point. In an earlier draft the second half of his melody had been like this—

—which would have been good enough for most people. But no: he finally restrained those 5th and 6th phrases and kept them lower, and, by bringing in A♮, created that clinching cadence in the dominant key, making a springboard for the leap to the top. And then he revised the descent by checking it halfway down, as if to allow us a momentary backward glance.

So much, then, for Melodic Outline apart from other factors. Perhaps we can sum up by saying that the contour should be such as the mind can readily grasp and remember, and then the voice will be able to follow suit.

2. Rhythm

Our second main attribute of a hymn-tune—its Rhythm—can be a potent factor in success. Our appreciation of rhythm, and our facility in remembering and reproducing it, are not in themselves *musical* talents. Almost everyone has them, and musicians must have them; but even if you were tone-deaf you could still play a drum rhythmically. Rhythm is for us all.

A succession of regular pulses, all of equal strength, is not so much a rhythm as a rhythmic background, of little interest to the mind. But if you disturb a pulse here and there, or arrange that the pulses can be strong or weak, there can emerge a pattern that does begin to interest the mind. The rhythm of the great tune from the choral finale of Beethoven's 9th Symphony, popular in American churches as HYMN TO JOY, is on this basic level, and British hymnbooks still contain dozens of lines of melody, in various metres, that are composed of equal notes. They have the alternation of weak and strong pulses, but are without any variety of short and long—without real rhythm.

This equal-note style was not characteristic of the early Reformation tunes which set the pattern for much of our hymnody. No Reformer would have expected success with such a dull style. It evolved from the late 17th century onwards, where the earlier psalm-tunes came to be sung (certainly in Britain) at an unbelievably slow pace. Each note became an event in itself, and the original rhythm was lost in the slowness. Everyone grumbled about it, including Isaac Watts; and unfortunately, when the tempo picked up in the mid-19th century, many composers and editors continued to think of equal notes as a norm. This was true of Anglican books and their imitators, but I would guess that the habit was less prevalent in America. The record was held by *Hymns Ancient & Modern* (1861), which presented the tune OLD 113TH as a succession of ninety-six equal minims. Almost the only thing that can be said for the equal-note style is that it helps to accommodate, by ironing out, any irregularities of stress or punctuation that an author has allowed himself in certain stanzas.

Tunes in triple time were well liked, especially in the 18th century, because instead of simple equality they could substitute a lilt. In John Wesley's collections WINCHESTER NEW appeared first in duple time as we know it, but was later changed to triple, and a similar conversion overtook MARTYRDOM in the early 19th century.

A dull equality of pulse can be relieved in various easy ways, as the better 19th century composers well knew. Selected syllables can last for two pulses instead of one, and (assuming the unit is a crotchet) you can bring in simple patterns like:

131

Such things give life to tunes like Gauntlett's IRBY, S. S. Wesley's HAREWOOD, and Elvey's ST GEORGE'S, WINDSOR.

Today's mainstream tune-writers are rhythmically free, and looking back we can see that their freedom was heralded by the two celebrated settings of "For all the saints"—Stanford's ENGELBERG in 1904 and Vaughan Williams's SINE NOMINE in 1906. Both are in G major, both are largely for unison singing, and the first may have helped to inspire the second. We have only to imagine either of these melodies reduced to equal notes to see what rhythmic freedom means. In SINE NOMINE, especially, the free melody floats above an equal-note bass, a device well known to Baroque composers, as for example in the tenor aria "But thou didst not leave" in Part Two of Handel's *Messiah*. SINE NOMINE requires rhythmic adjustments in certain stanzas, and this is a point to be watched by both authors and composers. Composers, who are always tempted to write a tune that is fine for stanza 1, must keep in mind the rhythmic needs of other stanzas, and if possible avoid specific adjustments. The words-writer, on the other hand, is asked to accept some loss of poetic freedom, and to remember that a hymn-text is not a poem but what has been well called a *libretto* for practical singing by a largely unskilled congregation. And the best situation of all is when author and composer can co-operate, and are ready to make mutual adjustments.

There are two rhythmic devices that might seem, at first sight, to offer difficulty. One is when a composer suddenly alters the number of pulses in a measure—say from 3 to 2, or 3 to 4. This is what the famous music-critic Ernest Newman once called "the limp" in the new music of his day; but it has, in fact, good classical ancestry. Do you find any difficulty in this melody from Brahms's trio, op. 101?

It is intriguing, but perfectly smooth. For a congregation the question is only whether the change of time feels right, and is not like a limp or a hiccup. Caryl Micklem has recently contributed to *New Church Praise* (1975) a most appealing hymn-and-tune which we are glad to be allowed to reproduce here. Its time-changes are so easy that time-signatures are superfluous. Notice, too, the close matching of melody and text, and the elegant economy of the harmony:

132

ALL KINDS OF LIGHT   5.88.55.
Unison

Caryl Micklem (*b.* 1925)

1 Father, we thank you for the light that shines all the day,
2 Father, we thank you for the lamps that lighten the way;
3 Father, we thank you for the friends who brighten our play;
4 Father, we thank you for your love in Jesus today,

for the bright sky you have given,
for human skill's exploration
for your command to call others
giving us hope for tomorrow

most like your heaven; Father, we thank you.
of your creation; Father, we thank you.
sisters and brothers; Father, we thank you.
through joy and sorrow; Father, we thank you.

All kinds of light

1

Father, we thank you
for the light that shines all the day;
for the bright sky you have given,
most like your heaven;
Father, we thank you.

2

Father, we thank you
for the lamps that lighten the way;
for human skill's exploration
of your creation;
Father, we thank you.

133

Father, we thank you   Father, we thank you
for the friends who brighten our play;   for your love in Jesus today,
  for your command to call others   giving us hope for tomorrow
  sisters and brothers;   through joy and sorrow;
    Father, we thank you.   Father, we thank you.

The other possible difficulty is that of Syncopation, which also has long ancestry. To 16th century musicians, and—from the evidence of the psalters —to their congregations too, it was no more of a problem than it is to younger people today. In those days you learned to sing *off* the beat almost as soon as you had learned to sing *on* it, giving composers a resource which was called "driving the notes". We meet this especially in the hymn-tunes of Orlando Gibbons (1583–1625), the best known being SONG 34 (ANGEL'S SONG) from *Hymnes & Songs of the Church* (1623), which we mention now because of misapprehensions about it. Here (with note-values halved) is the melody, for a single stanza by the poet George Wither:

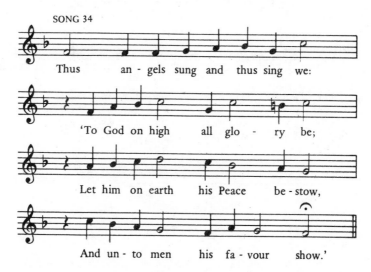

SONG 34

Thus an - gels sung and thus sing we:
'To God on high all glo - ry be;
Let him on earth his Peace be - stow,
And un - to men his fa - vour show.'

All the evidence is that we should think in terms of what we now call 2/4 time, controlled in those days by the "tactus" or down-and-up motion of the hand. The bar-lines serve to mark the ends of lines of words, and the first line is straightforward enough. Thereafter, following an erroneous lead in the early 20th century, some editors—ignoring the one-pulse rest—have presented the

remainder of the tune in triple time, instead of leaving it as intended in duple-time-with-syncopation, which is much more subtle and appealing. (I well remember the pleasure of a school choir when they were first shown this, and realised that their ability to syncopate was needed in a tune more than 300 years old!) Other tunes in which we meet such syncopation include COMMANDMENTS, SCHMÜCKE DICH and AVE VIRGO VIRGINUM.

There is a good deal of syncopation in modern hymnody of the lighter kind, and it must not be allowed to sound cheap and conventional. It is certainly appropriate in a lively little piece called *Communion Calypso*, with words written by Fred Kaan (b. 1929)for a Jamaican folksong. The arrangement is by Doreen Potter, with whom Erik Routley had worked so closely on the international hymnbook *Cantate Domino*. She died in 1980, having just been able to see the full music edition through the press. This piece has a most infectious quality:

Communion Calypso

135

1. Christ is spo - ken and seen and heard.
2. love in word and in deed ex - press.
3. God - im - man - u - el ev - ery where!

Je - sus lives a - gain,

earth can breathe a - gain, pass the Word a - round: loaves a - bound!

© Copyright 1975 Agapé.

3. Harmony

We come now to our third main attribute of a hymn-tune, passing from the melody to the Harmony that accompanies it.

The worshipper may enjoy attempting his or her part in the harmony; but we find, as we stand in the pew, that the harmony is something that happens all around us, in which we and our singing are immersed. Its contribution is a potential bonus, and we do not need to learn or memorise it. Harmony will be accounted successful if it enriches the melodic experience, and if it is helpful, if only subconsciously, to the singer.

Let us remember, however, that several classes of hymn-melody were originally intended for singing unaccompanied in unison. There are the medieval plainsong tunes such as PANGE LINGUA. There are the 16th century tunes of Genevan origin, including the OLD 100TH itself. (Sing this slowly to

136

yourself, preferably in the original rhythm, and note how balanced and satisfying its outline is.) And there are the so-called French Diocesan Tunes of the 17th and 18th centuries, of which ISTE CONFESSOR is a good example —Catholic in origin and preserving a little of the spirit of plainsong. And lastly a category that has proved particularly fruitful in our own century—folksongs borrowed to serve as hymn-tunes, of which examples are numerous on both sides of the Atlantic. All such melodies, in their earliest use, would have been sung unaccompanied, and it can be a helpful experience in today's worship if we sometimes treat a stanza or two in that way. In general, however, our congregations expect harmonies to be added, and we have to see that these are appropriate. The best compliment that such harmonies can earn is that they make the melody "sound right".

In most of our successful hymn-tunes there will be a close link between melody and harmony. Sometimes the harmony will play a special part, as we shall see, but in general its purpose is to facilitate and interpret the progression of the melody. If the two were allowed to be seriously at odds you could find yourself with something as bizarre as:

Such mistaken attempts at "modernity" have been seen in print.

But we must look in more detail at the interaction between melody and harmony. A melodic transition such as a rising 4th within the same harmony is easy for the mind and therefore easy for the voice, as at (a).

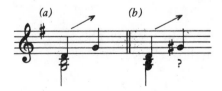

Recall the first three chords of the tune MENDELSSOHN, or the first five of REGENT SQUARE. But it would be much harder to sing (b), whatever the chord for the G♯, because that note conflicts with the memory of the previous harmony and is therefore harder to imagine.

There is another interesting case when a melody-note is deliberately a discord with its own bass, as is the first note in each of the following pairs:

In such cases the sound of the discord *predicts* the next sound, and the tune is, for the moment, self-propelling without the aid of memory. Such propulsion is found in many tunes, a notable example being the old favourite AURELIA, which has the following pairs, as well as several others:

AURELIA

etc.

Rather similar is an example in REGENT SQUARE, where the harmony neatly warns us of a change in the melody:

Phrases 1 and 3 of this tune have the same melody except for their final notes at (a) and (b); but by changing the harmony as we approach (b) the composer has made it almost impossible for us to sing (a) by mistake.

Harmonic changes can be used to create interest when a melody is stationary, and we can see J. S. Bach doing this in three different ways at the start of the chorale HERZLIEBSTER JESU in his Passion Music:

The special chromatic treatment at (c) follows the clamour of the crowd for the crucifixion of Jesus, and thus responds to a particular mood. (American hymnbooks usually give this fine Crüger melody in its earlier and more modal form.)

Harmony can also induce, or hint at, a change of key even when the melody does not insist on it, as in that refreshing moment in the third line of IRBY, if you are using Gauntlett's original version. Similarly, the use of a particular harmony can create a momentary radiance in the melody, as in the opening of ADESTE FIDELES, which in many English books is now harmonised thus:

139

This seems to have started with Joseph Barnby in his *Hymnary* of 1872, and was picked up by the *English Hymnal* in 1906. The special warmth of the fifth chord is surely in the spirit of the Christmas invitation.

In a number of 19th century tunes, notably those of Barnby and Stainer, harmonic colouring was used as a distinctive feature, and it is rather curious that rich chords (such as those known to musicians as the "diminished seventh" and the "augmented sixth"), frequently used by Beethoven and later masters, are branded as sentimental when used in hymn-tunes. Barnby himself made this point forcibly. A good example of harmonic progression as a chief interest is found in Dykes's popular MELITA, where the melody of the penultimate line is:

No one would think much of this if they had to sing it unaccompanied, but they enjoy its effectiveness with the harmony as a driving force.

So—looking at any hymn-tune—we may ask: How well has the composer used the resource of harmony? Does the harmony help the singers and make the tune "feel right"? Is the harmony interesting without being odd or pretentious? And, of course, circumstances alter cases. If you want the carol-melody IN DULCI JUBILO to sound light and flowing, you will not use the harmonies of Bach, who, in the tradition of slow chorale singing, thought of it majestically thus:

And you must not try to speed him up: Bach's chorale harmonies were not meant to be speeded up.

In certain recent books, such as *The Church Hymnary, Third Edition* (1973) in Britain and *Ecumenical Praise* (1977) in the USA, there have been experiments in using "modern" and sometimes atonal styles of harmony. I

140

have insufficient evidence, as yet, of the reception these have had from worshippers.

4. Structure

The appeal of a graceful melodic outline, of a vital rhythm, and even of interesting harmony, will be consciously felt by a congregation. The appeal of our fourth attribute, the *Structure* of the tune as a whole, will be largely subconscious, but is no less important. Does the shape of the tune carry you through it in a way that "feels right"? Have you, after singing a complete stanza, had a satisfying experience? Does it stand repetition? And above all, does the tune readily go into your memory, because—in the end—the only really successful tunes are those that people can hum to themselves after a reasonable time of learning and use.

This question of memory gets more and more important the longer the tune is. Most people can easily memorise a single phrase of melody, even a fairly long one like the opening phrase of Gibbons' SONG I:

This is like remembering the first line of a poem, such as "Earth hath not anything to show more fair" from Wordsworth's well-known sonnet. But they may not easily remember how it goes on; and to remember an eight-line tune is comparable with remembering an eight-line stanza of verse. There is a point to be made here about all kinds of memorising—namely that the task is much easier if the thing to be memorised has *a structure that can be described in words*. Only then can our minds get to work on it, and this is as true of a hymn-tune as it is of a friend's telephone-number.

There is also the important general principle for musical forms, as well as for poems and plays and speeches, that each of them—for full success—must strike a balance between the claims of *Unity* and those of *Variety*. A successful hymn-tune will have features that unify it, such as repetition of phrase, or recurring rhythms; and it will also maintain our interest throughout, by variety of melody and rhythm and harmony, by possible change of key, and by an occasional special feature such as reaching a high point. And all this is especially true in a long or longish tune. Too much Unity, as in repetitive

141

"pop" music and in some religious songs, is tediously memorable. Too much Variety, as in an indulgent improvisation, may be fun while it lasts, but is not memorable. We must always be watching the balance between the two.

Looking first at some of the shorter tune-forms we find that in a four-line psalm-tune such as WINCHESTER OLD most people can think of it in two balancing halves, and the more so if their conventional endings seem to "rhyme". It is not often that a short tune overdoes the Unity, but there is a risk of this in the little tune INNOCENTS:

This has the same rhythm in each line, the same melody for 1st and 3rd lines, and the 2nd and 4th lines much alike. The saving touch of variety has to come from the harmony, which at (a) remains in the tonic key, and at (b) modulates to the dominant.

We may note that several well-known four-line tunes have their first line the same as the third—TALLIS'S ORDINAL, ST CLEMENT, and (except for one detail) Dykes's NICAEA. This plan gives us, through successive stanzas, the pattern *ABAC, ABAC,* . . . ; and if this seems rather short on Variety we must not forget that in each stanza the words are different.

There is also a satisfying pattern that was often used by the great composers, in which a short phrase is first balanced by another short phrase, and then both are capped by a phrase twice as long. A good example in hymnody is the well-known tune variously named BEETHOVEN, FULDA, GARDINER, GERMANY and WALTON, whose creator William Gardiner in 1815 claimed that he had taken it "from Beethoven" but could never remember where. This pattern is just right for a tune in Short Metre, such as ST THOMAS, or Stainer's little tune ST PAUL'S ("Lord Jesus, think on me"):

And if a stanza has this pattern twice in succession we have a satisfying form for a longer tune, with a half-time point as a useful landmark. A first-class example is the 18th century tune LEONI, and equally good from the next century is Elvey's DIADEMATA.

The claims of both Unity and Variety are met in the most basic fashion by the pattern A – B – A. (Make a musical statement, make a contrasting one, return to the first.) On a larger scale this is the pattern of many classical arias, and of movements of the Minuet–Trio–Minuet type. In the smaller forms of strophic melody linked with verse the pattern is more often A – A – B – A, the opening phrase being clinched by repetition before we move to B. This is the form of many hymn-tunes derived from folksongs, Welsh or English, such as LLANFAIR and AR HYD Y NOS and FOREST GREEN. The Welsh tune EBENEZER, though not a folksong, is in the same mould, and the reader may be interested to see in GWALCHMAI and ELLACOMBE two small but effective departures from it.

Consider, however, another popular Welsh tune—HYFRYDOL. Sing this through to yourself and note where it departs from the A – A – B – A form. Sure enough, we have the 8 measures of "A" and they are exactly repeated; and then "B" occupies another 8 measures. But then, instead of returning to "A", the rest of the melody continues as new material (with a helpful sequence) through to an ending rather more final than that of "A". In this tune the youthful composer R. H. Prichard (1811–1887) gave us (no doubt unwittingly) an example of a most important melodic form used in Germany from the time of the Minnesingers in the 12th century to that of the Mastersingers as late as the 17th. For rather obscure technical reasons theorists call it the "bar-form". In this form the opening "A" was a rounded phrase or paragraph ending in the home key. This was then repeated; and those two statements were known as the "Stollen" or "props" of the melody. Everything that came after was known as the "Abgesang" or "after-song", which sometimes ended by quoting from the ending of "A" itself. In Wagner's opera *Die Meistersinger* we are told how an aspirant to the rank of "master" in the Guild had to prove that he could compose a song in this form.

A considerable number of our hymn-tunes, mainly ones of German origin, are structured in this way. A short and simple example from the late 17th century is UNSER HERRSCHER (or NEANDER):

But to see the bar-form at its best we turn to such notable tunes as LOBE DEN HERREN, MIT FREUDEN ZART, ST THEODULPH, EIN' FESTE BURG, Nicolai's noble pair WIE SCHÖN LEUCHTET and WACHET AUF, and various tunes by the prolific Johann Crüger. Nor must we forget two very English carols—THE FIRST NOWELL and the SUSSEX CAROL, as well as the Dutch Easter carol VRUECHTEN. From this distinguished list we conclude that the historic "bar-form" has commended itself to worshipping congregations very widely, and continues to do so.

If the closing measures of a bar-form tune quote largely from its opening measures, the bar-form is evidently approaching $A - A - B - A$, and such is the case in LUTHER (one of the two tunes called NUN FREUT EUCH). The student may also like to consider the Welsh tune ABERYSTWYTH from this point of view. Other variants of these two forms have proved very successful, as in the case of ABBOT'S LEIGH ("Glorious things of thee are spoken") written by Cyril V. Taylor (b. 1907) in 1941 and in Britain the most popular new tune of its generation. In singing this, one has the general impression of $A - A - B - A$

form, but the first two "A" sections end only with half-closes, and the final section is a much altered and developed form of "A".

A further variant, associated with folksong, is found in the form A – B – B – A, as in the tune KINGS LYNN, arranged by Vaughan Williams for "O God of earth and altar"; and mention of this brings to mind a point of some importance. In KINGS LYNN there is a small but significant difference between the two "B" statements. Where the first has:

the second has:

Such a feature adds to the musical interest, and would have been no trouble to the elderly fisherman of Kings Lynn in Norfolk who sang the tune to Vaughan Williams in 1905—indeed he might have invented it. But, to a congregation, such small and apparently arbitrary differences are an obstacle, and are best avoided. The same applies to a feature such as a special tune-ending for the last stanza. By all means let the choir and organ do something special, but not the congregation, unless you arrange that it doesn't matter if they forget to do it!

All the forms we have mentioned maintain a balance between Unity and Variety and have provided ground-plans for many successful hymn-tunes. But we must now bring in another factor, and that is the influence of the hymn's *metre*. Metrical shape will itself help to dictate structural shape, and can add significantly to a tune's memorability.

George Herbert (1593–1632) printed his poem "The Altar" so that it looked like an altar on the page, and although this was only a poetic conceit, it is true that a stanza with a "shape"—with lines of more than one length—is more suggestive both to a composer and to a singer than one of regular metre such as L.M., 888888, 10 10 10 10, etc. Equality is not as interesting to the human mind as inequality, and the composer of a would-be-successful tune in, say, 888888 starts with a handicap. He must devise a musical structure that transcends the plainness of the metre. As editors know, it is in some of these regular metres that we are most short of successful tunes, which may be another way of saying that hymn-writers have fallen too easily into adopting them. Certainly, in Methodist circles, Charles Wesley's frequent use of six-8's remains a problem for tune-selectors.

For a very popular stanza-with-a-shape we need look no further than:

> Praise to the Lord! the Almighty, the King of creation!
> O my soul, praise him, for he is thy health and salvation!
>   All ye who hear,
>   Now to his temple draw near,
> Joining in glad adoration.
>
> Tune: LOBE DEN HERREN

An exceptional case, perhaps, but what a splendid shape! Its vital statistics are 14 – 14 – 4 – 7 – 8; and how satisfying it is when, after singing those two long lines of 14, we come to the short line of 4, with the high point of the melody. The very sight of the short line would remind us of its notes if we were unsure of them, so helping the memory in what is quite a long tune.

We can recall other hymns whose distinctive mix of long and short lines is strongly reflected in the structure of the tune, hymns such as "Come down, O love divine" to Vaughan Williams's DOWN AMPNEY; "All my hope on God is founded", well-known in Britain to Herbert Howells's (1892–1984) MICHAEL; and—for a simple example—"Jesus, still lead on" (translations vary) to the tune known as SEELENBRÄUTIGAM or ROCHELLE. To these, English Methodists would certainly add Charles Wesley's hymns in metres of 55.11.D and 555.11, which have a zest all their own.

The conclusion must be that though the traditional metres with equal lines *can* inspire fine tunes, *in*equality is (once again) more interesting. So today's authors may be encouraged to favour more varied metres, and to continue to experiment with intriguingly irregular ones, as the writers Brian Wren (b. 1936) and Caryl Micklem have successfully done.

We shall conclude our look at Structure and Memorability by considering a pair of fine and long melodies, one French and one German. Both of them, along with the OLD 100TH, came into the English tradition via the Anglo-Genevan psalter of 1560, of which the only known copy is at Manchester College, Oxford. Each melody has 12 musical phrases, and the phrases are grouped in threes. The French melody was for Clément Marot's metrical paraphrase of Psalm 3, in the metre 667.667.667.667., beginning "O Seigneur . . .". Books that now contain it use that name, or else call it OLD 122ND from its English use for Psalm 122 in "Sternhold and Hopkins". After a long period of eclipse it was revived in 1899 by Robert Bridges, who matched it very well with his own version of "When morning gilds the skies". Here is the melody, with note-values halved:

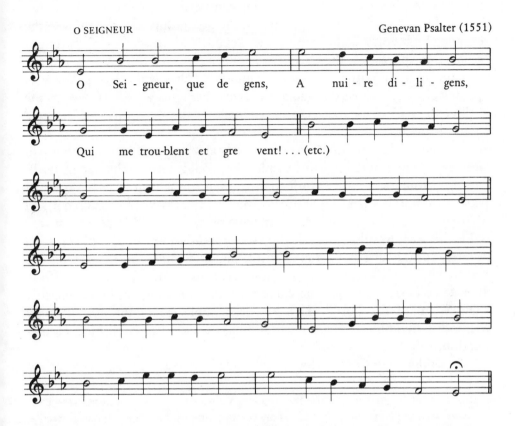

O SEIGNEUR   Genevan Psalter (1551)

O   Sei - gneur, que de gens,   A   nui - re di - li - gens,

Qui   me trou-blent et gre   vent! ... (etc.)

We have suggested that a memorable structure will be one that can helpfully be described in words. But there is scarcely anything you can say in words about the form here, beyond mentioning that the phrases go in threes. Within this constraint the tune has an engagingly improvisatory style. Of the 12 phrases no two are the same, and there are pairs of them, such as the 3rd and 6th, and the 8th and 11th, that can easily be confused. To sing this melody from memory, without prompting, is a considerable feat; and we must conclude that it will only be a rewarding tune for those who can read music, or who have exceptional memories—or, one must suppose, for a congregation under a musical discipline as strict as Calvin's at Geneva.

For a contrast in memorability we now turn to the German melody, first printed at Strasbourg in 1525 and reliably attributed to the young composer Matthäus Greit(t)er (*c.*1490–1550). It appeared with his own paraphrase from Psalm 119 in the giant metre 887.887.887.887., beginning "Es sind doch selig alle". As the reader will see shortly it is a fine example of the bar-form, and there is plenty in its structure that can be described in words. Easily memorable features are the repetition of the first group of three phrases, the recurring high notes as the "Abgesang" begins, and the sequential pattern of the last three phrases as they stride home. Big as the melody is, a congregation can come to terms with it in a very few minutes. (They will of course know its opening phrase, because this and one or two other hints were borrowed by the 17th century Catholic musicians at Cologne when they fashioned the tune LASST UNS ERFREUEN.)

To tell the full story of Greiter's melody and its continued appearance in German, French and English hymnbooks would need a chapter in itself. During its four and a half centuries it has been furnished with a wide variety of texts, including Watts's "I'll praise my Maker" and (as when Bach used it) "O Mensch, bewein dein Sünde gross". In what proved so sadly to be the last year of his life, Erik Routley was asked by the present writer if he would create a new text for the tune in its original form, and based on Psalm 119 as Greiter's text had been. His response was characteristically warm, and early in 1982, after some correspondence, he completed a powerful hymn under the title "The Word of the Lord". This has been published in the new (British) Methodist hymnbook *Hymns and Psalms* (Methodist Publishing House, London, 1983).

In sending a draft of the hymn Erik added:

It is a beautiful metre to write in—one feels almost any fool could manage it: I have used the *New English Bible* as my starting off point . . . [and] have allowed myself the odd echo from the NT, which I hope is legitimate.

And in a later letter he spoke of the inspiration for two particular lines in the first stanza:

The superb thing about Ps. 119 is that it is so personal and at the same time so concrete. That 96th verse—which was a favourite of [Bishop] Hensley Henson's, has long been a favourite of mine. (It was my starting point when I had to give the presidential address to the Congregationalists all those years ago). "I see that all things come to an end, but thy commandment is exceeding broad."

Erik's hymn, and the tune itself, shall now bring us that message afresh:

ES SIND DOCH SELIG ALLE' 88.7.88.7.D.

Original form of melody
by M. Greiter (*c.* 1490-50)
Harmonised by John Wilson, *b.* 1905

Unison or harmony

1. God speaks, and all things come to be;
2. Grant this to me, Lord, let me live
3. Bless'd are they all who hun - ger sore

God speaks, and Sa - tan's le - gions flee,
And, liv - ing, keep your word, and give
To see your righ - teous - ness once more

Scat - tered by love's brave splen - dour;
My life to gain its trea - sure.
En - throned in hearts and na - tions.

God speaks, and our for - give - ness seals;
Here but a stran - ger, let me trace
Bless'd are the pure in heart, who seek

God speaks, and gen - 'rous grace re - veals
My path to - ward a rest - ing place
To hear what God the Lord will speak

In pre - cepts wise and ten - der.
Where I shall find pure plea - sure.
In bliss - ful con - tem - pla - tions.

Though all I see must have an end,
Much kind - ness you have shown to me,
Bless'd be our God, who gives us light;

God's sta - tutes past all time ex - tend,
Pro - mise and pledge of joy to be,
Bless'd be the mer - cy and the might

By breadth and length un-boun - ded.
Con - tin - ue thus your bless - ing!
Which all the day at - tend us.

Though we are crea - tures of a day,
Wis - dom that mould - ed all my life,
Bless'd be the pro - mi - ses of grace,

Though heaven and earth may pass a - way,
Guide me, in days so full of strife,
Bless'd be the laws that still em - brace,

God's word is deep - er found - ed.
Gen - tly my heart pos - ses - sing.
En - ligh - ten, and de - fend us.

The Word of the Lord

1 GOD speaks, and all things come to be;
   God speaks, and Satan's legions flee,
      Scattered by love's brave splendour;
   God speaks, and our forgiveness seals;
   God speaks, and generous grace reveals
      In precepts wise and tender.
   Though all I see must have an end,
   God's statutes past all time extend,
      By breadth and length unbounded.
   Though we are creatures of a day,
   Though heaven and earth may pass away,
      God's word is deeper founded.

2 Grant this to me, Lord, let me live
   And, living, keep your word, and give
      My life to gain its treasure.
   Here but a stranger, let me trace
   My path toward a resting place
      Where I shall find pure pleasure.
   Much kindness you have shown to me,
   Promise and pledge of joy to be;
      Continue thus your blessing!
   Wisdom that moulded all my life,
   Guide me, in days so full of strife,
      Gently my heart possessing.

3 Bless'd are they all who hunger sore
   To see your righteousness once more
      Enthroned in hearts and nations.
   Bless'd are the pure in heart, who seek
   To hear what God the Lord will speak
      In blissful contemplations.
   Bless'd be our God, who gives us light;
   Bless'd be the mercy and the might
      Which all the day attend us.
   Bless'd be the promises of grace,
   Bless'd be the laws that still embrace,
      Enlighten, and defend us.

Erik Routley (1917–82)
based on Psalm 119

10

ERIK ROUTLEY AND THE EPISCOPAL HYMNAL 1982

Raymond F. Glover

Since the early 1970's the Standing Commission on Church Music of the Episcopal Church (SCCM) has been engaged in the lengthy and complex process of revising the Episcopal hymnal. Because this was also a period in which the Church was engaged in the revision of *The Book of Common Prayer*, the work of the Commission developed on two fronts: one, the creation of supplemental collections of hymns and service music to satisfy the immediate needs of congregations and the other, the development of long-range plans for the revision of the hymnal. In these activities the Reverend Dr Erik Routley was to play an important role.

In 1971 the SCCM, with Dr Lee Hastings Bristol, Jr as General Editor, published the first of its major supplements, *Songs for Liturgy and More Hymns and Spiritual Songs*. This was the first hymnal of the Episcopal Church to contain any of Erik's works; one of his best known texts, "All who love and serve the city," and the tune SHARPTHORNE. Five years later the Commission, recognizing Erik's gifts as a highly respected hymnologist, hymnal editor, theologian and teacher, invited him and the Rev. Dr Chad Walsh, a recognized and revered poet and priest of the Episcopal Church, to share their scholarship and vision with them.

The first working session of the Commission with the two scholars occurred on May 23, 1977, at the Virginia Theological Seminary in Alexandria, Virginia. On the day before Erik and Dr Walsh were to arrive, the Commission, after an intense discussion on the nature and function of hymns, produced a number of headings which were to form the outline of the symposium. They were: "What is a hymn?", "Is a hymn text different from a poem?", "Should the hymns in our hymnal conform to the Lectionary?", "Where do we find texts in a contemporary idiom which fit the needs of our new Lectionary?", "The artist as theologian and the theologian as artist," and "Style-ethnic hymns." The presentations and the dialogue between these two witty, articulate and very gifted men was electrifying, and I, as a fledgling member of the Commission, felt both stimulated and awed by their presence.

Dr Walsh defined a hymn as "a special kind of poem, a teaching vehicle. With music, a poem says more than it does by itself. Writing a hymn is limiting to a poet; he practices freedom with restraint. He sets limits and works within them."

Erik's response was a marvelous example of his cleverness in using words to express ideas in unforgettable ways. He saw "hymns as being poetry for people who aren't poets and music for people who aren't musicians." To this he added, "the duty of a hymn is to get the best out of people who sing it so they can respond to what the Lord has done."

On the art of writing hymns, Erik went on to say that, "Writing hymns is a specially pastoral craft; ordinary folk *own* hymns. Hymn writers must be practical."

On the nature and function of a hymnal, the two speakers presented varied thoughts. Chad Walsh felt that congregations should have freedom in the choice of hymns. He said, "We might have one general hymnal and some smaller supplements. Churches must constantly be experimenting."

Erik described a hymnal as "a body of practical divinity." As he developed his thoughts on the matter, he spoke on a favorite theme: "people should read their hymnal as poetry in addition to singing the hymns in church." In conclusion he reminded his listeners that "great Anglican hymnals have always been companions to the prayer book."

Erik's thoughts on a structure for revision became the thesis on which the text committee pursued its task of selecting hymns. He suggested that we "start with a lectionary structure and continue with important additional sections, dividing the work." As a result, our text Committee carried out a systematic analysis of the three year lectionary to ascertain the major biblical themes for which we needed texts. They determined the biblical themes of the hymns they were retaining from the *Hymnal 1940* and its supplements. By a comparison of the themes of the readings and the themes of the texts they had in hand, they were able to determine areas of need.

The subjects of style and ethnic hymnody elicited strong opinions from both speakers. Erik observed that "style is one thing, and the status of ethnic hymnody another." He asked, "What is non-ethnic hymnody?" In evaluating hymns, Erik cautioned us to "apply the same standards to all hymns." He continued, "Are Swedish, Mennonite, Welsh, etc., hymns ethnic? We must not use anything simply as a matter of duty." Chad Walsh observed that "style" is confusing; one should say "styles."

154

Although I had read many of Erik's books on music and liturgy and knew of him through the experiences of many of my friends, the Alexandria session was my first meeting with him. I was immediately aware of the sheer volume of knowledge he had amassed through his years of study and work; his directness; his incredible enthusiasm for the Church's song; his gregariousness and delightful sense of humor; his ability to be both practical and visionary.

Following the Alexandria meeting, the SCCM continued its preparation of supplemental materials for publication, including five books of hymns and service music. These collections were both practical and experimental in nature.

Hymns III, the largest of the two collections of hymns in the series, reveals significant contributions by Erik as author, music editor and composer. Among the texts is his paraphrase of Psalm 98, "New songs of celebration render," set to his adaptation of the Louis Bourgeois tune, RENDEZ À DIEU. As a music editor, he is represented by his edition of the tunes ELTHAM and MONTROSE, and as a composer by his very sensitive tune written for use with the Alfred F. Bayly text, "What does the Lord require." In this tune SHARP-THORNE, we have a fine example of Erik's ability to capture and illuminate in rhythm and harmony the essence of a text's meaning and mood and in the melody to underlay and support the natural rise and fall of the verbal structure of each line of the poetry. The end result is an ideal wedding of text and tune. These are the first of Erik Routley's efforts having a direct impact on hymnody in the Episcopal Church, and most particularly on the shape and content of the *Hymnal 1982*.

As a writer of hymnology and the theological implications of music in worship, as a spirited director of hymn festivals, as a leader of conferences and workshops and as a hymnal editor, text writer, and composer-arranger, Erik for many years has had a profound influence on many Commission members even though, like me, they did not know him personally.

However, several members of the Commission during the period of preparation for revision and the actual revision process did know Erik well, worked with him professionally, and numbered him as one of their cherished friends. Erik made himself readily available to them for consultation which clarified issues and led to sources of many texts and tunes. Directly and indirectly, he challenged us all to reconsider old values and to raise our sights toward new and expanding horizons.

The year 1981 found Erik once again working directly with the SCCM in their preparation of the *Hymnal 1982*. In January of that year, the Commission had progressed sufficiently with their task to seek from outside authorities advice and evaluation of works being considered for inclusion in the *Hymnal 1982.*

The three Reader Consultants selected were Erik (at that time a professor at Westminster Choir College, Princeton, New Jersey), The Rev. Dr Clement Welsh, then Warden of the College of Preachers, The National Cathedral, Washington DC, and the Rev. Dr Hays Rockwell, Rector of St James Church, New York City. Each Consultant was asked to read critically the proposed texts from the vantage point of literary style and integrity of textual alteration and to evaluate the historic and stylistic comprehensiveness of the collection. Fortunately, all three men accepted our invitation and subsequently offered wise and insightful comments which affected the contents of the collection as well as the final form of many texts used.

In Erik's comments on proposed texts, his vast reservoir of knowledge, the breadth of his theological understanding, his delightful sense of humor, and his ability to focus directly on issues all came to the fore.

For example, as a man of integrity, he came directly to the point about our inclusion of the hymn, "Amazing Grace," which gained such popularity with its revival in the 1970's. Erik wrote, "Are you including this because a lot of people have been persuaded by the media to want it?" In this query, Erik hit at a point of truth, for the text with the tune, NEW BRITAIN, had been included in response to the very strong appeal of clergy and laity throughout the church.

Stanza three of the W. A. Percy text, "They cast their nets in Galilee," raised a particular problem for Erik. This centered on the questionable identification of the "Young John who trimmed the flapping sail" with the writer of the *Book of Revelation* who "homeless, in Patmos died." Dr Rockwell wrote of this text, "A poem is not a piece of New Testament scholarship and I think Dr Percy is entitled to his license in verse 3." Erik felt differently and in his very distinctive way wrote, "Humph, no, sorry! I don't regard scholarship as the enemy of poetry. That will be because I am not a scholar. I regard imprecision as the enemy of poetry." I can almost see the gleam in Erik's eye and the set of his jaw as he stated his opinion. The text committee went along with Dr Rockwell's opinion and the stanza in question is in the book.

A similar delightful exchange occurred in response to the SCCM's plan to replace the third line of William Kethe's text based on Psalm 100, "Him serve with myrth, his praise forth tell" with "Him gladly serve." This alteration had been proposed because the archaic word "myrth" might not be understood by contemporary singers. To this Erik responded with emphatic gusto, "What in the name of fortune is wrong with 'Him serve with myrth'? Of course we know that Kethe wrote 'with fear' but the Scotsmen altered it to myrth, and if myrth is good enough for a bunch of 17th century Presbyterians, it's good enough for you." With that, "myrth" was restored!

In its philosophy for hymnal revision, the SCCM wrote, "The texts of the Hymnal should wherever possible use inclusive language which affirms the participation of all in the Body of Christ, the Church, while recognizing our diverse natures as children of God." To be specific on the use of sexist language they stated, "There are also a number of hymns couched in language that sounds so exclusively masculine that many of our parishioners are deeply troubled. The Commission believes that both the Church and the original authors will best be served by judicious modification of these texts to more inclusive language."

Erik had serious doubts about this and although "bowing humbly to the demands of the so-called anti-sexists" went on to write, "We are not going to please *everybody* if we delete words offensive to the 'anti-sexist' party." As a pragmatic solution he wrote, "I am going to suggest to our committee (the committee preparing the hymnal of the Reformed Church of which Erik was the editor) that we print the original version at the bottom of the page whenever we make this kind of alteration. I do not know whether I shall get away with it; but I give notice that I shall try."

Through these and many other significant comments, Erik contributed greatly to the refinement of the texts accepted for inclusion in the *Hymnal 1982*.

With Erik's sudden and untimely death, we were robbed of his further involvement in the *Hymnal 1982*, for we had planned to ask him to be a consultant on the tunes chosen for the music edition of the book. Despite this, the book will be a very tangible record of his gifts as author, composer, and editor. Included in the *Hymnal 1982* are two texts under his name—his metrical version of Psalm 98, "New songs of celebration render," and "All who love and serve the city." The list contains several entries representing his work as a composer and music editor—the haunting tune WOODBURY which he wrote for the Charles Wesley text, "Come, O thou Traveler unknown," LITTON, a spacious and stirring tune which he wrote shortly before his death for use with the John R. Peacey text, "Go forth for god," AUGUSTINE, written for the George Herbert text, "Let all the world in every corner sing," and SHARPTHORNE, with the Albert Bayly text, "What does the Lord require," already mentioned as appearing in two of the supplements produced by the SCCM. His work as an editor is represented by his adaptation of the tune, RENDEZ À DIEU.

157

In late 1985, the *Hymnal 1982* will be presented to the Church at a special service of dedication. At that time will be remembered the many men and women who gave generously of their time and talents. High on the roll will be the name of Erik Routley, hymnologist, poet, composer, theologian, teacher, and writer. His teaching helped shape the contents of the book; his criticisms and advice brought it to a high state of excellence; and his texts, tunes and tune arrangements add to its enrichment.

11

THE HYMN IN THE ANGLICAN LITURGY

James H. Litton

Liturgical renewal during the second half of the twentieth century has played a major role in the creative surge of hymnody during the past two decades. Most Churches have shared in the many changes brought about by Vatican II, especially through various adaptations of the three year lectionary, one of the major results of Vatican II.

In preparation for the *Lutheran Book of Worship* Lutherans in the United States placed emphasis on the "Hymn of the Day" as part of the various trial collections which paved the way for the LBW. This practice of having a hymn which is based on the Readings, and especially on the Gospel of the Day, sung each Sunday is, of course, a continuation of Luther's integration of hymns into the liturgical framework of worship on Sundays and on Feast Days. Seventeenth and eighteenth century German composers expanded this important Lutheran tradition through the development of liturgical concerted music, reaching a monumental apogee in the cantata cycles by J. S. Bach.

English hymnody began and was developed under different circumstances with diverse and often conflicting influences. Before we can focus on these developments and explore how they relate to late twentieth century English speaking (and singing) Christians, let us remind ourselves of the role of hymns in the pre-Reformation Church.

The Latin metrical office hymn became an important liturgical enrichment of the daily offices during the middle ages, and the sequence hymn became an important daily and seasonal part of the Mass. This liturgical hymn repertoire increased greatly and required "ecclesiastical" refinement when certain aspects of such hymnody became over developed.

As we probe beyond Latin hymnody, we find that liturgical integration was expected in the use of Greek hymns. These hymns were a necessary part of the liturgy and did not exist apart from their liturgical functions. A perfect example would be one of the earliest hymns, the *Phos hilaron*, which, as a candle lighting hymn, was as much a part of the Greek evening office as was the Sanctus a part of the Latin Mass. Seasonal Greek hymns, especially hymns

159

for the Great Fifty Days of Easter, were often dramatic expressions of the joy of the Easter Season. Many of these translated Greek Hymns form the core of the English Easter hymn repertoire.

Unlike the various German Church Orders of the sixteenth and seventeenth centuries, most of which continued Luther's liturgical role for the hymn in the proclamation of the Word, the English *Book of Common Prayer* of 1549 and the revised Prayer Book of 1552 made no provision for hymnody. Archbishop Cranmer did translate the *Veni Creator Spiritus*, a ninth century Pentecost office hymn, to be used as an important part of the Ordinal of 1550—English rites for the ordination of Bishops, Priests, and Deacons. This hymn became a part of the ordination services in the 1662 revision of the *Book of Common Prayer*.

During the politically, theologically, and liturgically confusing decades of the second half of the sixteenth century, English Christians had little opportunity to sing in church. The English liturgy of 1549 was intended to be sung, but by clerks or by the choir, and not by the congregation. "The service seems to have been conceived of as essentially a dialogue between priest and clerks or a monologue by the priest, with the congregation indicating its participation and assent in the "Amens". This limited participation by the people was non-musical, apart from singing the "Amens".[1]

Robin Leaver reminds us that hymns and metrical psalms were known in England during the mid sixteenth century and that Cranmer included office hymns in his reformed Latin Breviary (*ca.* 1538 to *ca.* 1545).[2] Leaver also solves the mystery of the English hostility towards hymns in the liturgy.[3] The fact that a group of English churchmen visited Zurich during the 1530's and 1540's and became influenced by Zwinglianism is an important key to the absence of liturgical hymnody in the English Prayer Book. "It is quite likely that Cranmer was silent on the question of congregational hymns in the liturgy because of the currency of Zwinglian views in the country: silence on the matter would serve to appease both conservative catholics who wanted to retain traditional ceremonial and music and also radical Zwinglians who wanted neither"[4]—a good example of Anglican compromise!

While the 1549 Prayer Book allowed for the continuation of the sung liturgy, the 1552 revision of the *Book of Common Prayer* makes it quite clear that the norm had become a spoken rather than a sung service—clearly an influence from Zurich.

Since this newly revised liturgy provided for little or no music it is obvious that parish churches, especially, could now dismiss clerks or choirs; and with the exception of a few parish choral foundations, the only choirs remaining were the endowed choral foundations in cathedrals, the collegiate chapels, and the Chapel Royal. It was the 1552 Prayer Book which brought about the development of the dual "cathedral service" and "parish church service" which has been a part of the English Church in various degrees since 1552. In view of the hostility toward music, it is remarkable that the "cathedral service" inspired composers such as Tallis, Byrd, Gibbons and many others to write a large amount of liturgical settings and English anthems which produced a "golden age" of English church music in the late sixteenth and early seventeenth centuries. The cathedral service was a continuation of the medieval choral service but sung, of course, to the liturgical texts of the 1552 Prayer Book. The parish church norm, then, became the said service, fertile ground for the future development of non liturgical hymn singing.

In order to trace the introduction of hymn singing into the English Church it must be remembered that metrical psalms and hymns, primarily from German and Danish Lutheran sources, had been translated into English since the mid 1530's. In addition, Thomas Sternhold published a selection of English metrical psalms in the mid 1540's, and these formed the beginning of "The Old Version" which became the primary and official collection of English metrical psalms. When first published these psalms were not sung in church, but, like their original French counterparts, were popularly sung at court.

The human urge to sing the praises of God in church, then, was a privilege of a few professional cathedral choirs, and before congregational hymnody in the form of English metrical Psalms could begin to enrich the largely spoken parish church services, several historic accidents must yet take place.

The accession of Queen Mary in 1553 and the concurrent return of the English Church to Rome caused many English protestants to flee to Germany and Geneva, where they came under the influence of Calvinist worship patterns and metrical psalm singing. The singing of these psalms made a profound impression on them. Upon their return to England after Elizabeth I had, once again, severed the ties with Rome, they began to introduce the singing of metrical psalms in English. "Whereas the French psalms were versified in many subtle French lyric meters, (the English metrical psalms) . . . were all in the meter of the old ballads."[5] This popular, almost folk meter, caused the metrical psalms to be immediately popular. But there were no provisions for this congregational hymnody to be used in the English liturgy. As compared to the liturgically integrated German hymn, the English hymn "was extra-liturgical . . . a . . . devotional song which was sung outside the Prayer Book offices."[6] In the Injunctions of 1559 Elizabeth I allowed the

161

singing of hymns (metrical psalms) before and after Morning and Evening Prayer, and by 1566 hymns could be sung before and after sermons. It is significant that metrical psalm or hymn singing still was extra-liturgical, and in no way related to the liturgical action.

A possible exception to this was the somewhat limited custom of singing hymns during communion in some parish churches and, perhaps, even in a few cathedrals. The 1549 Prayer Book provided for the singing of Agnus Dei by the clerks (or choir) during communion, but this was dropped in the 1552 Prayer Book. It is possible that, in some places, a communion hymn had begun to fill this lack of music during the communion of the people.

The history of the English hymn during the seventeenth and eighteenth centuries is well documented by Routley and others,[7] and need not be covered here. Erik Routley reminds us that "Dissenters played an important part in the development of English hymns. The reason for this lay in their lack of a stable prayer book service and their traditional unwillingness to recite the Creeds. For them, hymns were all that the congregation could utter in the course of a service. It was therefore likely that the need of hymns would first be felt where the Prayer Book was not in use."[8] So we see that for the dissenters, hymns were their primary liturgy. The next great step in the development of English hymnody is provided by a free churchman, Isaac Watts. With the exception of certain works by Charles Wesley, most hymns written during the late seventeenth, eighteenth, and early nineteenth centuries were non liturgical and expressed individual or corporate Christian experience or interpreted scripture, often as a kind of sung sermon. In contrast Charles Wesley, rooted in the traditions of the English Church, but deeply aware of the urgent need for reform, wrote many hymns based on the seasons of the Church year.

An important development for English singing Christians took place in the late eighteenth century following the Revolution in America. What was left of the English Church in the former Colonies had to reform itself as an independent Episcopal Church. The American Proposed Book of Common Prayer of 1785 included a large selection of metrical psalms along with 51 hymns in an appendix bound in with the Prayer Book. When the American Book of Common Prayer was ratified in 1789 it included the entire metrical psalter and 27 hymns.[9] Thus began the history of the Episcopal Hymnal in America which has always been a close companion to the Prayer Book. Additional revisions of the Hymnal took place in 1808, 1826, 1832, 1865, 1871, 1892, 1916, 1940, and 1982. Each early revision saw the inclusion of additional hymns to the standard metrical psalm collection, and the 1821 decision to make hymns "legal" in the Church of England affected the growth of new hymnody. In 1871 the hymn collection had grown so large that a separate, but still official collection of hymns became necessary. It is important to realize that even though it was published separately this collection of hymn texts was regarded as an extension of the Prayer Book; this and every Episcopal Hymnal since the original 1789 collection had to be approved by the General Convention of the Episcopal Church before the texts could be sung in Prayer Book services. The American Episcopal Hymnal, then, as an "official" companion to the Book of Common Prayer has paved the way for hymns to become a liturgical necessity in Episcopal worship especially in America.

Two nineteenth century developments in England had a profound effect on the slow evolution of the liturgical integration of hymnody in Anglican worship: the first was the Tractarian and Anglo Catholic movement which influenced the subsequent explosion of hymnody and led to the second influence, the publication of *Hymns Ancient and Modern* in 1861. This vastly increased repertoire of Anglican hymns was largely responsible for the first separate American Episcopal Hymnal of 1871, and *Hymns Ancient and Modern* influenced the Hymnals of 1892 and 1916. Routley reminds us that *Hymns A & M* was "arranged in a manner that recalls the Prayer Book",[10] and these two American Hymnals follow the A & M example by arranging the order of hymns to correspond to the order of the Prayer Book—morning, evening, church year etc.

Even though these nineteenth century liturgical directions in Anglican hymnody had become obvious, the fact that the English Prayer Book, with the same few rubrics regarding music, had not been revised since 1662 hampered any truly creative use of hymns in the liturgy. Officially hymns still were to be sung only before and after services or before and after sermons.

The first American Prayer Book continued this rubric, but made a major step toward the development of liturgical hymnody by providing for a hymn to be sung at the communion. This may have been the legalization of a common practice of singing communion hymns which, as we have seen, may have developed after the Agnus Dei was omitted in the 1552 Prayer Book. The American Prayer Book also allowed a "proper Hymn from the (Hymn) Selection" to be sung in place of the Gloria in excelsis. It is significant that both of these rubrics refer to the "Selection," or the appendix of hymns which was printed with the Prayer Book. This is a clear example of the use of appropriate hymns as a part of the liturgical celebration many years before "hymns of human composure" were legally allowed in Anglican worship.

The next step in the still slow but steady development of Anglican liturgical hymnody was the many nineteenth century translations of medieval office and sequence hymns as well as significant English versions of Lutheran chorales. *The English Hymnal* of 1906, which included a generous representation of these translated office hymns and German hymns, as well as many new hymn tunes, became an inspiration and model for many twentieth century hymnals, including the *Episcopal Hymnal 1940*. Departing somewhat from the Prayer Book format and beginning with seasonal hymns, this *Episcopal Hymnal*, in turn, has influenced most other American hymnals during the second half of this century.

Major liturgical and musical changes since 1960 have affected most Churches. Liturgical scholarship with roots in nineteenth century research has brought about the intensification of the liturgical movement, especially since World War Two. This has resulted in the greatest revisions in Roman Catholic worship since the sixteenth century, in trial liturgies for Lutherans and Anglicans throughout the world, the ecumenical and international study committees for English liturgical texts, and finally many greatly revised liturgies represented in collections and documents such as *The Lutheran Book of Worship*, The American *Book of Common Prayer, 1979* and the English *Alternative Service Book, 1980*.

New musical styles in hymnody and liturgical music were brought about by the Twentieth Century Light Music Group which began in England in the mid 1950's. Since the mid 1960's various study groups, conferences and individuals have been concerned with providing new hymn texts which speak of contemporary concerns and meet the needs of contemporary liturgical revisions.

The demand for new hymn music and new hymn texts has brought about a "Hymn Explosion" on both sides of the Atlantic. The immediate results of this explosion have been the publication of supplements to almost every major hymnal in England, the publication of the study/trial series which led to the LBW, and the following American hymn supplements: *More Hymns and Spiritual Songs, Ecumenical Praise*, Hymnal 1940 *Supplement II, Hymns III, Songs for Celebration, Westminster Praise, Cantate Domino* (Diocese of Chicago). The list continues to increase today, but after nearly two decades the supplements begin to give way to major hymnal revisions.

Alan Dunstan points out other historic "hymn explosions," especially those of the eighteenth century Wesley revival and the Oxford Movement inspired nineteenth century revival of Anglican Hymnody.[11] The current liturgical renewal or revival urges the modern Christian to sing about Baptism, various aspects of the Eucharist, The Great Fifty Days of Easter, The Lord's Day, as well as new themes and emphases for Pentecost, Lent, Epiphany and

Advent. The Eucharist causes us to go forth to love and serve, and to sing hymns which cause us to be concerned for the world—and the cities in which we live. These subjects and themes are clearly represented in recent hymnal revisions such as *The Lutheran Book of Worship, With One Voice*, and *The Episcopal Hymnal, 1982*, the English Methodist Hymnal and current *Hymns A & M* revisions. The soon to be published Hymnal of The Reformed Church in America, edited by Erik Routley, with his editorial work completed a few days before his sudden death, surely will include many examples of contemporary hymnody themes.

A survey of the *Episcopal Hymnal 1982* as compared to the *Hymnal 1940* reveals the following liturgical concerns:

		Hymns new to the collection	Retained from 1940 Hymnal
a)	Baptism	6	none
b)	Great 50 Day of Easter	19	15
c)	Pentecost	12	9
d)	Lent	7	4
e)	Advent	9	8
f)	Holy Week	3	9
g)	Lord's Day	5	1

This hymnal returns to the format of *Hymns A & M* and *The Episcopal Hymnals* of 1892 and 1916 by becoming, once again, a close companion to the Prayer Book with the first section providing hymns for the daily offices. In this section we find 15 hymns new to the collection for Morning Prayer, Noontime office, Evening Prayer and Compline, and 21 hymns for these daily offices retained from The 1940 collection. Many of these hymns are either classics or new translations of historic office hymns.

The table of contents for the *Hymnal 1982* is a detailed guide to the liturgical use of the hymns in the collection.[12] Not only are hymns for seasons of the Church Year clearly indicated but specific Sundays such as "The First Sunday in Lent, Year B" are assigned appropriate hymns. There is an expanded section of hymns for the Great Fifty Days of Easter with suggested hymns for each Sunday of Easter as well as for the entire Easter Season. The Hymns for Lent include texts which provide an expanded and enriched understanding of our preparation for the Easter Festival. Thomas Cain's hymn, "Eternal Lord of life, behold your church,"[13] is a good example of a hymn which expresses the pilgrimage through Lent to Easter, and includes Baptismal symbolism. New symbolism for the season of Lent was begun in the *Hymnal 1940* by the inclusion of the sixth century Latin hymn, "The glory of

165

these forty days," and continued in *Hymnal 1982* with Percy Dearmer's "Now quit your care" from the *Oxford Book of Carols*.[14] The inclusion of this text may be contrasted by the addition of the highly personal poem by John Donne, "Wilt thou forgive that sin."[15]

Enriched symbolism for the Day of Pentecost is evident in the inclusion of "A mighty sound from heaven" by G. B. Timms,[16] and by Timothy Rees, "Holy Spirit, ever living as the Church's very life."[17] It was discovered that many important liturgical themes could not be found in existing English hymnody, and it became necessary to commission new texts or to search through classic Lutheran hymnody in order to incorporate such themes. The Easter section is greatly enriched by the inclusion of "Christ Jesus lay in death's strong bands"[18] (*Christ lag in Todesbanden*) and by "Christ the Lord is risen again"[19] (*Christ ist erstanden*).

A vivid example of a contemporary Easter text is found in John Bennett's "Look there! The Christ, our Brother, comes resplendent from the gallows tree".[20] It is significant that the Holy Baptism section contains only hymns by contemporary writers such as Scott Francis Bremmer, John Arthur, Michael Saward, Mark Evans, John Brownlow Geyer or translations of classic Lutheran hymnody.

One of Luther's major contributions to liturgical German hymnody was the compilation of the *Deutsche Messe*, metrical hymns which could be sung in place of the Latin ordinary of the Mass. When the first American Prayer Book provided a rubric allowing a Hymn of Praise as a possible alternate for the Gloria in excelsis, the door was opened for the development of hymns in English as an alternative for the ordinary of the Service of Holy Communion. However, this creative possibility for English Eucharist liturgical hymns was never developed. When congregational singing of the Eucharist ordinary became necessary, composers were called on to create music for non metrical texts which could be quickly learned and sung by largely untrained singers —not an easy task.

The American *Book of Common Prayer, 1979* includes a rubric which allows, in certain circumstances, the singing of metrical versions of canticles and psalms in the liturgy. *The Hymnal 1982* provides a selection of metrical versions of canticles such as the Gloria in excelsis, Te Deum, Magnificat, First Song of Isaiah, among others. There is also a list of metrical psalms and psalm paraphrases which could be sung liturgically. *The Hymnal 1982* also includes at least one hymn for all Holy Days, The Common of Saints, Various Occasions and a greatly expanded General Hymns section which has a carefully detailed liturgical and topical index.

Unlike the *Lutheran Book of Worship, Hymnal 1982* does not include a list of Hymns for each Sunday of the Church Year, but the scriptual index makes it possible to find hymns which relate to the readings of the three year lectionary. Because of projected revisions of certain details of the lectionary it has been decided to issue lectionary hymn guides on a regular basis rather than risking the possible obsolescence of having such a guide being printed in the Hymnal. Hymn lectionary lists have been prepared by various groups and individuals and these provide a complete "hymn of the day" for the current three year lectionary based on hymns from *Hymnal 1940* and its various supplements. Publications from England provide comprehensive hymn selections for each Sunday and for the readings of the ASB lectionary.[21]

The *Alternative Service Book* and the American *Book of Common Prayer, 1979* both have greatly expanded the three or four classic Prayer Book rubrics regarding the use of music in worship. In the American Book the two rubrics from the 1789 Book which provided for hymnody within the liturgy have been expanded to scores of references which provide for a "hymn, psalm or anthem" to be sung after readings and at various other important parts of the services. It is interesting to note that the rubric of 1559 which first allowed hymns to be sung before and after services has been removed. A hymn, psalm or anthem may be sung (as an Introit) at the beginning of the service of Holy Eucharist, and *before* the Dismissal, but rubrics allowing hymns before and after any of the Daily Offices are not to be found in the *Prayer Book 1979.* Instead, the classic rubric which allows music to follow the set office collects has been included in the American Prayer Book for the first time for all the offices,[22] allowing a hymn or an anthem at this place in the service. In addition, the Prayer Book lists four specific hymns as necessary components of liturgies: Palm Sunday procession—"All glory, laud and honor"; Good Friday Liturgy —"Sing, my tongue, the glorious battle" and in ordinations—either *Veni Creator Spiritus* or *Veni Sancte Spiritus.*[23]

It is clear that these revised Anglican liturgies now recognize music and especially hymns as an integral and necessary part of worship in the Anglican tradition. "In other words, we are now presented with the opportunity of drawing on the Lutheran emphases with regard to the place of music in the liturgy which were never taken up in the sixteenth Century."[24] Thus nearly 450 years after the first Book of Common Prayer and nearly 500 years after Martin Luther composed, arranged, and commissioned the large repertoire of liturgical hymns for the revised Lutheran services, hymns now are a recognized and essential part of Anglican worship.

It is hoped that clergy, church musicians, and all who plan for liturgical celebrations will carefully study hymn texts so that choices from the many hymn possibilities for a service can be made with the greatest sensitivity as to the place of a specific hymn in a service and to the hymn's appropriateness for the occasion during which it is sung. Hymns are no longer extra liturgical, but have become necessary for late twentieth century liturgical celebrations. The creative possibilities are great for future hymn writers, composers of hymn tunes and other liturgical music. For the first time Anglican Prayer Books now have embraced music as a necessary and integral aspect of worship, and our response should be one of great joy and enormous creativity. If we and future generations respond to the musical challenge of our revised liturgies it is certain that the future of the Singing Church will be celebrative and creative.

NOTES

1 R. A. Leaver, *The Liturgy and Music*, Bramcote [Notts.] 1976, p. 4.
2 *Ibid.*, pp. 5–8.
3 *Ibid.*, pp. 9–13.
4 *Ibid.*, p. 10.
5 E. Routley, *English Hymns and their Tunes*, privately printed by The Hymn Society of Great Britain and Ireland, 1981, p. 3.
6 Leaver, *op. cit.*, p. 25.
7 See appended Selected Bibliography.
8 Routley, *op. cit.*, p. 6.
9 M. Martens, "Four Centuries of Anglican Hymnody in America" in *Hymnal Studies One*, Church Hymnal Corporation, New York 1981, p. 16.
10 Routley, *op. cit.*, p. 10.
11 A. Dunstan, *The Hymn Explosion*, London 1981.
12 See *Hymnal Studies Two*, The Church Hymnal Corporation, New York 1982.
13 *Proposed Texts for the Hymnal 1982*, No. 114, Church Hymnal Corporation, New York 1982.
14 *Ibid.*, No. 121.
15 *Ibid.*, No. 123.
16 *Ibid.*, No. 182.
17 *Ibid.*, No. 413.
18 *Ibid.*, No. 164.
19 *Ibid.*, No. 165.
20 *Ibid.*, No. 148.
21 See appended Selected Bibliography.

22 The 1928 BCP allowed for an anthem to be sung at this point in Evening Prayer only.
23 The inclusion of ordination hymns is a continuation of the rubric from the ordinal of 1550 and the BCP 1662.
24 Leaver, *op. cit.*, p. 30.

SELECTED BIBLIOGRAPHY

F. Blume, *Protestant Church Music*, New York 1974.

A. B. Bushong, *A Guide to The Lectionary*, New York 1978.

A. Dunstan, *The Hymn Explosion* [RSCM Handbook No. 6], Croydon 1981.

M. J. Hatchett, *A Manual for Clergy and Church Musicians*, The Church Hymnal Corporation, New York 1980.

M. J. Hatchett, *Commentary on the American Prayer Book*, New York 1980.

M. J. Hatchett, *The Making of the First American Book of Common Prayer 1776–1789*, New York 1982

R. A. Leaver, *Hymns with the New Lectionary*, Bramcote [Notts.] 1980.

R. A. Leaver, *The Liturgy and Music: A study of the use of the Hymn in Two Liturgical Traditions*, Bramcote [Notts.] 1976.

E. Routley, Erik, *A Short History of English Church Music*, Mowbrays, London and Oxford 1977.

E. Routley, *An English-Speaking Hymnal Guide*, Collegeville [Minn.] 1981.

E. Routley, *A Panorama of Christian Hymnody*, Collegeville [Minn.] 1981.

E. Routley, *Ecumenical Hymnody*, London 1959.

E. Routley, *English Hymns and Their Tunes*, The Hymn Society of Great Britain and Ireland, London 1981. (Printed for private circulation.)

E. Routley, Erik, *Hymn Tunes—An Historical Outline* [Study Notes No. 5], Croydon *ca.* 1960.

E. Routley, *Hymns and The Faith*, London 1955.

E. Routley, *The Music of Christian Hymns*, Chicago 1981.

E. Routley, *Words of Hymns—A Short History* [Study Notes No. 6], Croydon *ca.* 1960.

M. K. Stulken, *Hymnal Companion to the Lutheran Book of Worship*, Philadelphia 1981.

N. Temperley, "The Anglican Communion Hymn: From Wither to Wesley", *The Hymn*, Vol. 30, No. 1–4.

N. Temperley, *The Music of the English Parish Church*, Cambridge 1980.

A Hymn Guide for the Sunday themes of the New Lectionary, London and Oxford 1981.

Hymns III, Church Hymnal Corporation, New York 1979.

Hymns Ancient and Modern, London 1875.

Hymnal Studies One: Perspectives on the New Edition, The Church Hymnal Corporation, New York 1982.

Hymnal Studies Two: Introducing the Hymnal 1982, The Church Hymnal Corporation, New York 1982.

Proposed Texts for the Hymnal 1982, The Church Hymnal Corporation, New York 1982.

The Book of Common Prayer, 1789, together with Selections from the Psalms of David in Metre with Hymns suited to the Feasts and Fasts of the Church and other occasions of Pubíic Worship, New York 1853.

The Church Hymnal, Boston, 1894.

The Hymnal 1940, The Church Hymnal Corporation, New York 1943.

The Lutheran Book of Worship, Minneapolis 1978.

The Prayer Book Guide to Christian Education, New York 1983.

12

BEGINNINGS AT DUNBLANE

Ian M. Fraser

"I know that Erik looked back and found Dunblane unique, something he did not manage to recapture elsewhere." Thus Alan Luff, Precentor of Westminster Abbey, looking back on his personal experience of the "unique creative atmosphere" which marked the Scottish Churches House hymn-writing initiative. "It was from the Dunblane enterprise that the world 'hymn explosion' took off" I am told on all hands. The beginnings? It was given to me to load a starter's gun and to Erik to fire it. All I said was "Let's stop moaning and get down to the job". All Erik said was "Let's; now!" We were off.

It was 1961, as far as existing records can help us. Scottish Churches House was just beginning to find its feet as a house of the co-operating Churches in Scotland—a place held in common which gave them opportunity to move, together, into fresh fields. During a free period between sessions of a consultation on evangelism, some participants exchanged harsh comments on some "modern" hymns recently published in a Church magazine. Their criticism was mainly that these retained all the old stereotypes. For the umpteenth time, the cry went up "Nobody's getting down to writing the hymns for our time". On this occasion, the cry was heard.

Erik became the real catalyst and inspirer, while I acted as back-up. He cheerfully described my role as that of gauleiter—I was to prepare the working sessions, and produce reports: but especially was to breathe down the necks of those who had agreed to do some portion of the work, and see that it was made available in time. Did you ever happen to notice Erik's hands? He had sticky fingers for work but buttery fingers for praise. Credit directed to him was always diverted to someone or somewhere else. But the flow of ideas and encouragement came quite specially from him.

Dunblane 1961–1969
When it was agreed that we get down to the job I was asked first of all to take soundings; then, if these proved positive, to bring a consultation into being in

1962. Reggie Barrett-Ayres, Head of the Department of Music in Aberdeen University, acted as convenor, and Erik became Secretary.

1962

The first consultation took place in early October 1962. Jock Wilson, reporting for the *British Weekly*, put it on record that two dozen ministers and organists of the Church of Scotland the Congregational Church and the Episcopal Church met to "take a radical look at Church music today."

Ian McKenzie, now of the BBC, then Scottish Secretary of the SCM, opened the consultation. He likened the tension between high-brow and middle-and-low-brow music to that between creation and redemption and made the plea:

> As our Lord consorted with publicans and sinners without making any demands that they should first of all change, so we should open ourselves to the young people of today and let them bring what they are and what they have . . .

At a later session, Erik applied C. S. Lewis' literary criterion to the work of judging new music (he illustrated with a number of tape recordings), i.e. "the capacity for receiving all the best the reader can give." Later he reminded the consultation that it is always the immediate past which we want to scrap and the contemporary which appears revolutionary. He warned against two stock phrases: "I don't like it" (said because "it" has impressed us as fascinating and dangerous and has threatened our self-preservation) and "only the best is good enough" (which he called "almost idolatrous"). David Hamilton observed that, since singing had become about the only thing left to the people themselves, it was no wonder that they resisted innovation.

Reggie Barrett-Ayres was asked to take the final session. He spoke of:

> . . . the polyphony of the 16th century, . . . its sense of unity: the forthright music of the Lutheran tradition, where new reform with economy illustrated strength; and, finally, the folk element in hymnology, that part of our humanity, "the milk of human kindness" which is Love. Unity, strength and love were the three vital virtues which were worth keeping alive." These were then illustrated from compositions by students and staff of his University's Music Department, concluding with a Cantata by Reggie himself . . .

It was observed in discussion that a great deal of strain stemmed from the tension between the "establishment" in the Church and the creative artist.

At that very first consultation, the possibility of an ecumenical hymn book was mooted. An alternative was also advocated—John Cheyne put forward the idea of a loose leaf publication (so that pieces could be tried, affirmed, changed, discarded until what was wanted and needed was found) rather than a new hymn book which would "solidify the conventional set-up".

A further consultation was agreed on for October 1963, and the agenda proposed as follows:

(a) Evidences will be looked at from churches already "on the job". This session will give opportunity to participants to share insights, needs and fruitful lines worked on locally.

(b) Composers are being approached and asked to be prepared to be associated experimentally with a local church. What link up will prove most effective? What kind of experimentation is likely to prove significant and where? We must share ideas on these.

(c) Re folk-songs and folk-song groups: a contribution is being sought from Sydney Carter regarding the social and musical significance of such groups and music forms. Consideration should also be given to the place of "disposable music".

(d) Is good music a bourgeois cult? Erik Routley will raise this question.

(e) What are the prospects for an Ecumenical Hymnary? Anglicans and Presbyterians meeting in Scottish Churches House recently were agreed that fresh confessions or even the revision of existing confessions *undertaken denominationally* no longer make sense. Is this equally true of denominational hymnaries?!

1963

The 1963 consultation illustrated features which became characteristic of Dunblane gatherings, namely: a) seminal contributions from people on the march; b) specific tasks (such as the project of producing a new *Church Hymnary*); c) plans for getting more people creatively involved.

The report records:

In a sparkle and fizz of bright images Erik Routley presented the thesis that good music was a bourgeois cult. Hymns, it was said, had to be by great composers, and there had to be an exactness in producing the music according to the best traditions! The reality is that many of the composers of hymn music remain anonymous, and would have had no great mind about whether this or that way to play their work was the right one! What "better" music demanded was attention: one had to gather one's faculties and do justice to it. But Bach, Brahms and others did a bread-and-butter job—they turned out the music which was required for the immediate purpose which faced them . . .

Modern Protestantism is pretty firmly in the "good music which requires and deserves serious attention" tradition. Most people who do not have our background and do not have their minds trained as we do, either enjoy music in a different way or feel that their way of enjoying it is inferior—and want to move up a grade so that they can at least appear to enjoy it the way we do! There is no reason for believing that the common enjoyment of music is of less value than "appreciation of good music". The ordinary chap and his missus relish a bit of moderate background noise in a restaurant, since it provides them with a bit of privacy and at the same time saves them the awkwardness of silence. They love a good crowd sing. Do we try to go where they are? Or do we try to get them to come where we are? Is there some point or points of common meeting? Or is this all we can say—that we must be much more humble and teachable before an enjoyment of music which is not of the same kind as our own? . . .

Tom Keir introduced the question of producing an ecumenical hymnary:

He noted these factors which had to be taken seriously within a general ecumenical concern such as he himself held: (a) there were financial considerations, particularly with churches which had produced new Hymnaries in recent years; (b) a book produced commonly would lose its point if it were not used commonly: the ecumenical advantage would be lost. The 1650 Psalter was intended to serve this purpose but the Anglicans did not pick it up, so that no common purpose was served; (c) There were theological difficulties. Would Baptists happily have in their Hymn Book hymns which understood infant baptism as a proper form of Christian baptism? Would Anglo-Catholics want a transubstantiation slant to Eucharistic hymns? Could the Feast of the Blessed Virgin Mary be included without alienating certain Churches: or excluded without alienating others? We would arrive at a very lowest-common-denominator level if we rejected hymns which might offend one Church or another; and would produce a very small hymnary indeed; (d) We already used the Psalms in common. We had a common structure in Holy Communion basically. We needed a common lectionary—which would appear to be a more profitable next step. And we needed to avoid standardisation which curbed vitality. (e) We had to watch our timing, and the time did not seem to be ripe at the

174

moment. Churches are only now discovering their brethren and discovering themselves in ecumenical debate. This must go on for some time.

The report proceeds:

> Erik Routley was essentially of a different mind although he appreciated in a new way certain of the points made. There seemed to him to be a Scottish culture which transcends denominational boundaries and a Scottish Churches' Hymnary would be welcomed.

But we were persuaded to stay on safe ground rather than risk skating on the thin but inviting ecumenical ice of that time. I believe we followed the logic of the situation; and I believe we failed to produce fruits before our time —something we were called to do in face of the logic. From this point, a definitive Hymn Book was not on the cards. Supplements to Hymn books and loose-leaf items of praise were concentrated on. The consultation planned forward thus:

> Erik Routley was encouraged (and any help that was needed was offered to him) to proceed with the linking up of composers with congregations to undertake experimental work. If this could be developed, it would produce a very useful ferment which could help other things of musical interest to sprout.

A Working Group was set up comprising Reggie Barrett-Ayres, Erik Routley, Jock Wilson, John Currie, John Cheyne, Stewart Todd, Tom Weir and Ian Mackenzie. They were asked to find/produce twelve hymns with thirty-six tunes by February 1964, the projected first meeting date of the Working Group. Items wanted fell into two categories, a) hymns which the group identified in the *Revised Church Hymnary* whose words deserved better tunes b) new hymns, particularly on themes which were not dealt with adequately in the hymnaries. Among themes suggested under (b) were baptism in relation to Christ's baptism and baptism as incorporation; the Church militant in the Communion of Saints; eucharistic hymns; marriage hymns; hymns dealing with the mission, ministries, reconciling work of the World Church; the mystery of the Godhead; the Holy Spirit in exciting Pentecostal manifestation and in the corporate action of the community; eschatological hymns; processional hymns for various occasions.

It was planned that this material then be tried out in congregations, between the time of its evaluation in February and the autumn consultation.

Tapes of the material could be circulated to help any interested minister or organist to interest, in turn, congregation and choir.

1964

Before the October 1964 consultation, all participants received a sizeable batch of hymns, songs, words, tunes—assembled by the Working Group—to try out, criticise, amend, replace or whatever. The names of the composers of the music were concealed. Participants were asked themselves to contribute: and material they supplied was also sent out beforehand. The early part of the 1964 consultation was given over to the evaluation of work submitted.

Links were made, through Erik, with the proprietors of Hymns Ancient and Modern at this point, since they were eager to work along the same lines. The enterprise was becoming British, not just Scottish. Sydney Carter shared in the 1964 consultation.

> He took a session, and shared with us some of his experience. He pointed to the way in which submerged belief and unbelief were becoming articulate among groups he frequented. People wanted to make sense of life—and they could not get away from life! Folk Song groups brought together people of quite different convictions and backgrounds. Meetings in pubs or coffee bars created a fellowship which was in many senses like that of a church: from time to time, moments of unity were experienced and those present became all of one mind, almost as in an act of worship. A network of these circles existed all over the world. Wherever you went, you felt you belonged. Community was real: people offered hospitality to others freely when they could, and willingly shared what money they had.
>
> Folk music was experiencing a boom in the U.S.A. Twice as many came recently to a Folk Festival as came to the Newport Jazz Festival. In Britain a good deal of what was available came out through Radio Caroline [the pirate radio station].
>
> In Scotland traditional music never came to a full stop. There had been a clear break in England. An impetus at the beginning of the century, especially through such people as Cecil Sharp and Vaughan Williams brought a revival down south. It had quite a flavour of English nationalism about it. But then the whole thing "went educated", and lost a good deal of its impetus Some of the native stuff could not be put down on paper! It was introduced into schools and taken up enthusiastically by school ma'ams. As might be expected, words and music were emasculated.
>
> Skiffle brought something almost equivalent to a religious revival. One of the

176

useful things it did was to stop the word "folk" being a word of opprobrium. The word gained an acceptable image. An interesting thing about those who have developed it from that point, is that very many of them are visual artists whose interest has been captured by the possiblities music offers, rather than literary people.

What is it in folk music that grips people? For one thing, it is about honest things presented honestly. You get reality in the treatment of love and work, for instance, which you do not get in the Top Ten. Also there are elements of magic and poetry in it, of which many people are starved. It appeals particularly to the under-twenty-fives. Those who appreciate it often appreciate classical music and, surprisingly often, church music. But folk music is not really pure music—rather it is drama, to which the music (or even music and words) is secondary. And it may depend for its effect a great deal on the person who is presenting it. It has echoes of the most primitive forms of drama. It does not differentiate the arts but uses them in proportion. By word, sound, movement, vision a total assault is made on the senses. Musicians want to make the musical interest paramount: very properly they are denied this in folk music.

Out of this movement an approach has developed to music and song which is radical and almost (in relation to what musicians feel is their proper sphere) subversive. It attracts a motley company in which, for instance, Communists and Roman Catholics almost balance one another out for numbers.

To follow Sydney's shared perceptions, records were played—records of Bob Dylan on the Bishop of Woolwich and George Fox and a new setting of "Teach me my God and King". These provided an interval to reflect and absorb.

In the consequent discussion the question was raised whether it is possible to have religious songs which are anti-Christian, to provide a certain bite and realism in worship. It was also observed—some things which are needed are not singable in Church. Where truth seems to be emerging in some kind of drama form, does it belong properly to religious theatre rather than worship? In later discussion it was observed: "Folk is a root from which contemporary things can grow."

At the end of the whole gathering it was debated whether another consultation should be held. a) It was agreed that the process of creating, judging, making available material for songs and hymns of our time cried out for further investment of time and energy. b) Jazz still had to be looked into. c) Colin Day suggested that there be a contribution to the Perth Kirk Week 1965—and that would require further work. A fresh Working Group comprising Erik Routley, Margaret Dickie, George McPhee, Douglas Galbraith, John Geyer and John Currie was appointed to carry the work forward.

Deliberately it was decided to draw on the experience of unbelievers too. Some common thinking was also to be done with the Corrie Trio (later to become the famous folksinging group) and with Ian Menzies and the Clyde Valley Stompers.

A fruit of the Group's work was a first publication, produced early in 1965, *Dunblane Praises No. 1*. Music was hand-written, and the whole production deliberately suggested an unfinished, non-status, try-it-and-see approach.

1965

By now a groundwork of common perceptions had been laid. Keynote contributions tailed off. Time was more and more occupied with producing and gathering material, trying and testing it out. The wording of the heading of the next consultation, given in the letter of invitation, makes this clear: "Forty-eight Hours of Composition and Consultation on Music and Words to catch the ear of our time." It was promised that "most of the time will be occupied with hammering out words and music on the spot in small groups or solo—it will be essentially an experimental, working come-together."

An undated flier from Erik, designed to stimulate thinking especially on the part of those who had recently been drawn in, was probably issued as a preparatory document for this consultation. He raised in it questions about the respect and/or disrespect due to existing liturgical traditions. I extract a few points:

Worship is made up of both certain acts and implied doctrines—what are these? (Do different traditions have a common mind on the essentials, he would seem to be asking).

Thinking of folk song as Sydney Carter had presented it, do ironic words, descriptive of actual human situations, have a place in worship—say, related to the confession of sin rather than to proclamation?

Since antiphony "is for some reason repellent to people of the reformed religious culture" do Gelineau and Catholic liturgies provide possible clues for re-examining our hang-ups? Two sections and the summary, I feel, should be given in Erik's own words. They show how he probed and questioned, shook people up, got them exploring:

SPONTANEITY?

One of the evocative words among many Christian groups is "spontaneity". The idea of anything in public worship being prepared or rehearsed is strange to most people. Try out some questions like these:

(a) To what extent is it proper to treat a congregation as people joining in a play, charade, or a kind of socio-drama?

(b) If it is, in this sense, proper—and the central act of all worship suggests that in some sense it must be—then must not some kinds of congregational activity be regarded as "preparation" or "rehearsal" for the drama. Is this a profane way, or a creative way, for example, of looking at "Preparation for Communion"?

(c) If that kind of approach—which includes anything from a congregational practice to a spiritual "rehearsal" or "preparation"—is legitimate: if the learning of the Book of Common Prayer responses and Catechism, for example, makes the public conversation and communal acts come naturally to Anglican worshippers—is there on the other hand any place for the "pentecostal" in worship? Jazz music depends on improvisation, which must correspond in some way to the improvised, spontaneous element upon which the left wing of the Reformation placed such reliance. Is this right?

SIN

It is very necessary to try to come to some common mind on the question whether experiments with worship are or are not found to be vitiated by a spiritual pride that takes too much in human creative ability for granted.

(a) Is liturgy (controlled drama, if it be drama at all) a necessary safeguard against the consequences of sin?

(b) Exactly what outward activities in worshippers ought to be controlled in this or any other way?

(c) On the other hand: is a rigid adherence to principles itself a refusal to commit ourselves to the needs of the time and to the duty of responding to them?

SUMMARY

The Consultation will do something very useful if it can, through corporate thinking and discussion, help artists to see just how far they ought, in writing words or music for the Church, to regard existing liturgical customs as a framework within which they must operate, and how far they are permitted to present material whose use would involve considerable (if temporary) change in liturgical habits.

There is one very great danger, a sense of which has prompted these notes: namely, that Sunday Morning and Sunday Evening become divorced from each other and lead to an aesthetic and social schism in the local community. How much may the informed and responsible bearers of the church's tradition insist on? How much is dispensable? How much requires translation?

179

1966

The 1966 Consultation did groundwork which allowed the Working Group, in December of that year, to produce *Dunblane Praises No. 2*, which (still adopting a provisional form) was published in 1967.

By that time, the whole enterprise was taking off in a larger way.

A BBC "Songs of Praise", introducing new words and music to the public was broadcast on February 12th, led by Dunblane Cathedral Choir with Peter Youngson as soloist and Erik as conductor.

Material was by now being requested for children—the first steps were taken towards what was later published (still keeping to a provisional form) as *Dunblane Praises for Schools: 1 Juniors*.

Choirs, groups and individuals of Aberdeen University (under Reggie Barrett-Ayres) and Manchester Cathedral (under Alan Luff) prepared joint work with the aim of recording a disc to introduce fresh material to a wider public.

Plans were laid for the first publication deliberately given more definitive form, *New Songs for the Church* 1 and 2, as a supplement to hymn books (published by Galliard and Scottish Churches Council). Childrens hymns, scrutinized by a professional child psychologist, were included.

The introduction ends: "we hope that the use of this book may inject into public worship a new kind of sincerity and gaiety which are the constituents of the real seriousness of the Christian faith". Erik's words.

The need for fresh consultations was not now commanding, and the work flowed into a variety of different channels. Alan Luff has shared with me his own regret that he was not able to develop more of his work on chants and canticles in association with the group which met at Dunblane—he saw no other group which was as creative and had as sure a touch. Otherwise, people seem to have been content that, with a basic work done, they should follow whichever lines most interested them.

One line of development, however, needs special mention. Many of us in the Dunblane group were worried at the number of childrens' hymns which served as adult control devices—suggesting that God's great desire was to keep children in line and get them to be meek and mild like Jesus; tidy, colourless conformists.

It was thanks largely to the energetic work of one member, Gracie King, and the co-operation of an Iona Community Family Group that the first volume of children's hymns was produced. Two criteria were set for work which could be published—either children supplied the words or children said "yes" to them. The introduction explicitly states "the present volume consists

180

partly of ideas and words provided by children, integrated in form with the help of an adult, and partly works of adults which had been tried out with children. One tune was composed by children."

The new book was firmly in the Dunblane tradition:

This is a try-it-and-see book for junior pupils. Day schools and Sunday schools are asked to bring it into use, allow time for children to familiarise themselves with words and music, and judge what meets the mind of children and speaks truly of the faith, and what does not.

They are asked to enter further into the spirit of experiment which produced this book. Is this note or that theme missing? Why not get children to share their thoughts about it and shape these into verse? Or let an adult try to frame words and music which catch the imagination of children. As *Dunblane Praises 1* and 2 were try-it-out publications which led to the more definitive *New Songs for the Church* (Galliard Press 7/6) so we hope for a ferment of creation of schools praises. Original words and music can be forwarded to Mrs R. M. King, c/o Scottish Churches House. Out of what stands the test, when tried out with different groups, a more definitive volume of new praise could emerge over the years.

Gracie King culled musical and spoken ideas from individual children, some of them ESN (educationally subnormal) pupils, and sometimes from a whole class working on a "round robin" basis; she would then clothe the ideas in useable form.

The resulting song would then be tried out in a variety of classes and schools. Wherever class after class made the same "mistake", Gracie would correct *the song*, not the singers—thus speeding up the "folk process". The final version would then be used in a variety of town and rural schools for school worship. The song would at that point be rested. Only those songs which were remembered and re-requested in several schools or Sunday Schools would be submitted for consideration for a *Dunblane Praises* publication. Those songs that were not asked for again were jettisonned. In this way child creativity, adult experience and popular acceptability were married to form child folk hymns.

Some years later a sign and outcome of the Dunblane approach to worship happened in a small rural church. Gracie King was asked if she could "do something with the children" for the church's centenary. The result was a service "Praise through the Ages". The items were linked by bible readings and commentaries on local history given by the teenagers. By the time the (conventional) congregation were asked to sing Tallis in canon (unrehearsed)

181

they quite took it in their stride. They had gained confidence to be active music makers themselves.

The Dunblane Method of Working

In working through the documents, it struck me that aspects of "the Dunblane approach" were registered quite clearly.

1. The aim was to get people involved in finding new words and music, and not to do this for them. In preparation for the 1963 Conference, Erik set out the mind of himself and his colleagues in the following words: "we are looking for a new simple music, without a traditional ecclesiastical accent, perhaps making use of instruments other than piano or organ (recorder, trumpet, clarinet, strings?) of which we could say 'Try this'". He adds that it must be free of copyright "so that it could be freely used at once".

In a letter to me a year or two before he died, Erik speaks in some astonishment regarding the extent to which early productions of members of the group found favour in different parts of the world and made their way into a variety of hymnaries. What we turned out was not thought of as substantive in itself. It had the aim of getting people goaded and encouraged into creative action. Members of the group would have been quite content if the fruit had been people who said "I could do better than that", and went on to do so.

2. The whole enterprise was undertaken in community. No doubt there were individuals who had set out to break the mould in earlier years (cf. hermits and the Celtic church). But, as far as I know, no such ecumenical "intentional community" existed previously. The accent was on gifts brought together to serve one another and build one another up in a common initiative to which all sorts contributed. In the preface to *Dunblane Praises No. 1* it was said: "Hymns and tunes which carry the reference 'Dunblane' in these pages, instead of the names of their authors or composers, are often the result of communal thinking and criticism". In the report of the 1963 Consultation, those who were prepared to turn out words and music were asked to hold their hand before giving their work a final finish. They were invited, instead, to "give it a run", testing it out in experience, and exploring, with others, possibilities which might emerge only from actual production and use. Once a communal mind has been brought to bear, the rounding off could be completed more effectively.

It was quite customary, when the Working Group met, to take material which had been sent in and say "Here is a bit of music with possibilities which have not been quite realised", or "Here are words which need a good working over to give them full effectiveness"—and hand over the item to a member of the group to work on for an hour or two hours, and then bring back for group judgement. Even if the author were present, the assumption would be that he or she stood too near to the product; that someone else might provide a fresh perspective on it.

It was this way of working which goaded Erik to write words for a hymn for the first time in his life. Alan Luff can tell the full story, because he was the miscreant who unwittingly challenged Erik to move into new fields:

> We had a session to identify gaps in the existing hymnaries. A hymn or ballad which would be useful in a Christian Aid context was called for. We were all sent packing to see what we might be able to produce. It turned out that Erik and I had been given adjoining rooms.
>
> Now, I had never written any kind of hymn, ever before. I wondered how to start, and began looking up biblical texts. I landed on the feeding of the five thousand and the words in the New English Bible translation "Where can we find bread to feed these people". I made that the first line of the song or ballad or hymn. Then I found that the only way I could work was by creating a thread of tune on which I could string the words. So I hummed over and over and over again this little bit of a tune as I looked for the words I wanted. Poor Erik, next door, was put entirely off the task of writing his own tune. He gave up, in the end, and went on (and I say, "Praise the Lord"!) to write his magnificent hymn (the first for him as well) "All who love and serve your City".
>
> I was sorry when I found the frustration I had caused him. But, in the end, I rather feel more proud of my humming and doodling next door to him, because it expanded his own creative work.
>
> I think there was something of Dunblane in this whole incident. Coming into the group, you did not think you had anything to give. Yet you were challenged or encouraged or whatever was needed, to meet the situation. Somehow the Holy Spirit was abroad and things happened. The whole thing could come out, as in the case of Erik, in a way quite different from anything which was intended.

3. Whatever was produced was floated on the waters. The copyright remained in the hands of the author, while freedom was afforded to interested parties to try things out. Only when a publisher secured copyright was an item withdrawn from general circulation.

Techniques were sought to get musical life flowing. In the letter already mentioned in preparation for the 1963 consultation, a particular possibility is presented:

We think that the most fruitful way of making such an experiment would be to put you in direct touch with a source of demand that lay near to where you live, so that if you wished you could personally supervise the initial production of what you wrote. A demand might come in from, say Drumchapel: and we might write to one of you and say "Here is the demand: here are the resources: would you care to write something, fairly quickly, that they could try out?" What you sent would have to be sent without prejudice. We should have to face the possibility that it might not come off. But would you please let us know whether the principle of the thing seems to make sense to you, and whether the idea of participating appeals to you?

People were also encouraged to work on new types of musical production. The report of the 1964 consultation includes the following: "The good songs at present are those of seekers not of finders: and for this the 'cabaret' song is a fine vehicle". When Mrs Margaret Dickie stressed the need to keep such experimentation clear of the disciplined march of eucharistic worship, there came the following counter-assertion: "If the liturgy has in it basically the re-enactment of the works of creation and redemption, then it could be that the 'cabaret' material could be a vital disturbing explosive preparation for the eucharist or the sermon."

4. Those who responded to the invitation to produce material were encouraged to believe that what they attempted could have merit even if it were of a limited or transitory character: "The intention is not necessarily that the music should have a long life: it may well be used for a time and then discarded. Do you think it is possible to have a 'disposable' music that is free of the pretentiousness of 'pop' as it is normally understood? We think that there is a legitimate relation between this idea and that of (say) film music". There was quite a debate about this at one point, on the part of those who thought that they were being encouraged to write ephemeral stuff. There was no such intention. What was meant is illustrated by a conference I shared with Methodist Laymen in Swanwick, where a hymn was produced which spoke to the people of the conference but would not have spoken to those who could not share what they had experienced in the conference. "Write it on toilet paper" I used to suggest for such occasions "When it has fulfilled its purpose it can be flushed away."

5. Straight speaking was promised and, from the start, was a feature of the group's way of working. If members of the group and others associated were to have taken umbrage when their work was criticised, there would have been no possibility of giving it more effective form. Introducing a session of the 1963 consultation, Reggie Barrett-Ayres proposed that the Working Group be

set up to produce new tunes to existing words and create altogether new hymns. He went on: "These would be submitted to the most rigorous criticism in terms of their theology, thèir music and their capacity to communicate with congregations and to be sung with understanding and spirit by congregations. They could be worked at experimentally over a period between the time in the year and the autumn consultation." In that consultation itself, members recognised the need for self-criticism and balance. Thus, from the report (Erik's words, I'd guess):

> We have to be aware of the adjective "Christian". So often it has meant a form of lasso with which we hope to capture things within reach which appeal to us, and dress them up our way . . .
>
> Humour is a way of acknowledging one's insufficiency. The medieval carols made this point. It might be that the person who can write hymns is the person who can write good light verse—verse which is light but deep, making an immediate impact which gains the attention and then reveals level upon level of meaning.

6. People themselves were to be the judges—congregations, groups who wanted a good crowd sing, all sorts of folk using their own judgement and depending on whatever was their musical taste. That included children. Confidence was given to ordinary folk to create and to evaluate.

I may illustrate from my own experience the way in which those who had never thought of themselves as possible contributors to the musical praise of the Church were drawn in. What happened may be expressed thus: awareness of the potential of church praise-forms, as vehicles for words and music, began to take up residence *in the forefront* of people's consciousness instead of staying in the background. Add to that that the Working Group bestowed, in a very direct way, a reassuring and encouraging sense that many non-specialists could perfectly well have a stab at this work. That the group would criticise it rigorously was also encouraging: it meant that second and third rate productions would not be allowed to pass.

Thanks to the influence of a perceptive English teacher at school, I was given an early habit of savouring words, rolling them around on the tongue of the mind to appreciate their flavours. I gained the habit of experimenting with words, phrases, ideas to see how they could be set in creative relationship.

When the Dunblane Group started its work, three phrases were interacting in one magnetic field in my mind. There was Jesus Christ as "the Sun behind all suns". There was Blake's "Tyger, tyger burning bright". There was

T. S. Eliot's "In the juvenescence of the year, Came Christ the tiger". Previously, the fruit of that interplay might have been expressed in an article, a sermon, or simply some doodles. Now it sought a poem/hymn form. All I could bring to the task in terms of knowledge of style was to say things as clearly, tellingly and economically as possible. On the way to a Presbytery meeting of all things, I found myself with two lines which began to create a basis of new perception:

> Christ, burning
> past all suns

I saw Christ as the Lord of the world's jungle, flaming through its thickets of darkness, lithe and powerful, fierce in his love for his own. But he is not only a jungle-presence, I had to remind myself. Risen and ascended, he is in control of the whole created order, above all the jungles of the Universe, over the Universe itself:

so

> Stars beneath your feet
> like leaves on forest floor

came next.

It is in contrast to his burning love and might that our human predicament is to be seen. We have dangerous longings to act and be "as gods", to take absolute charge of our world—who were meant to take charge *with God*. Yet it is the will of God that we be curious, satisfy our thirst for knowledge, exercise power! The next lines came out:

> Man, turning
> spaceward, spurns
> knowledge incomplete
> fevered to explore*

Realism required me now to set the hope for the creation represented in Christ dialectically over against the threat we human beings pose to creation.

*NB Note the rhyming scheme where the second 4-lines answer, in contrast, the first four lines—EDS.

186

Christ, holding
atoms in one
loom of light and power
to weave creations life:

Christ, festive
in quick bird
rush of river flood
glances lovers dart:

man, moulding
rocket, gun
turns creation sour
plots dissolving strife

youth, restive
seek new word
beat of life in blood
ashes in the heart

What relationship is there between the mighty work of Jesus Christ in and over the universe and our human ability to use the gifts and power entrusted to us to destroy or spoil the marvellous work? I had to find some correspondence. It came in Christ's determination to take our side, whatever the consequences. That was the root of hope.

Christ, humble
on our side,
snatching death's foul keys
cramping Satan's scope—
we gamble
on our Guide,
inch our gains of peace,
work a work of hope.

(From the first roughcast to the finished product took months, off and on).

I even got courage, as someone who had no musical training, to attempt my own tunes. I became annoyed at the way in which musicians developed their musical creations and attempted to tack them on to my words. My only resource then, as a musically uninstructed person, was to live with the rhythm of the words for some months until they declared their own tune to me.

"Christ burning" did not catch on. Another Dunblane gift—I had now a perspective for such an eventuality. Maybe my work was not all that good, or did not communicate. Maybe it was more authentically presented as a poem than as a hymn (Erik wrote at one point to say that he could not get Americans to appreciate my *poetic* hymns; and I myself believe that good verse provides the usual vehicle for hymns). Someone else might be stimulated by it to do better. The time for the hymn might be in the future rather than in the present. "Work in as imaginative and disciplined a way as possible; then sit lightly by your work" was one of the lessons learned by those who came to Dunblane.

*　　*　　*　　*

187

New people were drawn in every year during the 60's. Probably a hundred at least were involved directly. It is a fortunate accident that Erik felt it necessary, in preparation for the 1966 consultation, to share with new participants some of the main things we had been working at over a period. (By this time what had been initially called "the Dunblane Consultation on Music" was now called "the Scottish Churches' Music Consultation".) He wrote, tongue at times in cheek:

> We all tend to think (thus the contemporary creed)
>> that new kinds of church music must be looked for
>>> that they are waiting to be found
>>>> that if we look in the right places we shall find them:
>> that once found, scrutinised and agreed to be worthwhile,
>>> we must make them available so that people can try them:
>> that no musical form is regarded as taboo in itself, but
>>> that whatever form the music is in we want to find good music; that is to say, that we are jaded with second-rate "jazz" or "pop" or "pantomime" or what not, but, where anything in these styles—or any other styles —looks good music, we welcome it;
>> that sometimes a good thing comes of spontaneous composition in a "working party".

Dunblane Praises, No. 1 was the result of thoughts along these lines.

We have also had some considerable discussion on the question what is the proper place of new kinds of music in public worship, and have managed to distinguish the sort of material that goes better as a solo (such as Sydney Carter's songs) from that which goes better congregationally, we have even asked what might happen to worship if new kinds of musical expressions were introduced into it. This has provoked suggestions which have drawn down on the Consultation the frowns of some observers—and indeed some members. Never mind.

It seems pretty clear that the kind of music we look for, and, with luck, find, suggests a more dramatic view of liturgy than some of us are accustomed to. This is very bad indeed. But we soldier on.

Personalities

"The time would fail me. . . ." It is very difficult to select, from the many people involved, who should be mentioned particularly. Yet this whole enterprise depended on the drawing together of people with special skills and the ability to relate creatively to one another. I hope I may be forgiven for mentioning but a few and therefore leaving out many.

Reggie Barrett-Ayres was convenor. Reggie had quite an unusual gift for drawing musical quality out of very unlikely characters. His interest was in the area where music and drama met, and that was the direction he took off on, at the end of the 1960's.

Stewart Todd was deeply concerned that all church music should be subservient to the Word of God and serve the Gospel, not drawing attention to itself but being modest and humble in its service.

Peter Cutts joined the Group when his talents for clothing words with music were coming to full fruitfulness.

Alan Luff joined late, and brought gifts from that fact—as from his musical ability, and conviction that chants and canticles must find their place and the initiative of Gelineau be accepted as an encouragement to break into new territory.

Eric Reid's "Trotting, Trotting through Jerusalem" has found its way into hymn books in many parts of the world. His death in a car accident really bereaved the group. He was an immensely fertile composer who had a strongly academic and modern background, and a common touch. He had done his thesis in Germany on the work of one of the avant-garde Second Viennese School of Composers. Yet, at school where he taught, the development of brass band and other musical work put him in deep community with children and, from that, with ordinary folk of all kinds.

Alan Luff reminded me of the way in which, quite often, productions developed at Dunblane or in relation to it, took serious account of the violence in society. He noted that few of the hymn books or supplements picked up material which had life's rawness and crudity about it. For me, Peter Youngson's "Body and Blood" was the best neglected piece of writing in the whole Dunblane repertoire. Peter had been a Communist in his young days. He had a very powerful voice and heckled Donald Soper at Tower Hill unmercifully. At one point Donald stopped and commanded him to lose the power of speech. He went dumb. Early the next morning, he appeared at Donald Soper's door. What followed produced his conversion. He was parish minister in the territory of the gangs, Easterhouse, when he participated in the Dunblane enterprise.

John Geyer refused to allow us to ignore what was developing in teenage culture, or to dismiss new sounds if they did not fit in with previous ideas of harmony.

Caryl Micklem brought a feel for the music which best clothed words (e.g. "Christ burning") . . . And so on.

The Still Centre

Alan Luff: "I was always very much taken up with the worship in the little chapel cell up behind Scottish Churches House. It was the Iona forms of worship we were using, and that had a fresh heightening impact on me. The very simplicity of that place, as we sat around . . . It often had been all words and talk during the sessions. Simply to be there and to be very quiet, got deep into me. Then various people, Erik very often, led us—with few words, but very perceptively. The musical input in those services was very scant indeed —strange, considering what we were engaged in. But the acts of worship and waiting on God were very much the heart of what was going on at Dunblane. They were the still centre of the operation."

PUBLICATIONS

Dunblane Praises No. 1, 1965.
Dunblane Praises No. 2, 1967.
Dunblanes Praises for Schools 1. Juniors, 1970—all three provisional-style publications.
New Songs for the Church Book 1. Psalms, Children's Songs, Ballads, Hymns.
New Songs for the Church Book 2. Canticles published in 1969 by Galliard and Scottish Churches Council.

13

THE HYMN RENAISSANCE IN THE UNITED STATES

Russell Schulz-Widmar

In the United States we are experiencing something of a renaissance in hymnody. But the term "hymn explosion," an expression which accurately describes what has been happening on the other side of the Atlantic, carries with it the notion of surprise and excitement, uncontrolability—and even danger and loss. Although all these things can be said to apply to what we have been experiencing on both sides of the Atlantic, the term also implies a dramatic outpouring of new material. The United Kingdom has seen more of such a phenomenon than has the United States, and one of the moving forces behind our own hymnic reawakening has been the steady stream of new materials available to us from British writers.

On both sides of the Atlantic it is becoming increasingly difficult to speak of English hymnody and American hymnody as two different things. We have always shared a common language and have agreed upon most fundamental Christian concerns and aspirations, but now, more than ever before we also agree on how to realize those concerns and aspirations in words and music.

When the scene in the United States is surveyed as a whole—when all the facets of the art and practice of hymnody are taken together—then it can be clearly seen that something of significance has been happening here. We do, indeed, have our younger hymn writers as well as the old "professionals". Taken together they represent a remarkable variety of styles. We are also seeing some re-translation and text modification, and often the results are distinguished and desirable for contemporary usage. On the music side we have an impressive array of composers, arrangers, and researchers, whose influence on the practice of hymn singing will likely be viewed by our posterity as highly positive. In reviewing this productive creativity I propose to address two general areas: 1) Words—new texts, but also touching on translations and alterations of older texts; 2) Music—both newly composed as well as the altering or restoring of older material.

191

Authors

If we are to attempt a general survey of hymn writers we must start by confessing that this inevitably will be only a quick glance at the scene, and that a great many interesting and valuable landmarks will be left out. Furthermore, what you will be getting is one person's interpretation of the scene and you may not agree, or you may know better.

And if I am to be tour guide, before we start our tour, and in order to lengthen our perspective, I will insist on stopping first to pay suitable homage at the shrines of Martin H. Franzmann (1907–1976) and F. Bland Tucker (1895–1984). Both these gentlemen have been heroes in the field of American hymnody, exerting all sorts of positive influence on both our hymn producers and consumers.

Franzmann's masterpiece is "O God, O Lord of Heaven and Earth." See the *Worship Supplement*, 1969, for his work, and the *Lutheran Book of Worship*, 1978, for a modernized version. The modernizers dealt a couple of nasty blows, but the hymn survives, though with a limp very uncharacteristic of this writer. In this hymn he proclaims the gospel memorably and eloquently in four tightly structured stanzas. He wrote the hymn to commemorate the 450th anniversary of the Lutheran Reformation and it first came out on a flyer to be inserted in Sunday service leaflets. These sorts of things done by the Lutherans plant expectations, and to this day they continue to enjoy mightily the benefits of this kind of activity. Indeed it seems safe to say that no denomination enjoys more excellent hymn texts by their own writers than do the Lutherans.

Another Franzmann hymn that is extremely powerful with its proper music is "Weary of all Trumpeting", to the tune called both DISTLER and TRUMPETS. The tune by Hugo Distler had been associated with nationalistic purposes in Nazi Germany. There was always regret for this; indeed Distler never wanted to celebrate anything to do with Nazism. His pupil, Jan Bender, wanted to give the music a use that Distler would have wanted, so he asked Franzmann to write a new text to match the meter and mood of the music. All the gritty power that the composer put into his music has been nobly sanctified by these words and put into the service of Christ's cross. The hymn concludes with a dramatic call to servanthood and self-surrender:

> 3   To the triumph of your cross
>   summon all the living,
>   summon us to live by loss,
>   gaining all by giving,

suffering all that we may see
triumph in surrender;
leaving all, that we may be
partners in your splendor.

Franzmann was a poet of unusual gifts and he excelled in condensing theology in a profound way. But he was also an optimist. One of his early hymns—"Thy Strong Word Did Cleave the Darkness"—contains these glad sentiments:

3   Thy strong Word bespeaks us righteous;
        bright with thine own holiness,
    glorious now, we press toward glory,
        and our lives our hopes confess.

Bland Tucker died a few minutes into the New Year of 1984. His gifts and skill, coupled with a long life, had made him the dean of American hymnwriters. He had served on the text committees for both the Episcopal *Hymnal 1940* and the *Hymnal 1982*. (This latter book will come out in 1985; the hymnal is dated from the year the wordbook was approved by the church's General Convention.) Probably his greatest hymn is "Our Father, by Whose Name," which is one of the few twentieth-century hymns that is both important enough and well-known enough to be included on the list of recommended hymns prepared by the Consultation on Ecumenical Hymnody. His "Christ, When For Us You Were Baptized" first appeared in *Hymns III*, 1979, and from there it immediately crossed the Atlantic. It will appear with his own minor revisions in the *Hymnal 1982*.

For this same hymnal Dr Tucker made a major revision of one of his earlier hymns, and this revision demonstrates the kinds of changes that are becoming more acceptable to both hymnal editors and hymn singers. Here is his original hymn, based on Clement of Alexandria, with his revision next to it:

1   Master of eager youth,   Shepherd of innocence,
        controlling, guiding,   thou art our Confidence;
    lifting our hearts to truth,   to thee, our sure Defence,
        new power providing;   we bring our praises.

193

2 Though art our mighty Lord,
   our strength in sadness
the Father's conquering Word,
   true source of gladness;
thy Name we glorify,
O Jesus, throned on high,
who gav'st thyself to die
   for man's salvation.

1 Jesus, our mighty Lord,
   our strength in sadness,
the Father's conquering Word,
   true source of gladness;
your Name we glorify.
O Jesus, throned on high;
you gave yourself to die
   for our salvation.

3 Good Shepherd of thy sheep,
   thine own defending,
in love thy children keep
   to life unending.
Thou art thyself the Way:
lead us then day by day
in thine own steps, we pray,
   O Lord most holy.

2 Good Shepherd of your sheep,
   your own defending,
in love your children keep
   to life unending.
You are yourself the Way:
lead us then day by day
in your own steps, we pray,
   O Lord most holy.

4 Glorious their life who sing,
   with glad thanksgiving,
true hymns to Christ the King
   in all their living:
ye who confess his Name,
come then with hearts aflame;
let word and life acclaim
   our Lord and Saviour.

3 Glorious their life who sing,
   with glad thanksgiving,
true hymns to Christ the King
   in all their living:
all who confess his Name
come then with hearts aflame;
the God of peace acclaim
   as Lord and Savior.

He omitted his original first stanza entirely; in some ways this was a loss to both the hymn and to St Clement, but doubtless the hymn will have a wider application because of the change. St Clement or no, many people did not like the word *controlling* used as it was in the original. Furthermore, we now have a new and salutory opening line, strong and bold, that provides an image of Jesus that is quite different from that presented in many hymns. In the last stanza he made a change in the penultimate line in order to tighten the final lines to the preceding verses and to pack a little more punch.

Other changes consist of the modernization of *thee/thy* language to *you/your* language; this practice appears to be gaining ground in our hymnals especially in cases where rhyme is not affected. Finally in the new first stanza he altered *man's salvation* to *our salvation* in order to make the language more *inclusive.* This little change reveals the tip of an iceberg and one of the most widely debated controversies ever to impinge on English-language hymnody. To what extent masculine nouns and pronouns are acceptable for describing the human race or the Deity is a question being argued in a thousand different arenas. Certainly the whole matter does not appear to be a passing fad as many people had expected. The *Lutheran Book of Worship* was, I believe, the first major American hymnal to exhibit a considerable number of alterations on account of this issue, and since that time several more have followed suit. The Foreword to *Proposed Texts for the Hymnal 1982* (Episcopal) explained the issue as follows, (in part):

> In these closing decades of the twentieth century the Church, and indeed all our society, is becoming more and more sensitive to language that could be interpreted as either pejorative or discriminatory. In a medium as intense and intimate as congregational song—a medium which by its nature suggests as much as it says directly and communicates deep and abiding truths at many levels—the Church must make every effort to insure that the language used includes all its members and cultivates the spirit of acceptance and oneness exemplified by the life and teaching of our Lord.

Then, in addition to addressing language that sounds "so exclusively masculine that many of our parishoners are deeply troubled" the report touches on language that could be interpreted as condoning discrimination against the sick and handicapped, against blacks, against Jews, and against recipients of missionary activity. The report continues:

> The Commission not only acknowledges, but emphasizes, that the problems perceived in hymns such as these are totally outside the intent of the original authors. However, changes such as those we have proposed bear witness not only to the fact that language changes, but that we change, and that in change we strive always to proclaim gladly God's love for all of creation.

When the 1984 General Conference of the United Methodist Church authorized the development of a new hymnal, news releases were careful to explain that the use of inclusive language in the new hymnal was commended, but that the committee was also instructed to respect the language of "traditional hymns." This sort of decision represents a kind of middle ground where

195

many governing bodies eventually find themselves. The details of their solutions may vary, but it is probably safe to say that future editorial boards of mainline hymnals will not be able to remain untouched by this controversy. Hymnologist and editor Donald P. Hustad, of Southern Baptist Theological Seminary, Louisville, presented a moderate voice when he wrote in the October, 1983 issue of *Eternity*:

> Our worship principles and practices, like those of all Christian ministry, should be both prophetic and pastoral. We are prophetic in the use of language when we are faithful to biblical truth, including that which is wrapped up in the metaphoric words that attempt to reveal the numinous, ineffable God. We are pastoral when we make certain changes in established modes of expression—changes that are not in conflict with Scripture—because doing so will make worship more meaningful, and contribute to the unity of the body of Christ.

Having stopped to examine briefly the work of two principal hymn writers who, as much as anyone, provided the rich and attractive environment from which our present renaissance could spring, we will now begin our tour proper. We will limit our survey arbitrarily to six wordsmiths and six tunesmiths.

Jaroslav Vajda, born in a Lutheran parsonage in Lorain, Ohio, is a gifted hymn poet with the advantage of having a broad background in literature, music, and theology. Perhaps his most unusual hymn is "Now the Silence." It appeared in 1968 and is, in a way, the ultimate *rejectionist* hymn. Rather than rejecting or questioning some portion of the church's teaching (which would have been very ordinary in 1968 but uncharacteristic of this author) he embraces it and assumes it as a starting place. But then he rejects the very stuff from which hymns are made: normal grammar. This turns out to be by far the more interesting route. He presents us with a hymn of 71 words divided into 19 (or 21) lines. Every line begins with the word *Now*, which, we see in retrospect, is a very '60's word. More than a third of the hymn consists of the words *Now the*, and there is neither a finite verb to be found nor one speck of punctuation. But he does leave us with a tantalizing smorgasbord of impressions for our imaginations to work over. Sung to Carl Schalk's tune called NOW, this makes a very fine hymn.

> Now the silence
> Now the peace
> Now the empty hands uplifted
> Now the kneeling

196

Now the plea
Now the Father's arms in welcome
Now the hearing
Now the power
Now the vessel brimmed for pouring
Now the Body
Now the Blood
Now the joyful celebration
Now the wedding
Now the songs
Now the heart forgiven leaping
Now the Spirit's visitation
Now the Son's epiphany
Now the Father's blessing
Now Now Now

Vajda likes to make translations, and has done a good many from the Slovak. One of the best is "God, My Lord, My Strength" which comes from a seventeenth-century Slovak service book. This is a magnificent, rugged hymn of trust and determination.

God, my Lord, my strength, my place of hiding
and confiding
in all needs by night and day;
though foes surround me,
and Satan mark his prey,
God shall have his way.

Christ in me, and I am freed for living
and forgiving,
heart of flesh for lifeless stone;
now bold to serve him,
now cheered his love to own,
nevermore alone.

Up, weak knees and spirit bowed in sorrow!
No tomorrow
shall arise to beat you down;
God goes before you
and angels all around;
on your head a crown!

Vajda produced this hymn for the *LBW* and it is one of the treasures of the book. It is carried by a wonderful striding tune, and though the music is somewhat awesome at first hearing—a quality it probably must have if it is to carry this text—it is eminently rememberable and natural. What note could be changed in this splendid melody?

|Tune: PÁN BŮH

Another translation in the *LBW* exhibits some of the skills of Gracia Grindal. Here are her first two stanzas of *Es ist ein Ros* along with the corresponding originals.

<table>
<tr><td>

1   Es ist ein Ros entsprungen
    Aus einer Wurzel zart,
Als uns die Alten sungen:
    Aus Jesse Kam die Art;
      Und hat ein Blümlein bracht,
        Mitten im kalten Winter,
    Wohl zu der halben Nacht.

</td><td>

1   Lo, how a rose is growing,
    a bloom of finest grace;
the prophets had foretold it:
    a branch of Jesse's race
      would bear one perfect flower
        here in the cold of winter
    and darkest midnight hour.

</td></tr>
<tr><td>

2   Das Röslein, das ich meine,
    Davon Jessias sagt,
Ist Maria die reine,
    Die uns dies Blümlein bracht;
      Aus Gottes ew'gem Rat
        Hat sie ein Kindlein g'boren,
    Ist blieb'n ein' reine Magd.

</td><td>

2   The rose of which I'm singing
    Isaiah had foretold.
He came to us through Mary
    who sheltered him from cold.
      Through God's eternal will
        this child to us was given
    at midnight calm and still.

</td></tr>
</table>

Her translation reflects the German admirably, getting in almost everything and adding relatively little filler. Therefore it is a faithful translation. But it also is a good English text, which is its more important quality. Dr Grindal always votes on the side of cleanness and understandability when a choice has to be made between those and grandiloquence. In order to loosen things up to obtain this goal she handles rhyme very freely. In this case she dispensed altogether with the rhyme that in the original ties line 3 to line 1; some will criticize her for that but she made her decision knowing that. Then to gain additional elbow room she stretches rhyme a good deal, occasionally to the limit: later in "Lo, How a Rose" she rhymes *sang* with *ran*, *air* with *fear*, and *men* with *sin*, but she's willing to go much further than that! The results are hymn texts that congregations can understand while they are singing, texts that bear up under study but do not require it.

Dr Grindal has given a great deal of thought to alternative methods of textual organization in congregational music. "The Living Water" is a hymn that uses dialogue and word repetition to delineate form. It is taken from a collection entitled *Singing the Story* which she assembled in 1983 during a course she was teaching in hymn-writing. Many of the songs in this collection relate to Biblical stories involving women. Characteristically Dr Grindal wrote a very spare text, one that sounds as if continued usage had worn away everything that was not essential to the plot of the story or to the remembering of the story.

The Living Water

At Jacob's well, where Jesus sat
   a woman came for water.
"Give me a drink," the Savior said,
   "Give me a drink of water."

"But sir," she said, "how can you ask
   of me a drink of water?
I am a poor Samaritan
   and cannot give you water."

"Then ask of me," the Savior said,
   "Give me a drink of water.
And I will give to you a drink,
   a drink of living water."

"How can that be," the woman said,
   "You have no jar for water"
"Who drinks of me," the Savior said,
   "Will drink eternal water."

"Give me to drink," the woman said,
"I thirst for life, for water.
You are the way, the truth, the life,
the spring of living water."

Sometimes Dr Grindal builds on an idea that Heinz Werner Zimmerman was party to in the late '60's; he would take a verse straight from the Bible and set it to a congregational tune. Then his American publisher would get someone to write successive stanzas to fit what he had done. Dr Grindal has been condensing that process, or rearranging the steps, or making other changes in organization or procedure, and the results have been very stimulating.

Not only does Gracia Grindal write hymns, but she writes and speaks engagingly about the whys and wherefores, the joys and sorrows of hymn writing. As much as anyone could, she has made hymn writing something of a popular topic.

Omer Westendorf has been an important figure in hymnological circles as well as in wider church music circles, especially those of the Roman Catholic persuasion. He was editor of *Peoples' Mass Book*, 1961, which was the first full-size service book and hymnal to respond to the reforms of Vatican II. His hymn based on *Ubi caritas* was included in that book under the pseudonym J. Clifford Evers, and from there it has gone into a number of books, both Catholic and Protestant. As printed in the Presbyterian *Worshipbook*, 1972, the hymn begins and ends:

1   Where charity and love prevail
      there God is ever found.
    brought here together by Christ's love,
      by love are we thus bound.

6   No race or creed can love exclude
      if honored be God's name;
    Our brotherhood embraces all
      whose Father is the same.

His "Gift of Finest Wheat" was selected as the official hymn of the 41st Eucharistic Congress held in Philadelphia in 1976. This hymn includes as stanzas 3 and 4 the following:

3   Is not the cup we bless and share
        the blood of Christ outpoured?
    Do not one cup, one loaf declare
        our oneness in the Lord?

4   The mystery of your presence, Lord,
        no mortal tongue can tell:
    whom all the world cannot contain
        comes in our hearts to dwell.

Both hymns quoted here are characteristic of much of the new Roman Catholic hymnody in their faithfulness to the Bible or some other source. Often hymn texts are really just Bible paraphrases or a little more; unfortunately in the hands of many writers this has proven to be a painfully artless style. We are seeing in print some hymns that make all those old Calvinist paraphrases look absolutely inviting. And at least the Calvinists had the sensibility to temper the "plainness" of their words by providing a correspondingly modest tune.

An example of what I'm talking about is "I am the Bread of Life" by Sister Suzanne Toolan, a writer surely of many gifts and graces, but who missed the boat this time. At first this piece looks like a typical case of hymnological fundamentalism. These lines are of course from John 6 and are some of the most potent in scripture. Thus they are some of the most easily spoiled. They are a hot item, so to speak, and one must question the value of stretching these words over this melody. But if they are to be "handled," then they deserve, and really require, some kind of exegesis. In this case, the exegesis is provided by default by the debilitating tune of the verses and the sensational refrain. It turns out to be all wrong.

Contrasting something like "I am the Bread" with Westendorf's stanzas immediately reveals that one constitutes a real and valuable contribution to hymnody and the other does not.

Frank von Christenson, a retired Presbyterian minister, has made a number of significant contributions to the repertoire, including "Break Forth, O Living Light of God" and "As Saints of Old Their First Fruit Brought," which are from 1952 and 1961 respectively. (This latter hymn is also known as "As Those of Old . . ." and—originally—"As Men of Old . . . ," as well as "In Humble Gratitude, O God" which begins the shortened version used in England.) But perhaps he is at his best in "Eternal Spirit of the Living Christ" which was first published in 1974 and, after continuing adjustment, will be printed in definitive form in the *Hymnal 1982*. Sung to Carl Schalk's FLENTGE this hymn has started to make a remarkable impact. It is about prayer and what it means to be in Christ, things important to the piety of many today.

Tune: FLENTGE

1   Eternal Spirit of the living Christ,
        I know not how to ask or what to say;
    I only know my need, as deep as life,
        and only you can teach me how to pray.

2   Come, pray in me the prayer I need this day;
        help me to see your purpose and your will—
    where I have failed, what I have done amiss;
        held in forgiving love, let me be still.

3   Come with the vision and the strength I need
        to serve my God, and all humanity;
    fulfillment of my life in love outpoured—
        my life in you, O Christ, your love in me.

Jeffrey Rowthorn teaches at Yale, at the Divinity School and at the Institute of Sacred Music. In 1980 he, Bruce Neswick and Thomas Jones edited *Laudamus,* a supplement of hymns and service music for use at Yale. As one would expect, it is an exceptional collection and it is made all the more valuable by the inclusion of five of Rowthorn's own hymns. Several of them have taken off, especially "Lord, You Give the Great Commission" which puts in the mouths and hearts of congregations many good sentiments. A favourite of mine is "Earth's Scattered Isles," a solid hymn that takes its inspiration from Psalm 97. He wrote it in 1974, which makes it one of his earlier hymns. Though Rowthorn's hymns are usually packed full, they are never talkative. They are logically thought out and well constructed. Often there is one primary thought developed in each stanza, and the stanzas are linked together not only by their sense but by some simple unifying device: a refrain, a repeated word, or interconnecting words at the same place in each stanza. "Earth's Scattered Isles" has an excellent tune in MEADVILLE by Walter Pelz.

Earth's scattered isles and contoured hills
    which part the seas and mold the land,
and vistas newly seen from space
    that show a world awesome and grand,
        all wondrously unite to sing:
        take heart, take hope, the Lord is King!

God's judgment passed on social ills
    that thwart awhile his firm intent,
the flagging dreams of weary folk
    whose brave new world lies torn and rent,
        in painful form their message bring:
        take heart, take hope, the Lord is King!

203

The constant care which Israel knew
    alike in faith and faithlessness,
the subtle providence which guides
    a pilgrim Church through change and stress,
        inspire us gratefully to sing:
        take heart, take hope, the Lord is King!

The light which shines through noble acts,
    the quest for truth dispelling lies,
the grace of Christ received in us
    so love lives on and discord dies,
        all blend their song, good news to bring:
        take heart, take hope, the Lord is King!

Carl Daw also is emerging as a writer to watch. Formerly a member of the English faculty at the College of William and Mary, he was ordained a priest in the Episcopal Church in 1982. Doubtless his most popular piece—and indeed it is to be admired for its excellence as well as its popularity—is "Like the Murmur of the Dove's Song." He wrote it to be sung to Peter Cutts' wonderful tune entitled BRIDEGROOM. The tune had had been written in the late '60's to carry the Victorian paraphrase "As the Bridegroom to His Chosen." The editorial board of the *Hymnal 1982* had admired Mr Cutts' ingratiating music, but felt that "As the Bridegroom" became somehow a little fantastic when carried by it, that the fervency of the music turned the text from charming to a tad corny. Mr Daw wrote his text using a format similar to that of the original text, but kept things cooler, more conspicuously disciplined, and more liturgical. The result is a very happy marriage of text and tune and a very useful hymn.

Like the murmur of the dove's song,
    like the challenge of her flight,
like the vigor of the wind's rush,
    like the new flame's eager might:
        come, Holy Spirit, come.

To the members of Christ's Body,
    to the branches of the Vine,
to the Church in faith assembled,
    to her midst as gift and sign:
        come, Holy Spirit, come.

With the healing of division,
   with the ceaseless voice of prayer,
with the power to love and witness,
   with the peace beyond compare:
come, Holy Spirit, come.

A recent hymn by Father Daw begins "What Boundless Love, O Carpenter of Nazareth." Even if perhaps one does not completely admire every detail of this hymn, it is immediately obvious that the author is a person of skill, imagination, and theological scope. Perhaps what we admire more than a perfection of details are the larger perfections; for example, the way the hymn rolls so wonderfully into that excellent final stanza and the way that stanza then illuminates what had preceded it. This kind of hymn writing is much rarer than the kind where one or two good lines are trapped in a wallow of words.

What boundless love, O Carpenter of Nazareth,
brought you to earth to share our human toil?
Was there no task in heaven's vast infinity
fit for the hands that formed us from the soil?

Could Adam's fate, to earn his bread by sweat of brow,
be turned to blessing or less bitter made?
Yet for our sake the Word took flesh and sanctified
our daily labor by his humble trade.

Still in our midst, this Lord of shop and marketplace
prays through our work of body, mind, and strength,
and calls us still to labor for the common good,
led by his love that knows no breadth or length.

O come to him, you laborers who long for rest;
his yoke is easy and his burden light.
That mighty work he did for you on Calvary
forever gives you favor in God's sight.

Mr Daw also has an ear and an appreciation for resonance. When he thinks a situation can accept it he is not afraid to use that elevated kind of language that we conveniently label *hymnic diction*. He obviously believes that directness is not always best; he frequently likes verbal roominess. This can be dangerous in an era that admires economy, and indeed it can result in lumps in an otherwise delicious sauce. But good language and good art after all, involve spacing and timing, and release as well as pressure. Most encouraging, I think, is that Carl Daw has been writing hymns for only five or six years and he should have a long career ahead of him.

Composers

When we look at contemporary hymn music writers in this country, we inevitably turn first to Calvin Hampton. More than anyone else he has brought new sounds to the field and has been able to convince us that these sounds can work because of his remarkable gifts as a composer. In a fascinating article he wrote for *The Hymn* (vol. 35, no. 2, 1984, p. 7) he stated: "The listener must *want* to commit a tune to memory, and provoking that desire is a responsibility of the composer." So he is content to see himself more as a *pasticheur* than an inventor. In the same article he wrote of hymn music writers: "A composer is expected to make his string of notes 'tell a hundred stories to the soul.' We are not magicians—we are pick-pockets and grave robbers with trained memories." He declares himself to be a perpetual student, and his work therefore clearly exhibits both experimentation and evolution. He does not consider a tune to be finished until it has been sung for several years by a congregation, so that they might offer some "corrections."

Hampton's music (we must call what he writes *hymn music* for they most definitely are not just *tunes*) demonstrates very clearly a move among many newer writers toward using the organ in a variety of ways, not all of which could be called idiomatic if we define that word in the narrow sense. Indeed we must remember that the organ always has been in part an instrument for playing transcriptions. Most hymns are, after all, none other than easy four-part choral music, and much of the baroque organ literature is easily related to idioms developed on other keyboard instruments or to instrumental solos with orchestra accompaniment. Today we have a number of composers like Hampton who are producing congregational music with organ accompaniments that look more like instrumental transcriptions than choral music. This can be as old hat as the introduction of added voices or the insertion of bits of counterpoint, or as dramatic as some of Hampton's hymns which look for all the world like actual reductions of ensemble music. The style can easily go all the way from neo-classic (Hampton's MACDOUGALL) right over to neo-Broadway (his SONDHEIM, or, even more, REMEMBRANCE by Buryl Red). Frequently this route leads through neo-Langlais (Hampton's PIKE and

WYTON) and the effect and power accrued can be breathtaking! Thus it seems that many of our leading composers look at a variety of musical idioms in addition to hymn tunes when they are speculating on what might be useful for congregational singing. This raises the risk factor significantly, but the process is opening wide many doors that formerly had been opened only a crack.

Hampton's DeTAR—now almost a classic—demonstrates my point clearly. He named it for the renowned organist at the Church of the Ascension in New York's Greenwich Village. The music first appeared in a little collection put out by Concordia in 1973. This pamphlet along with the landmark *Ecumenical Praise* (published by Hope Publishing Company in 1977) served as some of the clearest signals that a significant regeneration of interest in hymnody was developing. Both have had an impact on hymnody in this country that is far beyond what their publishers ever could have imagined.

The obbligato which appears in the right hand of the organ part may be sung by the sopranos, or played on a solo instrument.

Tune: De TAR

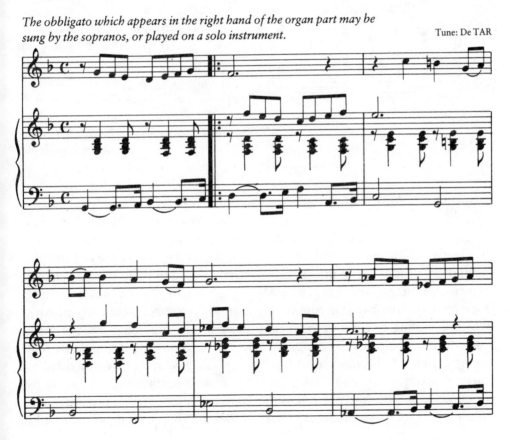

After stanzas 1-3 | After stanza 4

A - men.

David Hurd is rapidly gaining a national reputation among American hymn music writers. His earlier music showed the strong positive influence of Hampton, but with the *David Hurd Hymnary*, brought out by GIA in 1983, he clearly established himself as a major independent force. He is a prolific composer, producing many of his materials on commission or for use at General Seminary, New York, where he is Professor of Church Music. Writing for a relatively unchanging community that sings together frequently and one which is willing to offer opinions and criticism doubtless has been of great value to this composer. The most brilliant of his many hymns, and one that seems destined to become very popular, is MIGHTY SAVIOR. It was written to carry an exceptionally fine text reworked from a tenth-century original by Anne LeCroy, who teaches English at East Tennessee State University. The musical texture is essentially two-part. Under the characteristically song-like

1. Christ, might - y Sav - ior Light of all cre - a - tion,
2. Now comes the day's end as the sun is set - ting:
3. There - fore we come now eve - ning rites to of - fer,

you make the day - time ra - diant with the sun - light
mir - ror of day - break, pledge of res - ur - rec - tion;
joy - ful - ly chant - ing ho - ly hymns to praise you,

and to the night give glit - ter - ing a - dorn - ment,
while in the heav - ens choirs of stars ap - pear - ing
with all cre - a - tion join - ing hearts and voi - ces

209

stars _____ in the heav - en.
hal - low the night - fall.
sing - ing your glo - ry.

Text: Mozarabic, 10th cent.; tr. Alan G. McDougall; rev. Anne K. LeCroy (b. 1930) and others
(stanzas 4 and 5 are omitted)

melody that he, like Hampton, writes so naturally, he places a supporting bass—in this case a functional bass, but one in which melodic and rhythmic concerns are not subordinated inordinately to the harmonic. This bass does for song-hymns (if I may use that term) what walking basses did for Vaughan Williams' and Shaw's march-hymns: it provides counter-melody and rhythmic momentum. Richly textured chords bridge the space between the melody and bass. The methods are simple but the effect is electrifying.

Another of the younger composers who knows how to help a congregation sing well is Gerald Near. His LOWRY (1977) exhibits the careful manipulation and balance between melodic and harmonic attractiveness that characterizes much of his work. Quite clearly these two components were conceived to be interdependent, particularly at the striking movement from the end of line 2 to the beginning of line 3. Melodically the hymn is very simple and not particularly dramatic or inventive (which certainly is no criticism of a hymn tune!). Harmonically he breaks just enough rules to keep the ear interested. All told he is like a latter day Gauntlett or Billings: he writes music that is gratifying, but he has hewn it down so that its substance has integrity and the prospect of a long life.

Mr Near lives in Dallas where he has helped establish a publishing house and continues in his writing. In nearby Fort Worth at the Southwestern Baptist Theological Seminary, William J. Reynolds teaches in the church music department. Dr Reynolds has been an important figure in Baptist hymnody, both as composer and editor, particularly of the *Baptist Hymnal*, 1975. Before teaching at the seminary he was head of the Church Music Department of the

Baptist Sunday School Board. He has a wonderful gift for harmonizations of folkloric materials. His harmonizations scheduled to appear in *Songs of Zion*, a hymnal forthcoming from Keith Landis' Praise Publications, demonstrate this clearly.

Mr Reynolds often operates on the pop or gospel side of the stylistic spectrum and though I don't think this material holds up as well as his other work, it has been an appreciated component of the repertoire. I think his MORA PROCTOR, which comes more from the "folk-hymn" segment of his *oeuvre*, is an inspired piece, clearly revealing his ability to produce a persuasive melody and then harmonize it with skill and taste.

One of the abiding central figures of the contemporary American hymn scene is Austin Lovelace, now the Director of Music at Wellshire Presbyterian Church, Denver, and President of the Hymn Society of America from 1984 to 1986. He has had the advantage of working in a number of places around the

country and for institutions of various sorts: churches, colleges and semi-naries. He is a prolific author and composer. As well as being a composer of original tunes, he has distinguished himself as an arranger, often of American folk tunes. He excels in a very economical writing style; all the bases are covered but there's never a note too many.

His style of harmonizing American folkloric materials represents a kind of moderate position on how this sort of thing is to be done. On the one side are those who stick very closely to the original (or oldest) sources. They cheerfully reprint most or all of the parallelisms, retrogressions, non-functionalisms, and *non sequiturs* if they were there in the beginning. So this person is really more an editor than an arranger, and the effect of these "urtext" harmonizations is often characterized by congregations as beautiful, or haunting, or rugged, right down to amusing or even grotesque.

This approach is gaining considerable ground over against the opposite approach where the melody is seen as being much in need of laundering, or is merely a starting point for a new piece of music. First, radical surgery may be performed on the tune and then the revised product is made somehow more acceptable by means of a harmonization that pleases 1980's ears but may have little to do with the creative impulse that was behind the music in the first place.

Then there is the middle ground, represented so well by Lovelace (and, I hasten to add, a host of others; see the United Methodist *Book of Hymns* for examples). His goals are to exercise his rights as a composer but also to retain as much of the original spirit of the music as he can. He feels he has met success when the result of his labors is at once both new and respectful.

An example of this is his arrangement of DOVE OF PEACE from *Ecumenical Praise*. A glance at the bass line will reveal that it has very little ambition other than to compliment and support the melody; it could not be called a counter melody, and it does not indulge in self-advertising scalar motion as a kind of false counter melody—a favorite unifying device of the more "radical" arrangers, but one that can push harmonies where they do not naturally want to go. Lovelace's inner voices move mostly as a pair and, especially near the end, in sync with the bass. When choosing his notes the composer went for the most obvious ones, the ones that move most naturally from one to another, and always with the proviso that the resulting harmonies propel the music. Then he wrote in two E-flats at cadences, bowing momentarily to modality—a sound that has colored much of American folk hymnody and therefore is to be treasured.

Tune: DOVE OF PEACE

Our last example is a collaboration of musicians: the form of the melody (which is the chant *Gloria, laus et honor*) was determined by John Blackley and Barbara Jones, co-directors of the Schola Antiqua of New York. The accompaniment was added by Richard Proulx, Director of Music at Holy Name Cathedral, Chicago. The kind of thinking that produced this music could have far-reaching consequences as to how American congregations perceive chant hymns. As our example demonstrates, it has primarily to do with rhythm.

For decades American hymnals have been moving in the direction of printing chorales and psalter tunes in their original forms, which often included a variety of note values rather than strings of equal note values. For reformed churches the *cause celebre* has been OLD HUNDRED, and for the Lutherans it has been that plus EIN FESTE BURG. The matter as to whether today's congregations should sing the rhythmic forms can be debated, but often it is beyond dispute as to how the melody was conceived: all one has to do is check the sources.

Chant hymns in modern hymnals usually have been printed in equal values with occasional lengthened notes. Some scholars believed that they were conceived this way; others didn't believe that, but didn't really know how the music was to be performed because no one was sure of how to read many of the manuscripts. Over the life of this most enduring of musical genres many details had changed from place to place and from century to century, and notation systems—always and forever very inadequate right up to this very day—changed too. So chant hymns in modern congregational books have been printed in "equalist" style, giving pitches but almost no durations. Often the results have been very beautiful.

However, recent work indicates with increasing clarity that many chant hymns are not intrinsically "equalist." The controversy (of which there is plenty) begins when editors attempt rhythmic reconstructions. A question behind dozens of scholarly articles asks: "Who's he to say it goes this way when I have good reason to believe it goes this way?" Nevertheless the work goes on and it involves hard scholarship, experimentation, conjecture, and some witchcraft.

Tune: GLORIA, LAUS, ET HONOR

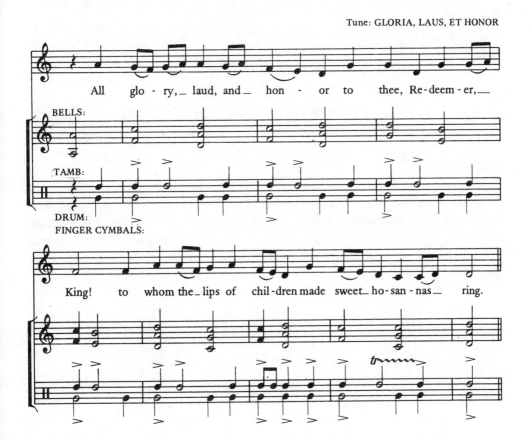

The Blackley/Jones form of GLORIA, LAUS is realized according to principles of proportional rhythm which they developed or reconstructed. With Mr Proulx's expert accompaniment it will be printed in the Episcopal *Hymnal 1982* as an alternative tune to VALET WILL ICH DIR GEBEN. (ST THEODOLPH). The effect is, in Mr Blackley's own words, one of "irregularity that feels regular," and in congregational performance with a cantor singing the verses, the hymn is superb.

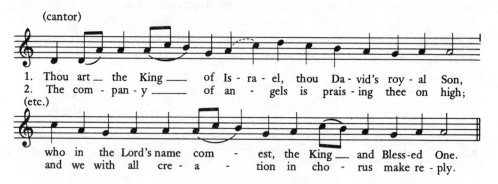

1. Thou art ── the King ── of Is - ra - el, thou Da - vid's roy - al Son,
2. The com - pan - y ──── of an - gels is prais - ing thee on high;
(etc.)

who in the Lord's name com - est, the King ── and Bless-ed One.
and we with all cre - a - tion in cho - rus make re - ply.

Conclusion

Our present renaissance grew out of both our immediate past and our more distant past. We are therefore in an opportune position to compare and contrast, to make choices, indeed, to enrich or reject. But the future is pressing in on us. We will be a little better prepared for it if we are both meticulous and charitable, if we educate ourselves and our congregations, and if we remain flexible.

14

NEW HYMNODY: SOME PROBLEMS
AND PROSPECTS

Fred Pratt Green
Fred Kaan
Brian Wren

Just a few days after Fred Pratt Green's 80th birthday, the three hymnwriters met in his home in Norwich on 6 September 1983. Robin A. Leaver was also there to act as arbiter and referee as these three men, whose hymns have been widely used and appreciated on both sides of the Atlantic—and further afield—over the past twenty years or so, thought aloud together and discussed their approach to and involvement in the difficult art of writing hymns. The following represents the substance of the conversation.

RAL: The first question most would want to ask the three of you is: How did you begin to write hymns and what was your original motivation? Perhaps we could begin with you, Brian?

BW: I began writing hymns when I was at theological college, Mansfield College, Oxford. I had for some time been using prayers in contemporary language, trying to write and speak in the language I would normally use, rather than in the archaic language of "thee" and "thou". I had written some youthful poetry, and had an ear for verse, so it was natural to try my hand at hymns. At that time there was a lot of new music around but very few new texts. So I wrote a hymn and sent it to Erik Routley, whom I had known earlier when he was teaching in Oxford. He wrote back and criticized it very tellingly. He also picked out one or two phrases he thought were good in it and said what he thought hymn writing was about. There was one phrase of his which has remained in my mind. He said: "The great glory of God and the contemporary need of humanity need to be made to collide in modern verse." I think that is one of the things I have tried to do since.

That's how I began. I did not write any more hymns for a year or so, then I

217

wrote two, in association with Peter Cutts. The first was *Lord Christ, the Father's mighty Son* and the other was *Christ upon a mountain peak*.

RAL: Were they written in response to requests or as the result of "inner compulsion"?

BW: *Christ upon the mountain peak*, on the Transfiguration, was specifically written for a conference. The other one came out of my experience of belonging to the Student Christian Movement. At that time it wasn't possible for Christians, Anglicans and non-Anglicans, to take communion together —*Lord Christ, the Father's mighty Son* came from the pain of this experience. That was in 1962 and I did not write anything further until 1968, partly because I was finishing a doctoral thesis and partly because I was "learning my trade" in the pastoral ministry.

RAL: So you began, Brian, in 1962. When did you make your beginning, Fred (K)?

FK: I started perhaps a year later, in 1963, when I was called to be the minister of the Pilgrim Church, Plymouth. All the writing I have done traces its origin back to that Plymouth experience, being the minister in a congregation which was very stimulating and which encouraged me all along the way to lead them in new ways of worship. In fact they had articulated very clearly in the letter which called me what they saw as the role of a Christian minister. One of these points was that of helping a congregation to express its faith in contemporary terms. They were all very much involved in the social and political life of the city of Plymouth and were anxious to see the worship reflecting this in their discipleship and witness, and also the other way round. So I would say that that was one main reason for starting to write hymns, and unlike Brian, I wrote very regularly. I got into a pattern whereby I almost produced a hymn for every Sunday morning service—not that they all survived—but it was certainly a regular discipline: it was part of my preparation for Sunday worship. But the other reason I ought also to confess is that, obviously, becoming a hymnwriter had its origins in the frustration created by what I could not find in the hard-cover hymn book. There are so many areas that were not covered at all in *Congregational Praise* (which by any standards is a pretty good book). For example, among the first texts I wrote were post-communion hymns; there were so few hymns enabling us to make the transition from breaking bread at the table to sharing bread in the world. But then, of course, there were also the other gaps which come under the heading of our social and political involvement in the world. There were no specific hymns about living in a modern city and an urbanized society. There were so few hymns which spoke about the glory of our humanness, so few hymns which emphasised the humanity of Jesus.

RAL: But what did you do with these hymns? You wrote them for your own church initially, so how did they begin to go wider afield?

FK: This was obviously home-spun hymnody. I produced these hymns late on Saturday night; that was the regular pattern. After I had written some, I took the liberty of sending them to Erik Routley on loose pieces of paper. He sent me a fairly cool letter back saying that it had all been written before! I was, I remember, a little crestfallen at this. But then after a few years we sifted all this material and put it together in a printed collection, a booklet called *Pilgrim Praise*. I sent a copy to Erik and the very texts which he had regarded with a cool eye earlier on he now commented on in a very positive way, and in fact, helped to promote them in connection with one or two hymn book committees. But it was an interesting experience and I am grateful for the ability in Erik's mind to change his opinion.

RAL: Could that have something to do with the fact that the earlier loose-leaf format was clearly temporary whereas a printed edition implies something more permanent?

FK: Perhaps. Although I would hate to think that only because it is printed it gains credibility. I should like to think that the hard-cover hymn book and the loose pieces of paper, which you can either discard or retain, could live side-by-side with each other in peace, supplementing each other. I think if I were asked to describe myself, I would say that I am a supplement writer, putting things alongside that which is already available and enjoyed in the church.

RAL: Fred Pratt Green, it is interesting that although you are the oldest of the three hymnwriters here, you are, in fact, the youngest in terms of actually writing hymns—both Brian and Fred had made a beginning before you turned your hand to crafting hymns. How did you begin?

FPG: Well, I have to confess that I wrote one hymn when I was chaplain to a girls boarding school because the headmistress asked me to do it. I also wrote two hymns for a Sunday School hymn book, on request. And then for very many years I wrote nothing at all in the way of hymns. I think it is true to say I somewhat despised hymns. I was fond of poetry and had written quite a lot in my middle years. I was very much in love with the modern poets, especially T.

S. Eliot, and the language of hymnody didn't appeal to me. However, I was put on a committee to produce a supplement to the *Methodist Hymn Book* (1933) which was eventually called *Hymns and Songs* (1969). I was put on this committee because of my literary interests in order to vet the new material, to see if it was worthy of inclusion. It wasn't very long before the committee said to me: "We want a text for the tune CHRISTE SANCTORUM. You call yourself a poet; you go away and write it!" So with the encouragement of John Wilson, and others, I did as I was told and wrote *Christ is the world's light*. After that I was asked to write hymns to fill gaps, as, for instance, on the relationship of Sunday and Sabbath—*The first day of the week*. Later I was asked to write new texts for other tunes, such as ENGELBERG, for which I wrote *When in our music God is glorified*. Almost from the beginning I had Erik Routley's critical encouragement. That's how it began and it has gone on ever since—I haven't been able to stop!

RAL: But your writing has been different from Fred Kaan's which grew out of a weekly concern to express the needs within a particular congregation. In contrast, you have responded to particular requests from many different congregations and from hymn book editors. I wonder, is there any distinction which can be drawn between the request that comes from the particular congregation and the request that comes from the editors? In other words, do the editors always really know what they are looking for? What do you think, Brian?

BW: I haven't responded to many requests from editors until recently, because the ones I've had—and I don't think I've had as many as Fred (PG)—have left me somewhat puzzled as to what they were on about. Or, the question has been posed in an unspecific way: "We are looking for new hymns on the life of Christ"; either that or the question is too specific "We need a hymn about St Lawrence"—neither of which actually grabs me very much. There isn't enough there for me to work with.

FPG: I'm quite different. I've had a number of requests for hymns on saints I had never heard of, or only vaguely heard of, like Boniface and Ninian. I have been drawn to look into their lives and have been attracted to write something about them.

RAL: Were these requests from editors or a congregation?

FPG: These were definitely for specific occasions, such as the thirteenhun-dredth anniversary of the birth of Boniface for which I had a request from Crediton, where Boniface is thought to have been born.

RAL: Is there a difference then between a request from a particular congregation with a particular need, and a request from hymn book editors, who tend to think in terms of general rather than specific needs?

FPG: Yes, and many of my hymns are therefore occasional pieces. But on the other hand I have had quite a number of requests from editors who have been specific in what they have wanted. They have often mentioned lectionary themes, such as, The Suffering Church. This so deeply moved me. I wrote *Pray for the church, afflicted and oppressed.*

FK: I think there is a difference in the nature of the request, isn't there? The editor is in a position to overview the work he is doing on behalf of his constituency, and he is perhaps rather analytical about what he is doing. Therefore he is able to identify specific needs. But the request that comes from the congregation is a request in which you yourself are involved. If you are the pastor of a local congregation, the request is not put to you in an analytical or academic way, but you grow with the people making the request. It is a *quest* rather than a request in which you are involved, and, because of your worship experience and your experience in Christian witness, you discover together what needs to be written.

BW: Could I add to what I said earlier? When I was on the *New Church Praise* (1974) committee I wrote several hymns not exactly in response to requests from the committee, but out of a common feeling we expressed, for instance, "We don't have too many good hymns on the Bible."—a statement left hanging in mid-air, and one or two of us would go away and write something. It is what Fred (K) was saying, that it is part of a common quest that we are engaged in.

FPG: We all felt the need for new hymns, didn't we? I so disliked many of the old ones that I was impelled to write some new ones!

RAL: So what you are all saying is that wherever the request has come from, you cannot respond to it until you are able to put yourself alongside that request and feel an affinity with it. Is that what you were saying, Brian?

BW: Yes, but this may well have to change because I am now more consciously looking for commissioned work, whereas until quite recently I have not had the time to respond to such requests.

FPG: That's just where I have been very lucky because all this happened to me just at the time I was retiring—I couldn't have done it when I was in the active ministry. One also had the feeling that it was a very great honour to write hymns to be sung in worship, for worship is of the utmost importance to our Christian life.

FK: Could I identify another area which has stimulated me? When I left the local pastoral ministry and went into an international, somewhat bureaucratic, aspect of ministry, I found myself often writing hymns, that were either triggered off by something said at a big assembly or consultation—a throw-away line by a speaker—or (and here again I come back to the negative prompting which sometimes sets you off) I have written some of my best texts in the most boring meetings! So much went on in the debate and discussion that seemed so terribly irrelevant to the real issues facing the Christian church, that I simply switched off and did the very opposite of what was going on in the meeting.

FPG: May I make a comment here? What we have been doing is exactly what Watts and Wesley did. Watts wrote hymns for his congregation because he had had enough of metrical psalms, and Wesley used the great opportunities of the revival to write hymns which expressed Christian experience.

RAL: Does that mean that the role of hymnody is simply to catch the experience that is already shared within the congregation, or to create the experience that should be there among the people?

FK: Unhesitatingly it must be both. Hymns both reflect the experience of the church and are also part of that quest to try and find new ways of expressing the faith; and that must be a conscious effort.

FPG: We are part of the age in which we live. It isn't that we have to feel a sudden inspiration to do something but do it because we are a part of a community which shares a common need or concern.

BW: And it works if what we write is something which is in tune with the hearts of those within the community. It doesn't work if we write in a way that is too far away from people's experience or searching. Then the words will not ring true and will have no meaning. I've found, having just been in the United States going round introducing a number of hymn texts, an amazing response to the new words. This suggests that a lot of what we write is near people's experience. It also suggests that a lot of it is fresh in the sense that many people haven't found their particular experience or questioning reflected in words written previously.

RAL: Is that therefore also a criticism of the hymnody that people have been singing, that they have been singing out of habit and formality, mouthing words which, because of their familiarity, they have not really come to terms with?

FPG: I am bound to say that I think this is rather true of the Wesley hymns. I think we have been singing the Charles Wesley hymns in the Methodist Church now for many years without the experience that created them.

FK: I think there is also a sense in which the melodies of our hymns sometimes get in the way of what the hymns are trying to say. It was, I think, Nathaniel Micklem who took the vesper hymn and twisted it:

> Lord, keep us safe this night
> Beneath the stars and moon,
> Pay thou no heed to what we say,
> We only like the tune.

There's a lot in that. The introduction of a new text to a new tune irritates people far more than the introduction of a new text to an existing tune.

FPG: You were very fortunate in not knowing so much about music that you used the old tunes!

FK: I think another area where perhaps I'm fortunate is that a) English is not my mother-tongue, and therefore I use English as something of a new discovery, and b), I didn't grow up as a Christian. I never set foot in church from the day I was baptized until I was in my late teens. So, I didn't grow up with the traditional language of the church, and even if I had, in making the transition from one country to another, from one language to another —Dutch to English—I was not familiar with the traditional expressions of the faith.

BW: I'm very interested to hear that, because one of the things I like about your hymns is the way you so often reveal a wealth of meaning in an everyday colloquial phrase. Is that something to do with English being a second language?

FK: Oh yes. It has become first language now, of course, but it is still fresh. One of the things I always do (and I suggest this to my colleagues in the ministry, too) is that before I start preparing myself for preaching by going back to the original Greek and Hebrew, I go to the English dictionary of etymology. I look up the meaning of the words in English and I trace them right back in English usage, and it is incredible what you find! It's just fantastic! Sometimes you get the whole of your sermon material presented to you through etymology—by simply looking up what the words mean.

RAL: What then is the hymnwriter's linguistic task?

BW: I think each hymn writer is like a musician. A musician has an instrument, a singer has their voice, and they tune and develop their instrument or voice in order to get the best out of it. The only instrument we have is ourselves, our own personality and experience—it's a kind of keyboard, a personality keyboard, through which one is able to write, through which, for instance, Fred (K) is able to see the English language in a new light. So you have to tune and explore that keyboard. My way of doing so is to ask—and keep asking—Who am I? What do I know, experience, and believe? Who am I in society? What is my social position? Am I one of those who benefit or suffer from injustice? Another basic question is: Who am I as male or female? By asking these questions of myself I find the subject matter of hymns and the direction in which I want to go. One emerging issue from such questioning is the question of sexism in hymn language. By a process of discussion and listening to what other people are saying, I have come to the point where first of all, it seems to me, quite straightforwardly as a matter of usage, that the words "man" and "men" don't really now suggest "people" in general, but have a clearly "male" or masculine sound. It is interesting when you talk about etymology, Fred (K), because etymology is past history, and present-day meanings have changed. The word "man" was originally a noun of common gender and was used as such in early English. For example, Aelfric, about the year 1100, speaks of a woman called Elen as "a full of faith man", without any inconsistency. But common usage has changed: there are a number of research surveys which tend to confirm this. If we want to communicate clearly, we can't go on using "men" to mean "people". It is therefore necessary to change this kind of language in my hymns as I have now done. But the second and more profound area is in how we understand and think about God. Again, through listening to what others are saying, particularly some writers in feminist theology, I have become convinced that we need to expand our ideas about God. I do not want to stop calling God "Father" because it is an important personal and Biblical image—but I now know that I can worship the Creator of male and female as my Mother, or Sister, as well. If we look at some of the biblical passages where God is actually thought of in feminine terms, as, for example, the Mother who picks up Ephraim and teaches him to

224

walk in Hosea, or as giving birth to new things, we find biblical precedents for thinking about and understanding God which are, for want of a better word, feminine. And this will enrich our faith.

RAL: Fred (K), where are you on the inclusive language issue? Has it been a factor for your hymnody?

FK: Yes it has. I think I ought to say of myself that I'm going in the same direction as Brian, only I haven't advanced as far as he has. I have also re-written my texts although they have not yet been published in this revised form, but that will happen soon. I have more difficulty perhaps than Brian with God-language as opposed to people-of-God-language, and I am still wrestling with it. I take every point that he makes and I am sympathetic to it, but I have to work it through in my own experience. Where I would draw the line, and this is perhaps where I have had some unhappy experiences in Canada and the United States, is that people have even begun to write about Jesus as if he wasn't really male, where they avoid speaking about him as "him". I think that this is where we have to be very careful. Our response to the Godhead is certainly a response which we ought to re-live and re-experience, but our response to Christ, both as an historical figure and as a real presence today, I think is something with which I could not tamper.

BW: Yes, I would agree with that. I've not had occasion to meet anyone who has done this, so I don't know the reasoning behind it. My understanding would be that we meet God in Jesus and inevitably there is certain restriction and particularity about it. To be fully expressed as a human being God had either to be male or female.

FPG: And he chose to be male!

BW: Well, I think it's a question of whether you make that a question of historical or normative importance. It would have been impossible for a woman to get a hearing in the patriarchal society of ancient times—not even enough of a hearing to be crucified!

RAL: Where do you stand on this issue, Fred (PG)?

FPG: Well, being the grandfather of the three it can be assumed that I am rather more conservative, though I would certainly go along with a great deal of what has been said. I do think that the use of "mankind" and "man" is extremely misleading in hymnody. My only trouble is that where I've got them in one or two of my hymns I can't do anything about it. "Humankind" doesn't fit with the metre and therefore one has to leave it as it is. I do think that to go

225

too far in this direction is going to destroy something that belongs to the tradition of the church from the beginning. It is likely to create difficulties for a great number of people and will tend rather to weaken Christianity in the end than to strengthen it. I feel this quite strongly. What must logically follow, surely, is the rewriting of the Bible, as well as of hymns?

FK: Fred, I have a problem with the concept by which you seem to suggest that tradition is something unalterable. Isn't tradition a living process in which we ourselves are involved, and therefore it doesn't arrive on our desk, so to speak, or on our lectern, as a rounded-off gift?

FPG: O yes, I agree that tradition changes and we come into something which is a revised tradition. But this approach seems to me to be suddenly extremely radical and, I would feel, for many people, deeply disturbing. God is neither "he", nor "she" nor "it". God is "God" and that says it all.

BW: Can I make one observation? We are four *men* in this room discussing this and our conversation is bound to be conditioned by that limitation. I take the point that some people are disturbed by changes of this sort, and some, indeed, are disturbed by change of any kind. But I also have friends who are equally disturbed by the "maleness" of Christianity.

FK: There are people who cannot cope with change, but I think there is a growing number of people who cannot cope with no-change, and they cannot cope with the unchangeableness of what has been handed down. I think that it is of the essence of the Christian faith that it is a *live* tradition which is in the process of being handed on. And what we are handing on is a Person. I think we ought to be on the side of those who are looking for creative changes in the way in which we experience and express our faith.

FPG: Yes, I'm all in favour of people being taught to think of God in much larger terms than we have usually thought of him in church. But if you are going to take a hymn and replace the "he" with something else, what is that substitute to be? You cannot put "he/she"; there is a sense in which God is "it" but this is difficult. It seems to me that you are going to write some very, very peculiar hymns.

BW: My response to that is that the issue goes beyond the single hymn text to the overall selection made by hymn books. I would like to see a selection of hymns which enabled us to worship the eternal being of God in both masculine and feminine terms. So that in one hymn you might be speaking of God as "Mother" and in another as "Father".

226

FPG: In other words, you are quite prepared now to write a hymn in which you use "he" for God?

BW: Yes, but it must be admitted that we have plenty of those already! I found 287 male pronouns of the first 80 hymns of the *Methodist Hymn Book* (1933), so it's a question of redressing the balance.

RAL: Isn't this the problem that new hymnody has always faced, that it is different from existing hymnody and an "either/or" confrontation occurs? New hymnody, rightly understood, is not intended to displace the best of the old but to add to it. Isn't this what you are trying to do, Brian, over this question of inclusive language?

BW: Inclusive language is one area I am exploring. But I also try to explore Christian themes which are quite "traditional", and which I want to look at in a new way—or re-discover something "traditional" which seems to have been forgotten. Fred (K) has spoken about hymns he has written during boring meetings. I have written at least one hymn because I was so annoyed with a sermon. It was a thoroughly "traditional" text in both form and content: *I am worthy, full of worth*.

FPG: You wouldn't alter the great hymns of the past in which "he" is used, or would you?

BW: I think I would take them on a case by case basis. Hymns do get altered and some need to be. Even John Wesley altered other people's hymns, though he didn't like his own being changed. But I don't know of any computerised rules for doing it. One hopes that when it is done it is done sensitively. There are some great hymns of the past which perhaps can continue unchanged. There are some which would be enhanced by some careful revision. There are probably a great many in the middle ground which, when you ask "Do you really want to sing this today?", "Is it worth revising?", the answer is, "No".

FPG: And you can trust people to alter these great hymns of the past? There have been alterations made lately which seem to me to be scandalous.

BW: I think there are some crass alterations going around at the moment. It is likely to be a hotly-contested area. But if a hymn is something which is written for a community, one must expect it to undergo change.

FPG: There's one thing about this whole argument that seems to me so strange. A hymn book gives you the life of the Christian church from the beginning. Therefore you don't want to change the hymns of the past into something that represents the present, because that destroys a sense of the history of the faith as it has come to us from earlier generations.

FK: I wouldn't go as far as Brian does. I think that the traditional hymns, the way they have been handed on to us, are texts with which we ought not to tamper. What right have we to re-write these hymns? What right have we to re-write Shakespeare? You wouldn't do that, or would you?

BW: I don't think it's the same kind of thing. It is difficult to think of examples, but I think that if you look at a number of hymn texts which we would regard as being classical, and go back to the originals, then as likely as not you will find that they *have* been altered. In many cases they have been altered because some particular words changed their meaning and became obscure or offensive.

RAL: However, whatever the pros and cons, the future of hymnody is not going to be in the rewriting of old texts but in the writing of new hymns.

FPG: But I would ask the more radical question: Is there a future for hymnody? We are moving now into a world which is going to be totally different from the one I've known.

FK: The answer is bound to be "yes". But it may be going in a direction which is perhaps different from the one we expect, and that is the direction in which we begin to learn musical and poetic idioms from cultures other than our own. This is where I think we in the West ought to listen far more carefully to our brothers and sisters in the Third World, for instance. We should learn to share their experiences, which is bound to include oppression, poverty and so on. We need to see life, the longing for human dignity, as expressed by those for whom this is a real struggle. In this way hymnody can probably be saved, if it *is* a matter of saving. I don't think it will peter out, but we will learn to sing hymns in idioms which hitherto have been strange to us.

RAL: Well, perhaps this is the point to add the colon: we therefore wait to experience how the sentence on future hymnody is to be completed.

*   *   *

Most of the hymns of Fred Pratt Green can be found in *The Hymns and Ballads of Fred Pratt Green*, with commentary by Bernard Braley, Carol Stream & London 1982; those of Fred Kaan in *The Hymn Texts of Fred Kaan*, with an introduction by Bernard Braley, Carol Stream & London 1985; and those of Brian Wren in *Faith Looking Forward. The Hymns & Songs of Brian Wren with many Tunes by Peter Cutts*, Carol Stream & Oxford 1983.

A BIBLIOGRAPHY OF
THE WORKS
OF
ERIK ROUTLEY

Ray Robinson

BIBLIOGRAPHY

CONTENTS

INTRODUCTION

THE LIFE WORK OF ERIK ROUTLEY

The writing career of Erik Routley (1917–1982) spanned a period of forty-three years. His first published writing appeared in *The Spectator* in February 1939—Letter to the Editor—and his final essay, "Hymn story: 'What does the Lord require?'" was published in the Trinity Church (Princeton) weekly leaflet *Tidings* on October 22, 1982, two weeks after his death. In the years that unfolded between these two publications, Erik Routley was impressively productive. Probably no one will ever know exactly how many articles and reviews he wrote, simply because he would write almost at the drop of a hat, for anyone, anywhere, and at any time—usually by return mail. Many of his essays appeared in periodicals which have passed out of existence, some surfaced in church bulletins and church newspapers which are not catalogued in any standard reference source, and still others were published in various school publications, college newsletters, and seminary periodicals.

In the relatively short space of forty-three years Erik Routley produced (in round numbers) 50 books and monographs, 4 hymnal companions, 600 published articles, 10 unpublished book-length manuscripts, 150 unpublished items (articles, critiques, lectures, etc.). In his lifetime he also served as editor for seven books and participated in the editorial decisions involving 15 hymnals. In addition, he composed something like 110 hymn and other tunes and about 70 original compositions (comprising 38 opus numbers). His hymn tunes and texts appear in more than 90 hymnals and hymnal supplements in America, England and other countries of the world. Between 1948 and 1974 he was editor of and contributor to the *Bulletin of the Hymn Society of Great Britain and Ireland* and, for a period of nineteen months (March 1958 –September 1959), he served in a similar capacity for *Congregational Monthly*.

One of the finest sources of his writings is found in *The British Weekly* to which he was a regular contributor between 1951 and 1970. In the early years his writings appeared in a monthly column entitled "Routley at Random." Between 1955 and 1970 he served as one of the periodical's regular reviewers,

233

often covering as many as eight to ten new books or new musical compositions (mostly choral or organ pieces) within the space of a single article. These writings would be supplemented from time to time by full-length feature articles on timely topics of interest ranging from musical topics to social and theological issues. Often these articles appeared on the paper's front page.

This staggering output of literary activity is simply amazing when one considers that writing was not a full-time vocation for Erik Routley; thirty-one years (1943–1974) of his adult life were spent in the ministry of the Congregational Church (the United Reformed Church after 1972) and eight as professor of church music at Westminster Choir College.

A short time spent studying the bibliography which follows will reveal a clear pattern in Erik Routley's creative output. The writings of the early years (1948–1959) are concerned almost exclusively with the hymnody of the church. His appointment in 1944 to the editorial committee of *Congregational Praise* (1951), which was also the first hymnal to include his hymn tunes, and his assuming four years later the editorship of the *Hymn Society Bulletin*, confirmed this interest. Of the 12 books which were published during these years, all but two deal with some aspect of Christian hymnody. The same pattern is found in the periodical articles which appear between 1944 and 1959; less than a dozen of the approximately 120 articles deal with a topic other than hymnody. However, near the end of this period he served as editor of *The Congregational Monthly* and for the first time in his public writing career his thoughts concerning the broader issues of religious life begin to appear in print.

The pastoral appointments in Edinburgh (1959–1967) and Newcastle-upon-Tyne (1967–1974) were of considerable influence on his writings during the second period (1959–1974). The eleven years just prior to the move to Scotland had been spent in the highly-charged academic environment of Oxford, where he could afford the luxury of confining his writing to the narrow field of his interest. However, once he returned to parish life he was forced to deal with the theological and social issues which are a regular part of the ministry of a large city church. It is thus not surprising that these concerns are present in his writings. Of the 17 books which were written during these years, 11 explored subjects other than musical. The same pattern emerges in the periodical literature as well.

Whereas in the first period Erik Routley's articles appear primarily in three periodicals (*Hymn Society Bulletin*, *The Congregational Monthly*, and the *Mansfield College Magazine*), the years between 1959 and 1974 find his writings reaching a much broader audience. For example, his sermons appear regularly in the prestigious *Expository Times*. Articles also begin to show up in *The British Weekly, The Cambridge Review, Christian Century, London Churchman, The London Quarterly and Holborn Review, New Christian, The Scottish Congregationalist, Theology Today* and *The Union Seminary Quarterly Review*.

Two of the books which were published during this period grew out of lectureships which he gave in 1966 in the United States. The Stone Lectures of Princeton Theological Seminary provided the impetus for *Words, Music and the Church* (1969), while the Gheens Lectures at the Southern Baptist Theological Seminary, Louisville, KY, produced the text for *Music Leadership in the Church* (1967). Two of his most influential books—*Into a Far Country* (1962) and *Twentieth-Century Church Music* (1964)—were the result of his work during the Edinburgh years.

The state of church music in the mid-1970s and the responsibilities related to his appointment as professor of church music at Westminster Choir College (1975) led Erik Routley to turn his attention in his later years almost exclusively to the field of church music. Of course, the interest in hymnody —the writing of articles, the editing of hymnals, and the developing of hymnal companions—continued during these years. The two volume series *An English Speaking Hymnal Guide* and *Panorama of Christian Hymnody* (1979), *The Music of Christian Hymns* (1981), and the recordings *Christian Hymns: An Introduction to their Story* (1980), all give evidence of his continuing interest in this field. However, another theme also seems to dominate his thinking after 1975: the worship practices of the American Church. Time and time again he challenges church musicians and ministers to consider the importance of "pattern, proportion and precision" in the liturgical life of the church. Two books—*Church Music and the Christian Faith* (1978) and *The Divine Formula* (1985), a posthumously published book written in 1976 —speak with conviction to this issue.

The matter of "inclusive language" was another new topic that surfaced in his periodical writings during this period; he was deeply concerned that this controversy would seriously damage the hymnody of the past as those charged with the responsibility of editing hymnals would change the poetry of giants like Isaac Watts, Charles Wesley and Phillip Doddridge.

It is interesting to note that all of Erik Routley's published books and most of his articles between 1975 and 1982 deal with musical topics. The one significant exception is a series of articles which appear monthly in *Reform* between February and December 1979 under the title "The Routley Commentary." In general, his writings in this periodical deal with subjects other than musical ones.

A few words should be written about the bibliography itself. The original impetus behind it was a desire to collect together as many Erik Routley writings as possible at Westminster Choir College. Its purpose was simple: to identify his literary output as a permanent memorial to his life and work. In addition, it was hoped that Dr Routley's personal library of books and hymnals could be secured and housed in the College's Talbott Library. With the publication of this memorial tribute and the decision of Margaret Routley to allow Westminster to secure the library, both goals have been achieved. The stage is now set for the establishment of a permanent Archive of the Routley literature at Westminster Choir College.

The task of identifying and organizing this material was facilitated by the fact that a complete collection of Dr Routley's books, pamphlets and many of his articles was therefore accessible. However, it was still necessary to visit a number of libraries to insure that this project was approached in as thorough a manner as possible. The search for periodical literature took place initially in Princeton at the Talbott Library, Westminster Choir College, and Speer Library, Princeton Theological Seminary. It was necessary to make two week-long trips to England to survey the extensive body of writings that appeared in periodicals which were published on that side of the Atlantic. For this reason visits to the archives of the Hymn Society of Great Britain and Ireland at Westminster Abbey, the British Library, and Dr William's Library were most helpful. Other items were secured at the Mansfield College Library in Oxford and the Westminster Music Library in London. Special thanks for their assistance are due to G. Edward Jones, Frederick Keay, Robin A. Leaver, Alan Luff, John Wilson, and Caryl Micklem in Great Britain; to Mary Benton, Jan Jacobson, Jane Nowakowski, Nancy Wicklund and Sherry Vellucci at Westminster Choir College; and to Margaret Routley for her invaluable help throughout the period of research.

As an introduction to the bibliography a few words about its organization seem appropriate. The bibliography begins with accounts of Erik Routley's life and work as they appear in reference works, collected biographies, periodicals and newspapers. The listing here is alphabetical by author or publication. Then there are sections in which his publications are listed according to the following categories: books and monographs, articles, hymnals in which he had an editorial role, hymn texts, hymn tunes, and original compositions. Apart from these musical works the items are listed chronologically with the articles within each category organized alphabetically. The third section deals with the unpublished writings, including theses, book-length manuscripts, articles, addresses, critiques, and lectures. At the end there is a short section which lists selected tape recordings: broadcasts, cassettes and video tapes.

Finally, a word about the hundreds of book, music and recording reviews which Erik Routley wrote during his lifetime but which do not appear in this bibliography. These important contributions to the review literature were regular features in periodicals like *The British Weekly, The Hymn, The Bulletin of the Hymn Society of Great Britain and Ireland*, and the *Mansfield College Magazine* and covered such diverse subjects as church music books, contemporary fiction, detective stories, hymn books, hymnological writings, social and theological issues. This is indeed a valuable resource of information; however space and time limitations simply made it impossible to present this material in the careful and comprehensive manner it deserved. Similarly, some of the smaller editorials in *The Bulletin of the Hymn Society of Great Britain and Ireland*, which deal with summaries of the contents of the issue concerned, or matters relating to that Society, have been omitted from this listing.

'A 3

DAYTON 7.6.7.6.6.7.6 1975

Composed for Westminster Praise, # 20

© Hinshaw

G. Schirmer Inc. New York   12 Staves   No. 5 - Printed in the U. S. A.

Abbreviations

AmOrg	*The American Organist*. The American Guild of Organists and the Royal Canadian College of Organists, New York.
BrWk	*The British Weekly*, London.
CamR	*The Cambridge Review*. St John's College, Cambridge.
Choir	*The Choir*, London.
ChorGL	*Choristers Guild Letters*, Garland, TX.
ChrC	*Christian Century*, Chicago, IL.
ChuMus (Lon.)	*Church Music*. The Church Music Association and the Society of St Gregory, London.
ChuMus (StL)	*Church Music*, St Louis, MO.
ChuMusQ	*Church Music Quarterly*. RSCM, Croydon.
CMSA	*The Church Music Society. Annual Reports*, London.
CongHS	*The Congregational Historical Society. Transactions*, London.
CongM	*The Congregational Monthly*. Congregational Church in England and Wales, London.
CongQ	*The Congregational Quarterly: a review of religious life and thought*, London; became *Reform* [Ref]
CongR	*The Congregational Review*, London.
Diap	*The Diapason*, Des Plaines, IL.
EngCM	*English Church Music*. RSCM, Croydon.
EpwR	*Epworth Review*, London.
ExpT	*The Expository Times*, Edinburgh.
HSB	*The Hymn Society of Great Britain & Ireland. Bulletin*, London.
Hy	*The Hymn*, Fort Worth, TX.
JCM	*Journal of Church Music*, Philadelphia, PA.
LCM	*Lancing College Magazine*, Shoreham, Sussex.
LQHR	*The London Quarterly & Holborn Review*, London.
MCM	*Mansfield College Magazine*, Oxford.
MCN	*Mansfield College Newsletter*, Oxford.
MethCMSB	*The Methodist Church Music Society. Bulletin*, Cheshire, England.
MethRec	*The Methodist Recorder*, London.
Mos	*Mosaic; a quarterly review of church music, liturgy and the arts*, London.
MusMin	*Music Ministry*, Nashville, TN.
MusOp	*Musical Opinion*, London.
MusT	*The Musical Times*, London.
NC	*New Christian*, London.
NYCSLB	*The New York C. S. Lewis Society. Bulletin*, New York.
Org	*The Organ*, Bournemouth, Dorset.
OrgR	*Organist's Review*. The Incorporated Association of Organists, Shawclough, Rochdale Lancashire.
Ref	*Reform*. United Reformed Church, London.

RL&M	*Reformed Liturgy and Music.* Joint Office of Worship of the Presbyterian Church (USA) in cooperation with the Presbyterian Association of Musicians, Louisville, KY.
RSCM	The Royal School of Church Music.
RW	*Reformed World.* World Alliance of Reformed Churches, Geneva.
SCM	The Student Christian Movement.
SC	*The Scottish Congregationalist*, Edinburgh.
SPCK	The Society for Promoting Christian Knowledge.
ThTo	*Theology Today*, Princeton, NJ.
URC	*The United Reformed Church*, London
USQR	*Union Seminary Quarterly Review.* Union Theological Seminary, New York.
WCCN	*Westminster Choir College Newsletter*, Princeton, NJ.
Wor	*Worship*, Collegeville, MN.

I. Accounts of Erik Routley's Life and Work

A. Reference Works

Dictionary of International Biography. Cambridge [Eng.]: Melrose 1976, 812.

International Authors and Writers Who's Who Cambridge [Eng.]: Melrose, 1976, 516–517.

Men of Achievement Cambridge [Eng.]: International Biographical Center, 1977, 535.

The New Grove Dictionary of Music and Musicians London: Macmillan 1980, 16, 278.

Who's Who London: A. & C. Black 1974, 2846.

B. Articles about Erik Routley (selected)

See also Nos 343, 582.

D. Armstrong, "Erik Routley's Debtors," Ref Jan 1983.

"The Books that Shape Men's Lives," ChrC 2 Nov 1977: 1010. A listing of books that influenced Erik Routley.

L. Dakers, "Profile 1980—Erik Routley," EngCM 1980: 55–57.

M. Dawney, "Hymnody: dead wood or living growth?" MusOp 100, Sept 1977: 579.

"Erik Routley—theological musician, writer, teacher . . . ," WCCN Dec 1978: 2.

"Honour for Erik Routley," BrWk 22 May 1969: 1. On his election as President of the Congregational Church.

W. J. Little, "Erik Routley—an appreciation," HSB 8/6 1975: 94.

"Minutes," CongM Aug 1970: 12–13. The minutes of the 138th Annual Assembly of the Congregational Church of England and Wales announcing Erik Routley's election as President.

R. Mitchell, "Erik Routley on Church Music," *Foundations* 11 Jly/Sept 1968: 268–270.

"Routley Leaves for the U.S.," BrWk 11 Jun 1971: 34.

L. B. Sateren, "More on the Display of Hymn Texts," Hy 30 1979: 116–118.

E. Thacker, "First Catch Your Jazz," Mos Oct 1965: 107–112.

F. B. Westbrook, "Erik Routley's Visit to Princeton as Visiting Lecturer," MethRec 5 Sep 1974.

C. Obituaries and Tributes (selected)

A. F. Bayly, "Erik Routley—Hymnodist Extraordinary—Dies in America aged 65," *The Link* Dec 1982/Feb 1983: 1–3.

G. & H. Betenbaugh, "Erik Routley: a tribute," Diap 74/3 1983: 3.

L. Dakers, "The Reverend Dr. Erik Routley," ChuMusQ 15 Jan 1983: 10.

"Dr. Erik Routley," *The Scotsman* [Edinburgh] 15 Oct 1982.

D. Duncan, "Fond Tribute to Erik Routley," BrWk 29 Oct 1982: 3.

"Erik Routley," ChrC 24 Nov 1982.

"Erik Routley (1917–1982)," *National Con-*

ference of Catholic Bishops Newsletter 19 Jan 1983: 4.

"Erik Routley (1917–1982)," ThTo 34 1984: 477.

G. Farrell, "In memory of Dr. Routley," Minstrel's Manifesto [Westminster Choir College Student Newspaper] 7/8 1 Nov 1982: 2.

E. Foley, "Review Rondeau," Pastoral Music Notebook Jan 1983: 6.

F. P. Green, "In Memory of Erik Routley" [Poem], MethRec 11 Nov 1982; reprinted Hy 34 1983: 18.

H. Hageman, "Erik Routley—in piam memoriam," The Church Herald 19 Nov 1982: 30.

D. Hinshaw, "Erik Routley; a personal view," Update; Hinshaw Mus. Pub., Chapel Hill, NC 3/1 Jan 1983: 2.

"Hymnal Editor Dies," The Church Herald 19 Nov 1982: 20.

"In Memoriam—the Reverend Dr. Erik Routley," Church Music Today Jan 1983: 1.

R. W. Lakins, Bulletin of St Paul's RC Church; Clifton, NJ. Nov 1982.

R. A. Leaver, "In Memoriam—Erik Routley," News of Hymnody 5 Jan 1983: 1–2.

R. A. Leaver, "The Routley Service at Westminster Abbey," Hy 34 1983: 110–111.

A. V. K. Malesky, "Erik Routley, 1917–1982," Pastoral Music 7/2 Dec 1982/Jan 1983: 6.

C. Micklem, "Erik Routley," Ref Nov 1982: 22.

C. Micklem, "Erik Routley 1917–1982: an appreciation," HSB 10/4 Jan 1983: 85–87.

C. Micklem, "Erik Routley, 31 Oct 1917–8 Oct 1982: hymnologist and ecclesiastical historian," United Reformed Church History Society Journal, 3 May 1983: 25.

"Nunc dimittis," Diap 73 Nov 1983: 11.

"Obituary," MusT 123 Dec 1982: 859.

"Obituary," Philadelphia Inquirer 9 Oct 1982.

"Obituary," Princeton Packet 13 Oct 1982.

"Obituary," Ref Nov 1982: 22.

"Obituary," ThTo 40, 1983: 477.

"Obituary," Town Topics [Princeton] 14 Oct 1982.

"Obituary," Yearbook URC 1984: 266–267.

"Obituary. The Rev. Dr. Erik Routley," Daily Telegraph [London] 13 Oct 1982.

"Rev. Dr. Erik Routley." The Times [London] 20 Oct 1982: 16.

R. Robinson, "A Tribute to Erik Routley," Hy 34 1983: 14–17.

R. Robinson, "Erik Routley (1917–1982); England's missionary to American church music," AmOrg 17/1 Jan 1983: 57.

R. Robinson, "The Westminster Abbey Service for Erik Routley," JCM 25/7 Sept 1983: 2–3.

J. Schreiber, "A Tribute to Erik Routley (1917–1982)," Presbyterian Association of Musicians Newsletter 4/2 Jan 1983: 3.

J. Wilson, "A Tribute," Hy 34 1983: 18–19.

C. R. Young, "Memorial Service," Hy 34 1983: 20–24.

D. Special Study

C. S. Pottie, A More Profound Alleluia! Gelineau and Routley on Music in Christian Worship, Washington [DC]: Pastoral Press 1984.

This is the published version of a Master of Arts degree thesis, Graduate Theological Union, Berkeley, 1980. The original title was The Theological Meaning of Music in Christian Worship. Two Views: Joseph Gelineau and Erik Routley. On pages 97–104 there is a working bibliography of 124 items, written by Erik Routley, which is misleading in a number of respects.

II The Publications of Erik Routley

A. Books and Monographs

1950

1 *The Church and Music: An enquiry into the history, the nature and scope of Christian judgement on music*, London: Duckworth 1950; revised and enlarged. London: Duckworth 1967; Boston: Crescendo 1967. The published version of his Bachelor of Divinity thesis; see No. 595. A small section was reprinted in *In Theory Only* 2 (1976): 26.

1951

2 *I'll Praise My Maker: a study of the hymns of certain authors who stand in or near the tradition of English Calvinism*, London: Independent 1951.

1952

3 *Hymns and Human Life*, London: Murray 1952, and New York: Philosophical Library 1953.
—— second edition, with new preface, London: Murray 1959; Grand Rapids, MI: Eerdmans 1959.

1955

4 *Hymns and the Faith*, London: Murray 1955; Greenwich, CT: Seabury 1956, Grand Rapids, MI: Eerdmans 1968.

1957

5 *The Gift of Conversion*, London: Butterworth 1957; Philadelphia: Muhlenberg 1958. [cp. No. 12].

6 *The Music of Christian Hymnody: a study of the development of the hymn tune since the Reformation, with special reference to English Protestantism*, London: Independent 1957. Partially based on his DPhil thesis; see No. 596.
7 *The Organist's Guide to Congregational Praise*, London: Independent 1957.
8 *The Wisdom of the Fathers*, London: SCM 1957; Naperville, IL: SCM Book Club 1957, Philadelphia: Westminster 1957.

1958

9 *The English Carol*, London: Jenkins 1958; New York: Oxford University Press 1959, Westport, CT: Greenwood 1973.

1959

10 *Church Music and Theology*, London: SCM 1959; Philadelphia, PA: Muhlenberg 1959.
—— second edition, with new preface, London: Waltham Forest Books 1965; Philadelphia, PA: Fortress 1965.
—— third edition: substantially rewritten, see No. 40.
11 *Ecumenical Hymnody*, London: Independent 1959.

1960

12 *Conversion*, Philadelphia: Muhlenberg 1960, Philadelphia: Fortress 1978; Derby: Peter Smith 1965. [Cp. No. 5]
13 *English Religious Dissent*, Cambridge

[Eng.]: Cambridge University Press 1960; Toronto: Macmillan 1960.

14 *Music, Sacred and Profane: occasional writings on music 1950–58*, London: Independent 1960.

1961

15 *Isaac Watts (1674–1748)*, London: Independent 1961.

16 *The Story of Congregationalism*, London: Independent 1961.

17 *Thomas Goodwin (1600–1680)*, London: Independent 1961.

1962

18 *The Ascent to the Cross*, London: SCM 1962; New York: Abingdon 1962.

19 *Beginning the Old Testament: studies in Genesis and Exodus for the general reader*, London: SCM 1962; Philadelphia, PA: SCM 1962.

20 *Congregationalists and Unity*, London: Mowbray 1962.

21 *Creeds and Confessions: the Reformation and its modern ecumenical implications*, London: Duckworth 1962, London: Darton, Longman and Todd 1966; Philadelphia, PA: Westminster 1963 [subtitle changed to: *from the Reformation to the modern church*].

22 *Into a Far Country: reflections upon the trajectory of the Divine Word, and upon the communication, in the affairs human and divine, of the imperative and the indicative*, London: Independent 1962.

1964

23 *Is Jazz Music Christian?* London: Epworth 1964.

24 *Hymns Today and Tomorrow*, New York: Abingdon 1964; London: Darton, Longman and Todd 1966.

25 *The Man for Others: an important contribution to the discussions inspired by the book Honest to God*, Derby: Peter Smith 1964; New York: Oxford University Press 1964. See also Nos. 312, 315, 323.

26 *Twentieth Century Church Music*, London: Jenkins 1964, 1966; New York: Oxford University Press 1964, 1966, Carol Stream, IL: Agape 1984.

1967

27 *Music Leadership in the Church: a conversation chiefly with my American friends*, Nashville, TN: Abingdon 1967, Carol Stream, IL: Agape 1985.

1968

28 *The Musical Wesleys*, London: Jenkins 1968; New York: Oxford University Press 1968, Westport [Conn.]: Greenwood 1976.

29 *Words, Music and the Church*, Nashville, TN: Abingdon 1968; London: Jenkins 1969.

30 *Into a Broad Land: Psalm 119 v 96 . . . being the substance of the address given to the General Assembly of the Congregational Church in England & Wales . . . on 4th May 1970 . . .*, London: The Congregational Church in England and Wales 1970.

1971

31 *Saul Among the Prophets: and other sermons 1963–69*, London: Epworth 1971; Nashville, TN: Abingdon 1972, abridged *The Upper Room*, Nashville, TN.

1972

32 *The Puritan Pleasures of the Detective Story: a personal monograph*, London: Gollancz 1972. The first chapter of this book has been translated and published in Japanese. An excerpt appears in *Twentieth-Century Literary Criticism*, Vol. 12, 1984, 19–20.

244

1973

33 *The Holy Pantomime: a sermon for Palm Sunday*, Leeds: John Paul the Preacher 1973.

34 *Lent '73*, St Albans: The United Reformed Church 1973. A series of Lenten readings.

35 *Truth, Growth, and Love*, Nashville, TN: *The Upper Room* 1973.

1975

36 *Exploring the Psalms*, Philadelphia, PA: Westminster 1975.

37 *Martin Shaw: a centenary appreciation*, London: E. M. Campbell 1975.

38 *An Organist's Companion to the Worshipbook* [New York: Program Agency, United Presbyterian Church, USA], 1975. Offprint from RL&M Vol. 9, No. 2, Spring 1975, 5–78.

1977

39 *Companion to Westminster Praise*, Chapel Hill, NC: Hinshaw 1977.

40 *A Short History of English Church Music*, London & Oxford: Mowbray 1977.

1978

41 *Church Music and the Christian Faith*, Carol Stream, IL: Agape 1978; London: Collins 1980. Substantially revised edition of No. 10.

1979

42 *An English-Speaking Hymnal Guide*, Collegeville, MN: The Liturgical Press 1979, Chicago: GIA Publications 1984.

43 *A Panorama of Christian Hymnody*, Collegeville, MN: The Liturgical Press 1979, Chicago: GIA Publications 1984.

1981

44 *English Hymns and Their Tunes: a survey* [edited by A. Luff], London: The Hymn Society of Great Britain and Ireland 1980. Part 1 comprises the historical introduction Erik Routley wrote for *Hymns for Church and School*, 1964 [see No. 54]; Part 2 was newly written and covers the years 1962–1981. The whole booklet was translated into German and issued as "Englische Kirchenlieder und ihr Melodien" in *Internationale Arbeitsgemeinschaft für Hymnologie Mitteilungen*, No. 5, Aug. 1981, 2–23.

45 *The Music of Christian Hymns*, Chicago: GIA Publications 1981.

1982

46 *Christian Hymns Observed: when in our music God is glorified*, Princeton, NJ: Prestige 1982.

47 *The Poetry of Worship*, London [Ontario]: Huron College 1982.

1985

48 *The Divine Formula*, Princeton, NJ: Prestige 1985.

Undated

49 *Hymn Tunes: an historical outline*, Croydon: RSCM [Study Notes Series No. 5] [*ca.* early 1960s].

50 *Words of Hymns: a short history*, Croydon: RSCM [Study Notes Series No. 6] [*ca.* early 1960s].

B. Books with Contributions by Erik Routley

1952

51 *The Organist and the Congregation: lectures and a sermon at the First Conference of Congregational Organists held at Mansfield College, Oxford, June 22, 23 and 24, 1951*, London: Independent 1952. Introduction by Erik Routley.

52 *Companion to Congregational Praise,* edited by K. L. Parry, London: Independent 1953. Erik Routley supplied the notes on the music.

1959
53 *Characters of the Bible,* London: Independent 1959. BBC talks by Erik Routley and Trevor Huddleston, broadcast 2–7 Feb.

1964
54 *Hymns for Church and School,* London: Novello 1964, reprinted 1966, 1970, with corrections 1973. Erik Routley wrote an introduction entitled "Hymns and their Tunes: An Historical Survey". It was reissued and brought up-to-date with a second part in 1981; see No. 44.

1966
55 *Dunblane Praises I,* Dunblane: Scottish Churches' House 1966. Erik Routley wrote the preface.

1967
56 *Christianity in its Social Context,* edited by J. G. Gerard and G. Irving, London: SPCK 1967. Erik Routley contributed a chapter entitled "1975".
57 *Dunblane Praises II,* Dunblane: Scottish Churches' House 1967. Erik Routley wrote the preface.
58 *Encyclopaedia Britannica,* Chicago & London: Encyclopedia Britannica Inc. 1967. Erik Routley contributed the following articles: ·
  "Chorale," 5: 682.
  "Hymn," 11: 986–991.
  "Isaac Watts," 23: 311–312.
  "Metrical Psalms," 15: 309.

1975
59 *English Church Music: a bibliography,* compiled by P. Yeats-Edwards, London & New York: White Lion 1975. Erik Routley contributed a preface.
60 *What Faith has Meant to Me,* edited by C. A. Frazier, Philadelphia, PA: Westminster 1975. Erik Routley contributed a chapter entitled "Something New Every Day".

1976
61 *Going to College Handbook,* Richmond [VA]: Outlook 1976. 30: 1—"The Standard of Excellence."

1979
62 *C. S. Lewis at the Breakfast Table, and other Reminiscences,* edited by J. T. Como, New York: Macmillan 1979. Erik Routley contributed chapter 4: "A Prophet": see also No. 65.
63 *In Memoriam: Howard Spencer Stanley (1901–1975),* Lindfield [Sussex]: privately published 1979. Erik Routley contributed a personal memoir.
64 *New Catholic Encyclopedia,* Washington & New York: McGraw Hill, 1979 17: 284–285—"Hymns and Hymnals".

1980
65 *The Pilgrim: a liturgical music-drama in the manner of a medieval matins drama for Eastertide,* for 6 or more soloists, SATB, orch. & handbells, by R. Proulx, Chicago: GIA Publications, G-2375, 1980. Erik Routley contributed a forward.

1982
66 *Hymns and Ballads of Fred Pratt Green,* with commentary by B. Braley, Carol Stream, IL: Hope 1982; London: Collins 1982. Erik Routley wrote the foreword.

1984
67 *In Search of C. S. Lewis: interviews with Kenneth Tynan, A. J. P. Taylor, Malcolm Muggeridge, and others who knew*

246

Lewis, edited by S. Schofield, South Plainfield [NJ]: Bridge 1984. Erik Routley wrote a chapter entitled "Stunning Effect"; see also 62.

68 *The Summit Choirbook*, edited by The Dominican Nuns of Summit, NJ 1984 [copyright 1983]. Erik Routley contributed the foreword.

C. Books Edited by Erik Routley

See also No. 51.

From 1964 Erik Routley acted as the general editor for the series *Studies in Church Music*. His own books in the series are Nos 26 and 28; the others are:

A. Hutchings, *Church Music in the Nineteenth Century*, London: Jenkins 1967; New York: Oxford University Press 1967, Westport, CT: Greenwood 1977.

P. le Huray, *Music in the Reformation in England*, London: Jenkins 1967; New York: Oxford University Press 1967; and Cambridge [Eng.] & New York: Cambridge University Press 1978.

B. Rainbow, *The Choral Revival in the Anglican Church (1839–1872)*, London: Barrie & Jenkins 1970; New York: Oxford University Press 1970.

C. Dearnley, *English Church Music, 1650–1750: in Royal Chapel, Cathedral, and Parish Church*, London: Barrie & Jenkins 1970; New York: Oxford University Press 1970.

D. Hymnals and Music edited by Erik Routley

1951

Congregational Praise. London: Congregational Union of England and Wales, 1951.

(Erik Routley served as a member of the editorial committee and general secretary for *Congregational Praise*). For Erik Routley's contributions to this hymn book, see p. 286.

1961

University Carol Book (UK)
Brighton: H. Freeman & Co. 1961; reprinted 1978.

1965

Dunblane Praises I
Scottish Churches' House, Dunblane, Perthshire, Scotland, 1965.

1967

Dunblane Praises II
Scottish Churches' House, Dunblane, Perthshire, Scotland, 1967.

1969

New Songs for the Church. (R. Barret Ayres, co-editor) Book I (Psalms, Children's Songs, Ballads, Hymns). London: Galliard, 1969.

New Songs for the Church. (R. Barret Ayres, co-editor) Book II (Canticles). London: Galliard, 1969.

1971

Eternal Light: 15 Hymn Tunes by Erik Routley. New York: Carl Fischer, 1971.

1973

St. James's Church Newcastle Upon Tyne Supplementary Hymns, 1973.

1974

Cantate Domino: An Ecumenical Hymn Book. Published on behalf of the World Council of Churches. Kassel: Bärenreiter 1974 [melody edition], London: Oxford University Press 1980 [full music edition]

Hymns for Celebration. (John Wilson, co-editor). Croydon: RSCM, 1974.

1976

Laszlo, Halmos, *Jubilate Deo*, with English text by Erik Routley, SATB unacc., Chapel Hill, NC: Hinshaw Music 1976, HMC 164.

Westminster Praise. Chapel Hill, NC: Hinshaw Music, 1976.

1977

Ecumenical Praise. Carol Stream, IL: Agape, 1977 (Erik Routley served as a member of the Editorial Board for *Ecumenical Praise*).

1979

Festival Praise. Chapel Hill, NC: Hinshaw Music, 1979.

1985

Rejoice in the Lord. Grand Rapids, MI: Reformed Church in America, Eerdman's Press, 1985

Undated

Behold Your King: A Devotion for Choir and Congregation. Croydon: RSCM.

Communion Hymns and Motets for Choirs, SATB. New York: Worldwide Music.

Singing on Saturday (Lionel Dakers, co-editor), Croydon: RSCM.

E. Articles

1939

69 "Letter to the Editor," *The Spectator* [Lon.] 163: 305.

1944

70 "A New Hymn-Book for Congregationalists: the principles that should guide us in our preparation," CongR 12: 338–343.

1945

71 "The Conference at Jordans," HSB 1/32: 1–4.

72 "Requirements in a New Hymn Book," HSB 1/30: 6–8.

73 "Some Modern Needs in Hymnody," HSB 1/32: 4–6.

1946

74 "The Bristol Conference," HSB 1/37: 1–6.

75 "Hymn-singing, an Aesthetic or Spiritual Pleasure?" HSB 1/37: 6–7.

76 "The Hymnal, 1940," HSB 1/34: 2–7.

77 "James Mearns, Hymnologist," HSB 1/35: 6–8.

1947

78 "Additional Note on Henry Vaughan as a Hymnodist," HSB 1/40: 3.

79 "English Hymnal and Ancient and Modern," HSB 1/38: 9–12.

80 "Hymns (1946) for the Use of the New Church," HSB 1/39: 6–13.

81 "Tunes for the 1946 New Church Hymn Book," HSB 1/39: 13–14.

1948

82 "Correspondence with an Anglican Who Disdains Hymns," *The Presbyter* 6/2: 15–20.

83 "Victorian Hymn Composers—I: Samuel Sebastian Wesley," HSB 2/1: 2–5; HSB 2/2: 4–11.

84 "Victorian Hymn Composers—II: John Bacchus Dykes," HSB 2/3: 1–8; HSB 2/5: 71–75.

1949

85 "The Bicentenary of Isaac Watts, 1948," HSB 2/5: 65–70.

86 "Julian," HSB 2/7: 97–100.

87 "Victorian Hymn Composers—IV: Arthur Seymour Sullivan," HSB 2/7: 103–110.

1950

88 "Hymns Ancient and Modern (1861)," HSB 2/9: 133–136.

89 "Hymns Ancient and Modern Revised (1950)," HSB 2/10: 145–159.

90 "Hymns Ancient and Modern (1950): Second thoughts," HSB 2/11: 172–173.

91 "Hymns for Young Methodists," HSB 2/11: 161–170.

92 "Music and Churchmanship," CongQ 28: 31–40.

93 "Sunday Half-Hour: Some Observations," HSB 2/11: 174–175.

94 "The Tercentenniary of the Scottish Psalter," HSB 2/12: 177–180.

1951

95 "A Hymn Tune Celebrated" [When I survey], HSB 2/13: 215–216.

96 "Church Music and the Gospel," BrWk 4 Oct: 3.

97 "Congregational Church Music," Minister's Bulletin 2/5: 5–16.

98 "Congregational Praise: Erik Routley on the New Hymn Book," BrWk 20 Dec: 2.

99 "Joseph Hart (1712–1768)," HSB 2/13: 196–208; cp. HSB 2/14: 230–231.

1952

100 "The Puritans and Music, 1952" [Church Music Supplement], BrWk 24 Jan: 1–3.

101 "Welsh Hymnody Today," HSB 3/3: 53–56.

1953

102 "A Christmas Sermon." The Scouter [The Boy Scouts Association] Dec: 295.

103 "Crimond—a controversy," HSB 3/6: 99–101.

104 "The Date of a Famous Hymn Tune," HSB 3/6: 101–102.

105 "Do You Want to Build an Organ?" BrWk 31 Dec.

106 "Editorial" [The coronation of Queen Elizabeth II], HSB 3/7: 105–106.

107 "Handel and Hymns," Choir 44: 155.

108 "In the Common Rooms" [A tribute to Nathaniel Micklem on retiring as Principal of Mansfield College], MCM 140: 161–162.

109 "The Principal of Mansfield," BrWk 9 Jly: 6.

110 "Snobbery" [Letter to the Editor], BrWk 2 Jly: 9.

111 "What Makes a Good Hymn?" HSB 3/6: 90–96.

1954

112 "The Boar's Head," BrWk 2 Dec: 1–3.

113 "The Book of Common Praise (1938) with Australian Supplement (1947)," HSB 3/11: 180–184.

114 "Charles Wesley and Matthew Henry," HSB 3/12: 193–199; reprinted CongQ 33: 345–351.

115 "The Lay Preacher and His Hymn Book," The Baptist Times Nov: 9.

116 "Letter," [Concerning his criticism of The Billy Graham Song Book], Choir 45: 162–163; see next entry below.

117 "To Billy Graham, on Reading The Billy Graham Song-Book," Choir 45: 106–107.

118 "We Need New Hymns for This Present Age," The Church of England Newspaper 29 Oct: 12.

119 "What Remains for the Modern Hymn-writer to do?" HSB 3/9: 148–153; reprinted CongQ 32: 322–327.

1955

120 Beginning with the August 11, 1955 issue of The British Weekly, Erik Routley was invited to write a monthly feature on a musical topic. This practice continued until October 1, 1970.

121 "Assessing the New Hymn Book" [Congregational Praise], CongM Nov: 127.

122 "The Date and Source of the Tune Dibdin," HSB 3/13: 213–214.

123 "Erik Routley on Music: Shanties," BrWk 13 Oct: 7.

124 "For Congregational Organists," *Church World* Jly.

125 "Hymnody in Canada and the U.S.A.," HSB 4/1: 1–5.

126 "Hymns and Youth," HSB 3/14: 222–227.

127 "Hymns New and Old," HSB 3/14: 233–235.

128 "Music in the College Chapel," MCN Jly.

129 "On the *Billy Graham Song Book*," Hy 6: 26, 36.

130 "Research and Piety," EngCM 25: 104–106.

131 "Routley's Romp: Ragtime!" BrWk 13 Oct: 7.

132 "Routley's Romp: a singular piece of musical folly," BrWk 10 Nov: 5.

133 "Routley's Romp: Chamber Music," BrWk 22 Dec: 5.

134 "Routley's Romp: Dance Music—Old Style," BrWk 8 Sept: 7.

135 "Texts for church musicians," Choir 45, Nos 1–12, Jan–Dec.

1956

136 Beginning with the January 1956 issue of *The Congregational Monthly*, Erik Routley wrote a short feature each month called "Sing up." Its purpose was to introduce a new hymn each month from *Congregational Praise*. This feature continued through December 1957.

137 "A Chamber Organ in the Chapel of Mansfield College, Oxford," Org 35: 200–203.

138 "A Delicate Question," HSB 4/1: 11–12.

139 "A Hymn Competition of 95 Years Ago," Hy 7: 105–110.

140 "Along A1: A68: B6320: A696," BrWk 26 Apr: 7 [issued anonymously].

141 "A Musical Jester" [Routley Romps Again], BrWk 26 Apr: 2.

142 "Anglican Chants," HSB 4/4: 61–63.

143 "Are You Looking for a Small Organ?" BrWk 30 Aug: 8–9.

144 "C. S. Lewis on the Frontiers," BrWk 20 Sept: 2.

145 "Editorial—English Hymnal 1906–1956," HSB 4/2: 17–26.

146 "Erik Routley on Music—I'm a dead Protestant myself," BrWk 15 Mar: 2.

147 "Erik Routley on Vaughan Williams," BrWk 28 Jun: 2.

148 "Geoffrey Beaumont's Twentieth Century Folk Mass," BrWk 20 Dec: 7–8.

149 "Give me my Beethoven neat" [Another Routley Romp], BrWk 27 Sept: 2.

150 "Hymnody in Canada and the U.S.A." HSB 4/1: 1–5.

151 "In Those Days There Was No King in Israel: Erik Routley on Nathaniel Micklem," BrWk 6 Dec: 8.

152 "Mansfield College, Oxford," [Letter to the Editor]. Org 36: 49–50.

153 "On Singing the Magnificat," BrWk 29 Nov: 10.

154 "Plainsong Isn't Respectable," BrWk 25 Oct: 2.

155 "The Proms," BrWk 30 Aug: 9–12.

156 "Routley on Mozart," BrWk 9 Feb: 5.

157 "Routley's Romp—holiday music," BrWk 26 Jly: 2.

158 "Sons of Nicholas," BrWk 26 Jan: 5.

159 "The trial of Thomas Cranmer," [Review of the play], BrWk 17 May: 2.

1957

160 "Beethoven's Credo," BrWk 19 Sept: 2.

161 "Cabbages and Kings," BrWk 4 Apr: 2.

162 "Charles Wesley, Junior (1757–1834)," HSB 4/7: 101–106.

163 "Charles Wesley Today: the Church's singer first and last," Choir 48: 227–229.

164 "Doctor Music," BrWk 28 Feb: 2.

165 "Editorial: A new development in hymn tune writing," HSB 4/6: 85–86.

166 "Hymns of Isaac Watts," CongM Jan: 5.

167 "Music: D and K (Deutsch and Köchel)," BrWk 24 Aug: 2.

168 "Music for Choir and Organist," BrWk 19 Sept: 2.

169 "Music for Fevered Seasons," [Bach's Brandenburg Concertos] BrWk 25 Jly: 2.

170 "The Musician's Sense of Humour," BrWk 31 Jan: 2.

171 "On Being a Self-taught Musician," BrWk 29 Nov: 5–12.

172 "On Stainer's Crucifixion," BrWk 30 May: 2.

173 "Only the Best is Good Enough," BrWk 27 Jun: 2.

174 "The Organ: atmosphere or truth?" BrWk 24 Aug: 2.

175 "Three Foreign Hymn Books" [*Innario Christiano*, 1953; *Ou de en Nieuwe Zangen*, 1954; *Evangelische Kirchengesangbuch, Ausgabe für die . . . Kirche der Pfalz*, 1951], HSB 4/7: 106–108.

1958

176 Beginning with the month of March 1958, Erik Routley became editor of *The Congregational Monthly*. His monthly editorials appear on the front cover and a column under the pen name "Fortunatus" appears on the inside back cover. Erik Routley edited the paper until October 1959. September 1959 was his last issue.

177 "The Art of Lexicography," BrWk 6 Nov: 7, 11.

178 "Ballet and Organ," BrWk 4 Sept: 2.

179 "Barth and Beethoven," BrWk 27 Mar: 7.

180 "Bartholomew," [Editorial]. CongM Aug: 86.

181 "Choral Music," BrWk 25 Sept: 2.

182 "Christmas and the Musician," BrWk 4 Dec: 3.

183 "The Church's Authority in a Vulgar Age," LQHR 183: 59–63.

184 "Clear speech" [Editorial], CongM Nov: 121.

185 "Covenant Sunday: the Bible and Philip Doddridge" [Editorial], CongM Oct: 109.

186 "Distemper and Variations," BrWk 4 Dec: 3.

187 "Easter" [Editorial], CongM Apr: 37.

188 "Evangelism and Modern Man," ChrC 8 Jly: 799–801.

189 "Hymns for Young People," CongM Oct: 6–7.

190 "Hymn Singing in the Reformed Church in Switzerland," HSB 4/10: 158–160.

191 "Kist O'Whustles," BrWk 28 Sept: 3.

192 "The late Dean D. F. R. Wilson," HSB 4/9: 123–124.

193 "Letter to the Editor" [About the hymn: "Father, hear the prayer we offer"], BrWk 16 Jan: 3.

194 "Lyra Germanica," HSB 4/11: 171–174.

195 "The Lord Protector" [Editorial], CongM Sept: 97.

196 "The Mystery of the 'Ninth,'" BrWk 12 Jan: 7.

197 "The New Lutheran Hymn Book," HSB 4/11: 174–180.

198 "O God the Protector of All" [Editorial]. CongM Jly: 73.

199 "On Playing Over," Choir 49: 221.

200 "Singing the Psalms for Pleasure," BrWk 31 Jly: 7.

201 "Temptations to Extravagance," BrWk 29 May: 11.

202 "That Wayward Metronome," BrWk 1 May: 7, 12.

203 "Trinity" [Editorial], CongM Jun: 61.

204 "Unfinished Task," BrWk 27 Feb: 7, 12.

205 "The Way Forward" [Editorial], CongM Mar: 25.

206 "Where Two or Three Thousand Are Met Together" [Editorial], CongM May: 49.

207 "W. H. Gladstone's Selection (1882)," HSB 4/10: 161–164.

208 "Dean D. F. R. Wilson." [Obituary], HSB 4/9: 133–134.

1959

209 "Antiquissima, Novissima," HSB 4/14: 213–219.

210 "A Babel of Names," HSB 4/14: 230–239.

211 "A Christian Theology of the Old Testament," BrWk 27 Aug: 2.

212 "Advent Hymns," CongM Dec: 143.

213 "A personal Note from the Editor [concerning Ralph Vaughan Williams and Martin Shaw], HSB 4/18: 185–188.

214 "Biblical Studies and Plainsong," BrWk 2 Apr: 7.

215 "George Wallace Briggs, (1875–1959)," HSB 4/14: 245–249.

216 "The Case Against Charles Wesley," HSB 4/14: 252–259.

217 "Consecrated Life," ExpT 71: 94–95.

218 "Controversy" [Editorial], CongM May: 58.

219 "Crimond Again," HSB 4/12: 195–196.

220 "Evangelism and Modern Man," ChrC 76 8 Jly: 799–801.

221 "For Choir and Organ," BrWk 15 Oct: 5.

222 "For Holiday Seasons" [Editorial], CongM Aug: 89.

223 "For Unity a Meditation," CongM Jan: 3.

224 "Forward Again" [Editorial about the new editor], CongM Sept: 101.

225 "Godly Quietness" [Editorial about the rebuilt organ at Mansfield College], CongM Jun: 65.

226 "Hymns for Children," CongM Jly: 85.

227 "Ministry" [Editorial], CongM Jly: 77.

228 "The Ministry of Women" [Editorial], CongM Apr: 37.

229 "Naughty People," BrWk 1 Jan: 7.

230 "On Singing Hymns," BrWk 5 Mar: 2.

231 "The Pleasures of Pop," BrWk 25 Jun: 2.

232 "Portrait of a Misfit," BrWk 19 Jan: 7.

233 "The Prophetic Pergolesi," BrWk 21 May: 7.

234 "What is it About Hymns 'A & M'?" BrWk 10 Dec: 5.

235 "When You Go to the Public Library," CongM Feb: 16.

236 "Where are the Organists?" BrWk 17 Sept: 2.

237 "The Wind Blows" [Editorial], CongM Mar: 25.

1960

238 "A Small Hymn Book" [Hymns for United Services], HSB 5/1: 13–14.

239 "Chopin and the Musical Graces," BrWk 18 Feb: 7.

240 "Conference of the Hymn Society of Great Britain and Ireland, Westminster College, Cambridge," HSB 5/2: 22–24.

241 "Consecrated Life," ExpT 71: 10–12.

242 "Contemporary Music for the Organ," BrWk 13 Oct: 10.

243 "Depart from Me," ExpT 71: 276–277.

244 "Edward Romilly Micklem" [Obituary], MCM 157: 23–25.

245 "I Believe in Carols," *Reckitt Colman Holdings Magazine* Dec: 23–25.

246 "The Impropriety of the Carol," *Incorporated Society of Musicians* 22 Apr.

247 "It is Sugar, Sugar All the Time," BrWk 21 Jly: 5.

248 "Letter from Edinburgh," CongM May: 77.

249 "Music in Church Today," BrWk 29 Dec: 7.

250 "Of Organs and Organists," BrWk 15 Sept: 5, 8.

251 "The Pilgrim Hymnal (1958)," HSB 5/1: 10–13.

252 "The Search for Positive Attitudes," BrWk 10 Nov: 7.

253 "Text for a Religious Aesthetic," ThTo 17: 192–199.

254 "The Trajectory of Faith," CamR 6 Feb: 333–335.

255 "Wanted—a new generation of novelists," BrWk 17 Nov: 7.

256 "Where Familiarity Breeds Corruption: Erik Routley and 'musica viva,'" BrWk 12 May: 7.

257 "Whither Hymnody?" HSB 5/2: 24–30.

1961

258 "Agatha Frances Micklem" [Obituary], MCM 159: 69–71.

259 "A Private Hymn Book from Scottish Congregationalism," HSB 5/4: 58–61.

260 "Carols—vulgar and demure," *London Churchman* Jan: 6–7.

261 "Consular Horse," ChrC 78: 343.

262 "Correspondence: editorial comment," HSB 5/6: 90–91.

263 "Handel's 'Largo' is Not for the Funeral," BrWk 23 Nov: 5.

264 "Let's Leave Out Lohengrin—and make the Wedding 'March' a matter for marriage-guidance," BrWk 26 Oct: 1, 12.

265 "Modern Idolatries," SC 57: 220–221, 235.

266 "Musicians of the Temple Church," HSB 5/5: 67–71.

267 "The New Irish Hymnal," HSB 5/3: 285–286.

268 "On Growing Quietly," ChrC 78: 727.

269 "On Ministerial Dress," CongM Jan: 11–12.

270 "Our Lord's Command," ExpT 72: 285–286.

271 "Our Response to the Cross," ExpT 72: 155–160.

272 "Resurrection is the Theme-music and the sacraments," BrWk 31 Dec: 40.

273 "Sir Thomas, the Preacher" [on the death of Sir Thomas Beecham], BrWk 23 Mar: 13.

274 "To the Chief Musician Upon_____?" HSB 5/5: 71–75.

275 "Unashamed Organist," BrWk 14 Sept: 5.

276 "What Theology has to Say" [about contemporary Church music] BrWk 5 Jan: 5.

1962

277 Beginning with the Apr. 1962 issue of *The Congregational Monthly*, Erik Routley wrote a series of six editorials under the pen name "Fortunatus" entitled "Letters to a Young Organist."

278 "All the Kingdoms," ExpT 73: 156–157.

279 "American Enthusiasm for Church Music," BrWk 13 Sept: 7.

280 "Editorial Comment" [On the *English Hymnal Service Book* and the *Baptist Hymn Book*], HSB 5/8: 120–124.

281 "Expediency or the Will of God?" LQHR 187: 197–201.

282 "Hiroshima in Music," BrWk 25 Oct: 7.

283 "Hymn Tunes, a practical survey," JCM 4: 2–5.

284 "'Jesus Shall Reign!': a matter of punctuation," HSB 5/7: 105–106.

285 "Kenneth Lloyd Parry (1884–1962)" [Obituary], HSB 5/7: 94–95.

286 "Maurice Frost (1888–1961)" [Obituary] unpaginated Supplement to HSB 5/6.

287 "Music and the Passion," BrWk 19 Apr: 10.

288 "The Old Hundred and Fourth," HSB 5/7: 106–107; see also No. 306.

289 "Whither music?" BrWk 5 Jly: 10.

1963

290 "As Hymnodus Sacer," HSB 5/10: 159.

291 "A Very Wicked Instrument?" [on church organs], BrWk 5 Sept: 2.

292 "The Chorale-Book for England, 1863," HSB 5/11: 173–186.

293 "Church Musician and His Faith," *Religion in Life* 32: 287–293.

294 "Faith and Charity," ExpT 74: 2.

295 "Frere Revised: A review and errata for 'Historical Companion to Hymns

Ancient and Modern,' " HSB 5/9: 138–141.

296 "Gesture Against Establishment: music at SCM Conference," BrWk 17 Jan: 2.

297 "Heavens Above!" [Letter to the Editor], BrWk 5 Sept: 5.

298 "How Bach Loved his Faith," BrWk 19 Sept: 5.

299 "Hymn Book" [Letter to the Editor], BrWk 4 Jly: 4.

300 "Hymns and Music in Church Worship," USQR 18: 235–242.

301 "Hymns: pop and square," *New Society* 24 Jan: 25.

302 "Is Music Ever Bad?" BrWk 4 Apr: 11.

303 "Living with Bach," BrWk 12 Sept: 2; reprinted in *St. Giles News* 31 (Autumn 1963); review of the complete organ works of J. S. Bach played by Herrick Bunney, organist at St Giles Cathedral, Edinburgh Festival, 1963.

304 "Music for the Choir," BrWk 21 Mar: 10.

305 "Musicians and Ministers" [Reply to W. H. Scheide], ThT 20: 274–276.

306 "The Old Hundred and Fourth: further perplexities," HSB 5/9: 138–141; see also No. 288.

307 "Renewal: music in God's new world," BrWk 5 Dec: 14.

308 "Scholar, Artist, Apologist," [a tribute to C. S. Lewis], BrWk 26 Dec: 3.

309 "The Theology and Practice of the Sect," LQHR 188: 99–104.

310 "This Do and Live," MusMin 4: 2–5.

311 "The Vocabulary of Church Music," USQR 18: 135–147.

1964

312 "An Analogy from Money" [Excerpt from *The Man for Others*; No. 25], BrWk 14 May: 5.

313 "An Extravagant Banquet" [on the Edinburgh Festival], BrWk 10 Sept: 7.

314 "Beer and Strawberries: a reply to the Bishop of Woolwich," BrWk 28 May: 5.

315 "Christ Out of Context," [Excerpt from *The Man for Others*; No. 25], BrWk 23 Apr: 5.

316 "Dancing Without Steps," BrWk 24 Sept: 5.

317 "Drunk at Nine in the Morning," ExpT 75: 218–219.

318 "The First Hundred," [Editorial], HSB 5/12: 193–197.

319 "From the 1964 Conference," HSB 5/13: 217–219.

320 "Golden Bells New Tun'd" [on the hymn book *Hymns of Faith*], BrWk 19 Mar: 2.

321 "Justice for the Organist," BrWk 31 Dec: 4.

322 "The Latest in Off-beat Church Music," BrWk 16 Jan: 2.

323 "Separated to Reconcile." [Excerpt from *The Man for Others*; No. 25], BrWk 30 Apr: 6.

324 "The Unnecessary Miracle," ExpT 75: 99–100.

325 "The Unreliable Masters," ExpT 75: 344–345.

326 "Waste and Danger," ExpT 75: 118–119.

327 "Worship Song (1905)," HSB 5/13: 225–234.

1965

328 "A Statement of Convictions," BrWk 11 Mar: 7.

329 "The Hymn Society in its Thirtieth Year: Conference 1965," HSB 6/2: 21–25.

330 "Hymns at the Mass," HSB 6/3: 51–55.

331 "Is God Standing at the Back?" BrWk 23 Sept: 5.

332 "Is the Anglican Chant the Best Medium for the Psalm in Worship?" Mos Oct: 98–105.

333 "Look Round in Anger," BrWk 16 Sept: 1.

334 "The National Anthem," BrWk 21 Oct: 3.

335 "On Hearing the Organ Works of Bach . . . Again," BrWk 25 Nov: 13.

336 "On the Demise of the Programme that Was Not So Much," BrWk 8 Apr: 7.

337 "Preacher and Artist," Mos Apr: 10–16.

338 "The Shaking of the Musical Foundations," CMSA: 11–20.

339 "Sing" [on modern hymns], BrWk 23 Dec: 4.

340 "Stephen Bell [1898–1964]," LCM: 6–7.

341 "William Healy Cadman" [Obituary], MCM 167: 243–245.

1966

342 "An 'Honest to God' Controversy, 1866," HSB 6/4: 66–71; reprinted Hy 18: 11–15.

343 "An Interview with Erik Routley," Chu-Mus (StL) 66/1: 34–36.

344 "Another Great Ecumenical Heave!" BrWk 7 Jly: 3.

345 "Another Scolding for the Church," BrWk 27 Jan: 1.

346 "Cambridge Conference, 1966," HSB 6/5: 77–80.

347 "The Church in Society"; comments on a series of volumes prepared for the World Council of Churches conference on The Church and The Modern World, July 12–26, 1966, BrWk 14, 21 & 28 Jly; 4 Aug.

348 "*Congregational Praise* After 21 years," CongM Aug: 18–19.

349 "Fasten Your Seat Belts" [report on a visit to America], BrWk 2 Jun: 5.

350 "For Choir and Organ," BrWk 13 Jan: 4.

351 "The Future of Congregationalism. Part I: The Ministry," BrWk 7 Apr: 5.

352 "The Future of Congregationalism. Part II: Worship," BrWk 14 Apr: 5.

353 "Hymns: probable and improbable," EngCM: 16–19.

354 "Letter to the Editor," NC 25 Aug.

355 "Lord of the Dance," BrWk 8 Sept: 7.

356 "More Memories of Music, People, Verse, and Worse," CongM Sept: 12–13.

357 "Music in Modern Worship," BrWk 29 Dec: 8.

358 "Music in the Tower [of London]," BrWk 8 Sept: 1.

359 "Music We Must Not Ignore" [a discussion of Karl-Heinz Stockhausen, the avant-garde composer of electronic music], BrWk 6 Jan: 5.

360 "On Christian Belief," three articles in *Aspire*, 1966–67.

361 "The Psalms in the Life of a Church Musician," JCM 8: 2–5; see also No. 381.

362 "Sex and Morality: ten people talking," BrWk 7 Nov: 6.

363 "Song for a Not-Quite Convert," BrWk 13 Jan: 5.

364 "That Song for Teenage Christians," BrWk 28 Aug: 5.

365 "Who Wants an Organist?" BrWk 15 Sept: 7.

1967

366 "A Curious Form of Service," BrWk 3 Aug: 12, 15.

367 "A Letter from Erik Routley," BrWk 14 Dec: 5.

368 "Centre of Musical Sanity," BrWk 25 May: 12, 15.

369 "The Church Explosion," BrWk 12 Oct: 6.

370 "Controversialists: History in the Hymn Book—(3): Samuel John Stone and John White Chadwick," BrWk 18 May: 6.

371 "The Disappearing Organist," BrWk 26 Sept: 4.

372 "Comments on The Methodist Hymnal 1966," Hy 18: 60.

373 "The Failure: History in the Hymn Book —(2): John Newton and William Cowper," BrWk 11 May: 6.

374 "Gifts Given and Received," ExpT 78: 220–221.

375 "The Highbrow: History in the Hymn Book—(4): Robert Bridges," BrWk 25 May: 6.

376 "Donald W. Hughes, (1911–1967), HSB 6/8: 165.

377 "Letter to the Editor" [rejecting the view that Jesus was an homosexual], NC 24 Aug.

378 "Letter to the Editor," NC 14 Dec.

379 "Letter to the Editor," BrWk 24 Aug: 2.

380 "New Season's Music," BrWk 12 Oct: 4.

381 "The Psalms in the life of a Church Musician" [second part of No. 361], JCM 9: 8–11.

382 "St. Giles Produced a Festival Statistic" [on Herrick Bunney's performance of all the organ works of J. S. Bach], BrWk 21 Sept: 7.

383 "Theological Protesters: Davis, Ainger, J. B. Phillips . . . and unity," BrWk 26 Jan: 5.

384 "Thomas Tiplady, 1882–1967," HSB 6/8: 163–165.

385 "The True Puritan: History in the Hymn Book—(1): Richard Baxter," BrWk 4 May: 6.

386 "Veni Immanuel," HSB 6/9: 113–118.

387 "The Vocabulary of Church Music," USQR 18: 135–147.

1968

388 "Bernard Manning is Back With Us," BrWk 8 Feb: 4.

389 "Calamitous" [Letter to the editor], BrWk 29 Aug: 6.

390 "Church Music and Theology," The Franciscan 10: 191–197.

391 "The Conspiracy of Joy," ExpT 80: 13–15.

392 "Crossroads, Roundabout, or Last Exit to Addington?" EngCM: 32–37.

393 "The Delusiveness of Immortality (especially in Church Music)," BrWk 28 Mar: 4.

394 "Erik Routley Sends . . . another postcard from America," BrWk 29 Aug: 7.

395 "Essentials of Remembrance," BrWk 19 Sept: 5.

396 "Evolution, Morality—and Mission," BrWk 25 Jly: 4.

397 "Faith, Folk and Clarity," BrWk 15 Feb: 6.

398 "The Field at Anathoth," BrWk 11 Jly: 4.

399 "From Traditional to Folk," BrWk 5 Dec: 5.

400 "Government by Friendship: Erik Routley contributes to inquiry into unity," BrWk 18 Jan: 6.

401 "How Shall We Celebrate Remembrance?" BrWk 12 Sept: 7.

402 *Hymns Ancient and Modern*: the 1868 supplement," HSB 6/10: 203–208.

403 "Hymns—the contemporary scene." *Canterbury Cathedral Chronicle* 63: 29–33.

404 "Introducing Malcolm Stewart," BrWk 27 Jun: 4.

405 "Leaving—and sticking to the church," BrWk 13 Jun: 7.

406 "New Church Music in the Alpha Class," BrWk 13 Jun: 4.

407 "Oh, Are You?" BrWk 18 Aug: 5.

408 "Organ Technology," BrWk 10 Oct: 7.

409 "Percy Dearmer, Twentieth Century Hymnologist," Hy 19: 74–80.

410 "Radicalism and Its Roots," BrWk 11 Jan: 4.

411 "Some Hymn Books and Modern Music," BrWk 1 Aug: 4.

412 "The St. Giles Organ," MT 109: 138.

413 "Theories of the Atonement," BrWk 29 Aug: 4.

414 "Tourist Theologians," BrWk 23 Apr: 4.

1969

415 "Amos was an Irishman," BrWk 4 Dec: 7.

416 "Behold the Man!" BrWk 6 Feb: 4.

417 "Charismatic Men," BrWk 18 Sept: 4.

418 "Death," BrWk 20 Mar: 4 & 27 Mar: 7.

419 "Ecumenicity: the musical opportunities," EngCM: 8–18.

420 "Editorial" [on his association with the Hymn Society of Great Britain & Ireland], HSB 7/3: 45–47.

421 "Henry Walford Davies," HSB 7/3: 54–61; see also No. 445.

422 "Hymns for Africa," BrWk 11 Dec: 4.

423 "The Interest in Liturgy," BrWk 21 Aug: 6.

424 "Letter to the Editor," NC 27 Nov.

425 "Letter to the Editor," NC 20 Mar.

426 "Making sense of Religion," BrWk 4 Dec: 6.

427 "Musical Prophet," BrWk 28 Aug: 7.

428 "New Hymns for Anglicans," BrWk 6 Nov: 4.

429 "New Songs for Methodists," BrWk 9 Oct: 4.

430 "Sir Hubert Parry: Hymnodist," HSB 7/1: 4–10.

431 "Powell, Politics and the Church," BrWk 25 Dec: 1, 4.

432 "Retrenchment or Revival?" BrWk 23 Jan: 5.

433 "Singing in the School," BrWk 2 Oct: 4.

434 "Take It All Seriously or Leave It Alone," BrWk 11 Sept: 5.

435 "Those Ghastly Occasions," CongM May: 7.

436 "Truly This Was a Son of God?" BrWk 3 Jly: 5.

437 "Words to be Eaten?" BrWk 14 Aug: 6.

1970

438 "A Damaging Idolatry—Celebrations (3)," BrWk 10 Sept: 4; see Nos 439, 440, 447.

439 "Celebration," BrWk 27 Aug: 1.

440 "Celebration Again," BrWk 3 Sept: 4.

441 "The Civilizing of Sex," BrWk 16 Apr: 6.

442 "The Controversialist," BrWk 2 Apr: 6.

443 "Fonthill in the Twenties," *Fonthill*

[150th Anniversary Celebration]: 49–53.

444 "For the Church Musician," BrWk 11 Jun: 4.

445 "(Henry) Walford Davies Addendum," HSB 7/4: 54–61; see also No. 421.

446 "Into a Broad Land" [An abridged version of the address delivered to the Assembly of the Congregational Church in England], BrWk 7 May: 6.

447 "Joy—On the Organ—Celebrations (4)," BrWk 17 Sept: 4.

448 "1969 Convocation Lecture Series by Erik Routley." *News Notes* [Fellowship of United Methodist Musicians] Apr & Jun; summary of the five lectures by J. Edward Moyer.

449 "O Ebenezer Prout," OrgR Jan: 9.

450 "Of God and Man," BrWk 9 Apr: 4.

451 "Recent Church Music," BrWk 14 May: 4.

452 "Rosemary Brown," BrWk 12 Mar: 3.

453 "St. Andrews Tide," ExpT 82: 45–46.

454 "True and False Simplicity," BrWk 4 Jun: 4.

455 "Twilight and Puritanism," CongHS 20: 350–360.

456 "What Shall We Remember?" BrWk 24 Sept: 3.

1971

457 "Geoffrey Beaumont, (1903–1970)," HSB 7/6: 65–70.

458 "Leslie H. Bunn, (1901–1971)," HSB 7/8: 165–166.

459 "From the President: the score at halftime," CongM Feb: 3.

460 "The Holy and Undivided Trinity," ExpT 82: 240–241.

461 "Hymns for a New Dispensation," ChuMus (Lon.) 3/12: 8–9.

462 "Improper Songs," MethRec 4 Mar.

463 "James Montgomery in the Church of Today," HSB 7/7: 129–132.

464 "Making Music in America," MethRec 2 Sept.

465 "The New Catholic Hymnal," HSB 7/8: 155–163.

466 "New Year—a time of hope," BrWk 1 Jan: 1.

467 "On Congregational Singing—the next chapter," HSB 7/6: 113–122.

468 "That Holiday Worship," CongM Nov: 19.

1972

469 "An Agreed Statement: a Protestant view" [on the Eucharist], ExpT 83: 360–363.

470 "The BBC Daily Service," OrgR Apr: 20.

471 "The Bristol Conference, 1972," HSB 7/11: 205–208.

472 "The Cause of Divisiveness," ExpT 83: 111–112.

473 "[Jesus Christ] Superstar—heretical and dangerous, doctrine matters—a personal view," MethRec 2 Mar.

474 "Greetings from Great Britain," Hy 23: 65.

475 "On Writing New Tunes," MusMin 4: 8–11.

476 "Otterburn Hall's Silver Jubilee," CongM Jly: 7.

477 "Some Recent Hymn Books," MethCMSB 1: 118–123.

478 "Traditional Statement" [Letter to the Editor about the URC merger], CongM Apr: 16.

479 "URC and Puritan Tradition: distinctive role of the new church," MethRec 24 Feb: 7.

480 "Who are the Folk?" MethRec 7 Sept.

481 "Words and Music in Church," OrgR Jan: 10–16.

482 "Young People and Hymns," ChorGL Jan: 93–94; reprinted HSB 8/1: 1–6.

1973

483 "The Barbaric Unison" (Letter to the Editor), MusT 114: 256–257.

484 "Cantate Domino (4th edition)," RW 32: 315–322.

485 "Contemporary Catholic Hymnody in Its Wider Setting" [a series of 4 articles], Wor 47: 194–211, 258–273, 322–337, 417–423; reprinted ChuMus (StL) 77/2: 1–22.

486 "Douglas Walter Langridge (1887–1973)," *Union Church Brighton* 10 Nov.

487 "Editorial" [On Wilfred Little], HSB 8/2: 21–22.

488 "Ferial and Festal," ChuMusQ Apr: 6–7.

489 "The Genuine Article," ExpT 84: 240–241.

490 "Hymns and Psalms with Understanding," ChuMusQ Jly: 4–5.

491 "Hymns Are Our Liturgy," MethCMSB 1: 182–186.

492 "On Singing Thankfully," EngCM: 25–29.

493 "Other Times, Other Manners," MethRec 1 Mar.

494 "Prayers We Have In Common: the musical implications," Wor 47: 137–143.

495 "The Prophet Lewis," NYCSLB Feb: 8.

496 "Recent American Catholic Hymnody," HSB 8/1: 19.

497 "The Root of the Matter," JCM 15: 2–8.

498 "Stunning Effect," NYCSLB 4. No 3 (Jan); reprinted *The Canadian C. S. Lewis Journal* 5 (1979): 1–5.

499 "Thornbury," OrgR Jan: 26.

500 "Those Hymns!" ChuMusQ Jan: 6–7.

501 "Where is it Going in the U.S.A.?" MethRec 6 Sept.

1974

502 [An article without a title] *Christian Celebration* Oct.

503 "A British Look at *The Worshipbook*," ThTo 31: 214–219.

504 "A New Book of Worship for a New Church," Wor 48: 413–420.

505 "Anniversary," Ref Jly–Aug: 8.

506 "Choices for Watts," MethRec 7 Mar.

507 "Church Music—the non-story of the 1970s" [Address given at the 71st regional convention at the AGO, Charlotte, North Carolina], OrgR Apr: 13–14.

508 "Contemporary Catholic Hymnody," ChuMusQ Jan: 6.

509 "Courtesy," Ref Jun: 29.

510 "Cunning and Innocent," Ref Dec: 12.

511 "The Eucharist Hymns of Isaac Watts," Wor 48: 526–535.

512 "Evening Services," Ref Jly–Aug: 36.

513 "Kenneth G. Finlay," [Obituary], HSB 8/4: 72–74.

514 "Gustav Holst—a composer for brave souls," JCM 16: 8–11.

515 "Have You Improved Your Leisure?" HSB 8/5: 89–90.

516 "Here Followeth The . . . ," ChuMusQ Jan: 4.

517 "Hymns, Stop The Plane, I Want to Get Off," EngCM: 10–17.

518 "Isaac Watts Takes the Chair," ChuMusQ Jan: 6.

519 "1973 Memorials," HSB 8/3: 51–53.

520 "Praise in Words," *Universa Laus Bulletin 1974*: 4–13, 22.

521 "Some Thoughts on the Carols of Advent, Christmas and Epiphany," ChuMus (StL) 74/2: 7–10.

522 "That Dreadful Red Book" [Hymns Ancient and Modern 1904 edition], HSB 8/5: 80–85.

523 "Tug of War?" ChuMusQ Oct: 4.

524 "Unconscious Sainthood," ExpT 86: 14–16.

525 "Your Zealous Enabler" [An article about Francis Westbrook], MethCMSB Jly; reprinted MethRec 5 Sept.

1975

526 "A National Hymnal?" Wor 49: 263–271.

527 "An English Reaction" [to the *Lutheran Book of Worship*], *The Chaplain*: 18–19.

528 "Eric Harding Thiman, 1900–1975: an appreciation," HSB 8/7: 117–120.

529 "Progress Report in Hymnody," Wor 49: 393–399.

530 "The tune 'McKee'," HSB 8/7: 124.

1976

531 "American Hymnody Here and There," MethCMSB 2: 75–80.

532 "Five American Companions" [to hymnals], HSB 8/11: 185–187.

533 "Routley in the U.S.A.," ChuMusQ 8: 7.

534 "The State of Music in American Churches: six contemporary viewpoints," ChuMus (StL) 76/1: 2.

535 "Things are Looking Better," Wor 50: 43–49.

536 "What's New from America?" HSB 8/9: 152–157.

1977

537 "A Hole in the Heavens," ThTo 34: 294–298.

538 "The Background of the English Renaissance in Hymnody," Hy 28: 64–66.

539 "Can We Enjoy Hymns?" MusMin 9/8 28–29.

540 "Christian Hymnody and Christian Maturity," Wor 51: 505–522.

541 "Contemporary Hymnody in its Wider Setting: a survey of materials," ChuMus (StL) 77/2: 122.

542 "Hymns as the Organist Sees Them," *Music* 11/4: 18.

543 "Hymn Writers of the New English Renaissance," Hy 28: 6–10.

544 "1976: A Vigorous Year in Hymnology," Wor 51: 120–126.

545 "Ought We to Sing Whittier?" HSB 8/13: 221–227.

546 "The Teaching and Promotion of Church Music in Britain and America," MusOp 100: 338–339.

547 "Theology for Church Musicians," ThTo 34: 20–28.

548 "Trends and Fads in Worship," *AD* Dec/Jan: 18–21.

549 "Two Silver Jubilee Hymns," Hy 28: 151–152.

550 "The Wet and the Dry," ChuMusQ 9: 5.

1978

551 "Hymns: a roundup for 1977," Wor 52: 108–120.

552 "Letter," HSB 9/1: 19.

553 "New Dimensions in Hymnody," WCCN Dec: 2.

554 "The New Lutheran Book of Worship: a preview of the hymns," Wor 52: 403–408.

555 "Victory of Life: an interpretation of the Book of Revelation arranged for dramatic reading with congregational participation," RL&M 12/1: 2–68.

1979

556 "Amen and Christian Hymnody," RL&M 13/1: 19–23.

557 "An Afternoon in the Attic," ChuMusQ Jan: 8–9.

558 "Church Music and Hymnody: browsing among recent books," Wor 53: 404–413.

559 "Church Music: the dilemma of excellence," *Pastoral Music* 3/5: 29–33.

560 "The 'Lutheran Book of Worship'," HSB 9/5: 73.

561 "On the Display of Hymn Texts," Hy 30: 16–20.

562 "The Routley Commentary," a series of 11 articles on various non-musical subjects in Ref Feb–Dec.

563 "Sexist Language: a view from a distance," Wor 53: 2–11; reprinted Hy 31 (1980): 26–32.

564 "Six Great Moments in Twentieth Century Hymn Music," ChuMusQ Apr: 4.

565 "The RSCM in Britain and Westminster Choir College in the USA—some comparisons," ChuMusQ Jly: 5–6.

566 "Three Anthems with Comments by the Composer," RL&M 13/3: 17–40.

567 "Two Notes on Hymn Tunes," HSB 9/5: 38.

1980

568 "A Hymn Festival in Germany," HSB 9/8: 44–45.

569 "Lee Hastings Bristol. Jr., 1923–1979," HSB 8/7: 135.

570 "Charles Williams: A comment from the Puritan Tradition, with some observations about 'He Came Down from Heaven' and 'The Desert of the Dove,'" *The Charles Williams Society Newsletter* 18: 4–11.

571 "Choosing Hymns," *Lay Preaching Matters* [URC Leaflet 4]: 1–4.

572 "Hymnody: our annual roundup," Wor 54: 446–455.

573 "Hymns Ancient and Modern: four supplements, 1889–1980," EngCM: 36–49.

574 "Outrageous" [a letter], Ref Jan: 30.

575 "Doreen Potter 1925–1980," HSB 9/9: 176.

576 "The Psalms in Today's Church," RL&M 14/4: 20–26.

577 "Reflections on Reading The Essential Question," Wor 54: 169–179.

578 "Robert Bridges: the meeting of poetry and hymnody," Hy 31: 285.

579 "Singing About the Cross," *Liturgy* 1/1: 65–68.

580 "The Unexpected Tune," ChuMusQ Jly: 8.

581 "A Wedding Song," RL&M 14/1: 47–49. See also M14 and H18.

1981

582 "An Interview with Erik Routley" [by H. Eskew], Hy 32: 198–206.

583 "Charles Wesley and his Vigorous Future," EpwR 8: 41–50.

584 "Holy Disorders," ChMusQ Apr: 1, 3; reprinted AmOrg 17/9: 41.

585 "Hymnody and Related Matters: our annual report, Wor 55: 518–528.

586 "Obligatory Praise—a review," *Church Times* 7 Aug: 4.

1982

587 "The American Solution" [Letter to the Editor], Ref Oct: 31.

588 "The Gender of God: a contribution to the conversation," Wor 56: 231–239.

589 "Hymnody 1981–1982: a quiet year," Wor 56: 503–512.

590 "Hymn Story: 'What does the Lord require'?" *Tidings* [Trinity Church, Princeton], 5/4: 3.

591 "Hymns by Accident" (their use and misuse in films and television), HSB 10/3: 79–81.

592 "Hymn Writers Today: Brian Arthur Wren," AmOrg 16/12: 26.

593 "Music at Lancing Fifty Years Ago," LCM.

594 "Spiritual Resonances in Hymnody," RL&M 16: 120–125.

III. The Unpublished Works of Erik Routley

A. Book Length Manuscripts

1946

595 "The Church and Music: An Enquiry into the Music, the Nature, and the Scope of Christian Judgment of Music" (Bachelor of Divinity thesis, Mansfield College, Oxford University, 1946). The substance of the thesis was issued as No. 1.

1952

596 "A Historical Study of Christian Hymnology: Its Development and Discipline" (Doctor of Philosophy dissertation, Oxford University, 1952). 769 pp. No. 6 is partially based on this thesis.

1978

597 "The Master at Work: A Study of the Six Miracle Stories in St. John's Gospel." Unpublished manuscript, 141 pp.

Undated

598 "The Christian Character." Unfinished manuscript, 47 pp.
599 "The Hymn Lover's Source Book." Unfinished compilation of historical and anecdotal items of interest to hymn lovers. 150 pp.
600 "Hymns Observed." This book-length manuscript, dedicated to John Wilson, was published in shorter form as No. 45.
601 "Morality." An unfinished manuscript, 120 pp.

602 "Random Thoughts about America and Britain." Unfinished manuscript. 55 pp.
603 "Theology of Major Choral Works." Unfinished manuscript consisting of notes mostly in outline form for a course at Westminster Choir College. 150 pp.
604 "What Goes on in Church." Unfinished manuscript. 56 pp.

B. Manuscript Addresses and Articles (mainly unpublished)

1952

605 "The Principles of Praise" (This article was the first of three that grew out of a series of lectures given at the summer school for ministers of the Eastern Province of the Congregational Union, Cambridge, England, June 25, 1952).

1955

606 "Charles Wesley's Debt to Matthew Henry" (An address given at the annual meeting of the Hymn Society of Great Britain and Ireland, 1955).
607 "Hymns and Human Life" (A lecture delivered at McMaster University, Hamilton, Ontario, by the invitation of the Vice-Chancellor, November 25, 1955). "The title, which I should not otherwise have used because I had written a book using that title, was prescribed by the Vice Chancellor."

1956

608 "The Church's Authority in a Vulgar Age" (Being the substance of an address given at the Methodist Luncheon, Central Hall, Westminster, December 14, 1956).

1957

609 "Devotional Life in the College" (An address given at a meeting of the Oxford Congregational Society, Hilary Term, 1957). "Hilary" refers to the Spring term.

610 "The Obstinate Victories of Mrs. Jellyby" (An address given at the Oxford Congregational Society Missions Group, February 5, 1957).

611 "On Being Saved" (A lecture given at a Richard Baxter Society Meeting, May 19, 1957).

612 "The Only Ground of Right Worship is Penitence" (A lecture given to the Junior Common Room, Mansfield College, Oxford, November 27, 1957).

613 "The Sacrament of Unity" (An address given at a Study Conference at Swanwick Student Christian Movement, July 20, 1957).

1958

614 "Images, Concepts and the Reformed Way of Life" (A lecture given at Kelham, an Anglican community, on March 15, 1958).

615 "On Christian Criticism of Music" (An address given to a Student Christian Movement Conference at Edinburgh, April 10, 1958).

616 "On the Misuse of the Bible" (An address given to the Congregational Society at Mansfield College, Oxford, on November 20, 1958).

617 "The Organist's Temptations (An address given at the Congregational Organists' Annual Conference, Mansfield College, Oxford, July 1958).

1960

618 "Edward Romilly Micklem (1892–1960)" (A sermon preached at the memorial service for Edward Romilly Micklem, Mansfield College Chapel, June 14, 1960).

619 "The Impropriety of the Carol" (An address delivered for a meeting of the International Society of Musicians, Scottish Branch, April 22, 1960).

1961

620 "The English Hymn: Its Literary History and Pretensions" (An address delivered at the English Association, Edinburgh Branch, November 10, 1961).

621 "The Use of Music in Schools" (A lecture delivered at the University of St Andrews, St Andrews, Scotland, July 27, 1961).

1962

622 "Academia and Ecclesia" (A lecture delivered at Sheffield Theological Seminar, February 19, 1962).

623 "The De Musica of St. Augustine: A Second Look" (A lecture given at the Theological Club, Edinburgh, December 11, 1962).

624 "How far are Hymns the Center of Congregational Liturgy?" (An address delivered to the Oxford University Congregational Society, November 25, 1962).

1963

625 "The Case for an Ecumenical Hymnbook" (An address to the Scottish Churches' Ecumenical Association, Edinburgh, December 11, 1963).

626 "Contemporary Church Music: Controversy or Counterpoint" (An address given at a meeting of the Incorporated Association of Organists, Edinburgh, Scotland, August 16, 1963).

627 "Jesus Lives in Music and the Arts" (A sermon delivered to the Oxford Uni-

versity congregation at St Mary the Virgin—the University Church—May 19, 1963).

628 "The Redemptive Obedience of Jesus Christ" (The Cadoux Lecture at the Northern Congregational College, 1963).

629 "Sacred and Secular in Church Music" (A lecture delivered at the Royal School of Church Music, Addington Palace, Croydon, England, July 31, 1963).

1964

630 "Saul among the Prophets" (An address given at the opening of the Edinburgh International Festival, 1964).

631 "Theology and Church Music" (An address to the Edinburgh Clergy Association, Edinburgh, Scotland, December 14, 1964).

1965

632 "Communication through Music" (An address given to the Airdrie Ministers' Fraternal, Carberry Tower, Scotland, September 6, 1965).

633 "The Economics of the Ministry" (A statement by Erik Routley while in Edinburgh, September 1965).

634 "Gowns and Choirs" (1965) (The occasion for this address is unknown.).

635 "Music and the Rising Generation" (A lecture given to the Music Masters of Scotland, October 9, 1965).

636 "The New Morality" (An address given to the Edinburgh Ministers' Fraternal, January 11, 1965).

637 "The Probable and Improbable in Hymns" (A lecture given at the Royal School of Church Music, Croydon, England, December 4, 1965).

638 "The Shaking of the Musical Foundations" (An address on contemporary church music given to the Church Music Society, May 20, 1965).

639 "Worship in Chapel" (A lecture given

to the Music Masters' Association, Oundle, England, June 30, 1965).

1966

640 "The Minister as Administrator" (An address delivered to the Edinburgh Ministers' Fraternal, March 6, 1966).

641 "Music in Worship [in Preparatory Schools]" (A lecture delivered at the Preparatory/Public School Christianity Conference, University of Sussex, Brighton, England, July 4, 1966).

642 "The Next Twenty-One Years: In Ministry and Worship" (An address delivered to the Church Office-Bearers Federation, Kirn, Scotland, April 2, 1966).

643 "What is a District Council?" (An address given to the Edinburgh District Council on the occasion of Erik Routley's induction as Chairman, February 22, 1966).

1967

644 "Key in Bach" (An address delivered to the Edinburgh Guild of Organists, Edinburgh, Scotland).

645 "The Minister as Director" (An address delivered to the Edinburgh Congregational Ministers' Fraternal, March 6, 1967).

646 "The Novelist as Prophet and Interpreter" (An address delivered to the Edinburgh Guild of Organists, Edinburgh, Scotland).

647 "Percy Dearmer—Hymnologist" (An address given at the Hymn Society Annual Conference, July 1967).

648 "The Shape of the Church" (An address given to the Ministers' Fraternal of Alloa and Dunfermline, Scotland, January 16, 1967).

649 "Where Angels Fear to Tread: Erik Routley on Methodist Hymns" (An address delivered at Kingsway in February 1967).

1968

650 "An Evaluation of *The Lutheran Hymnal* (1941)" (A critique prepared for Concordia Publishing House, St Louis, MO, July 1968). In this manuscript the author refers to a similar evaluation and critique of the Lutheran *Service Book and Hymnal* (1958).

651 "The Ecumenical Movement: A Comment from Protestant Dissent" (An address given at a meeting of the Newcastle Theological Society, March 21, 1968).

652 "Hymns—the Contemporary Scene" (An address delivered to the Friends of Canterbury Cathedral, Summer 1968).

653 "The Letter of James" (Two lectures given at the Ministers' Summer School, Cambridge, England, June 18–20, 1968).

654 "The Musical Opportunities of Ecumenicism" (The substance of an address delivered at the St Nicholas-tide celebration of the Royal School of Church Music, December 7, 1968, at the Royal College of Organists, London).

655 "Puritanism" (A series of three lectures delivered at the University of Wales, Bangor, November 1968).

1969

656 "Church Music in a post-Christian Age" (An address given at Exeter Cathedral, May 2, 1969).

657 "100 Hymns for Today" (A review of the hymns in this book, September 21, 1969).

1970

658 "The Free Churches and the RSCM" (A note by Erik Routley, President of the Congregational Church in England and Wales, Newcastle-upon-Tyne, April 28, 1987).

659 "From the President: The Score at Half Time" (An address delivered to ministers in conjunction with his responsibilities as President of the Congregational Church in England and Wales, 1970 –71). The exact date and occasion of this address are unknown.

660 "The Ministry: The Non-story of the Seventies?" (An address delivered to ministers, 1970–71). The exact date and occasion are unknown.

661 "Songs of Consolation" (An address delivered to the Bristol and District Lay Preachers, Hawkesbury, Upton, June 22, 1970).

662 "Three Lectures on Preaching" (Delivered at Perkins Theological Seminary, Dallas, TX, February 1970).

1971

663 "Church Music: The Non-Story of the Seventies?" (The substance of an address given to the 1971 Regional Convention of the American Guild of Organists, Charlotte, NC, June 16, 1971).

664 "Loneliness—The Spiritual Problems" (An address given to the Clergy-Doctors Association, Newcastle-upon-Tyne, May 27, 1971).

665 "On the Making of Music in Church" (An address given to the congregation of Trinity Congregational Church, Reading: "to celebrate the forty year service of Mr. Barkus, organist, undated but given during 1970–71."

666 "The Permissive Society" (An address delivered to the Yorkshire Congregational Union, Harrowgate, April 17, 1971).

667 "The United Reformed Church" (An article written for *The Methodist Recorder*, February 1971).

668 "Words and Music in the Church" (An address delivered to the International Association of Organists, Cambridge, England, August 2, 1971).

1972

669 "A Puritan Style To-Day" (An address prepared for the Mansfield College Association, June 22, 1972).

670 "Foreword" (written for *Gamut*, 1972).

671 "New Year, 1972" (A script prepared for a broadcast on Radio Newcastle, January 1, 1972).

672 "Ralph Vaughan Williams and Church Music" (written for Augsburg Publishing House, December 1972).

1973

673 "Duty and Delight are the Same Thing"; "The Joy of Discipline" (Two sermons preached at Independent Presbyterian Church, Birmingham, AL, as part of a Fine Arts Emphasis, May 20, 1978).

674 "On the New Prospect of Church Unity" (A sermon preached at St James Church, Newcastle-upon-Tyne, January 18, 1973).

675 "The Prophet Lewis" (Remarks delivered in New York City to C. S. Lewis Society, January 3, 1973).

1974

676 "Aspects of the Life and Works of Isaac Watts" (A commemoration lecture delivered at King Edward VI School, Southampton, 21 May 1974).

677 "Isaac Watts, 1674–1748" (Prepared for a service commemorating the anniversary of the birth of Isaac Watts —July 17, 1674, St James Church, Newcastle-upon-Tyne, July 31, 1974).

678 "Isaac Watts Surprised by Music" (An address delivered at the Royal School of Church Music, 1974).

679 "The Morality of the Detective Story" (An address delivered on February 18, 1974, occasion and location unknown).

680 "Two Music Makers: A Study in the Counterpoint of Tradition—Sidney Nicholson and Martin Shaw" (The Sidney Nicholson Lecture at the Royal School of Church Music, December 7, 1974).

681 "Your Zealous Enabler" (An article about Francis Westbrook, Methodist Hymnologist, 1974).

1975

682 "The Five Fingers of Prayer" (A narrative written for a recital of five Bach Chorale Preludes played by Lee H. Bristol, Jr, Princeton Theological Seminary, April 15, 1975).

683 "For the Dedication of the New Commons: Westminster Choir College, November 18, 1975."

684 "Music for Worship is Music" (An address given at the Church Music Editor's Conference, Westminster Choir College, April 1975).

685 "Music in the Service of the Church's Worship," (An address given at Princeton Theological Seminary, Alumni Day, June 2, 1975).

686 "Why Do You Stand Looking into Heaven?" (A sermon preached at a Service of Choral Evensong, Religious Arts Festival, Birmingham, AL, May 11, 1975).

1976

687 " 'Amen' and Christian Hymnody" (The outline of a lecture given at Westminster Choir College).

688 "Church Music: Dangers and Hopes" (The substance of an address given at a dinner in Richmond, Virginia, in honor of James R. Sydnor, April 2, 1976).

1977

689 "Britain and America: Partners in Hymnody?" (Written for the Hymn Society of Great Britain and Ireland, June 14, 1977).

690 "Britten Memorial" (A lecture given at Westminster Choir College, Princeton, NJ, May 19, 1977).

691 "Is Worship a Field for Experiment?"
(Although a similar article appeared in
AD [see No. 548], this article does not
appear in print).

692 "Reading-Drama for Church Use" (An
article written for the Episcopal Foundation).

1978

693 "The Continuing Crisis in Church
Music" (An address delivered in Water-
loo, IA, April 10, 1978).

694 "The Ecumenical Uses of Hymnody"
(An address delivered at Drew University, November 3, 1978).

695 Four addresses given at the AGO Con-
vention, Seattle, WA, 1978:
   I. "What the Twentieth Century Has
      Not Taught Us."
   II. "What is Happening to American
      Worship."
   III. "The Composer Today."
   IV. "The Contemporary Performer and
      Director."

696 "Informal Reactions to the Lutheran
Hymnal 1978" (prepared for the
Committee on the Lutheran Hymnal,
1978).

697 "Music for Today's Child" (An address
delivered to the Choristers Guild, Dallas,
TX, January 13, 1978).

698 " 'Sexist' Language: a view from a Distance" (An article similar in subject, but
different in content, from one that
appeared in *Worship* in January 1979
[see No. 563]).

699 "Worship without Music Does Not
Really Soar" (The AGO Convocation
Address, Seattle, WA, June 26, 1978).

1979

700 "Saint Nicholas" (An introduction to a
performance of Benjamin Britten's *St.
Nicholas*, First Presbyterian Church,
Bethlehem, PA, February 1979).

1980

701 "Creative Uses of the Hymnal" (A lecture prepared for the Wisconsin Educational Telephone Network, November
26, 1980). Due to technical difficulties
this lecture was not broadcast, but it was
subsequently circulated in manuscript
form.

702 "Hymnology: A Look into the Eighties"
(An address delivered to the Hymn Society of America, June 8, 1980).

1982

703 "The Church's Worship and the
Church's Life Style" (A lecture delivered
at the United Reformed Church, Somerville, NJ, January 31, 1982).

704 "The Life-Style of the Christian Church
Illustrated by Its Hymnody" (An address
delivered to the Litchfield Historical
Society, April 18, 1982).

705 "Music at Lancing Fifty Years Ago" (An
article written by Erik Routley upon
learning of the death of Jasper Rooper,
Director of Music at Lancing, 1934–
1980); see No. 593.

706 "On Hymn Playing" (A lecture delivered
at the Westminster Choir College Summer Session, 1982).

Undated

707 "A New Book of Worship for a New
Church (United Reformed Church)."

708 "A Paper Written to the Congregational
College (Edinburgh)" (Concerning the
reasons for a shortage of ministerial
candidates).

709 "BWV 565: A View from a Distance."

710 "Can the Organist Help Us to Enjoy
Hymns?"

711 "The Carols of Advent, Christmas and
Epiphany."

712 "Christian Vocation: Assurance or
Doubt?" (A handwritten incomplete
article).

713 "The Church Hymnary" (A Memorandum based on the revised edition of the 1937 Hymnal).

714 "Church Music and Theology" (An address delivered to the Society of St Francis, 1967?).

715 "The Communication of the Gospel."

716 "The Cross in Hymnody."

717 "Doctors and Detective."

718 "Evangelism and New Concepts of Man."

719 "Family Church and Its Problems" (An address about the Sunday School).

720 "Favorite Hymns."

721 "Global Pilgrim" (A profile of Fred Kaan, 1972).

722 "Gustav Holst and Church Music: A Composer for Brave Souls."

723 "Hymnody and the Lord's Supper".

724 "Hymnody and the Old Testament."

725 "Hymnody Reflecting Culture."

726 "The Hymnological Strategy of Scramdyke" (This article presupposed acquaintance with *The Screwtape Letters* and implied deep gratitude to that author).

727 "*Hymns Ancient and Modern:* Comments by Erik Routley."

728 "Hymns for the Present Age."

729 "Hymns in a Presbyterian Congregation" (written for American Presbyterian Congregations).

730 "Is Poetry the Enemy of Religious Truth?".

731 "Making Music in Church: The Dilemma of Excellence."

732 "Memo from Erik Routley: On 'You' and 'Thou' in Hymns and Liturgy."

733 "The Miracles and Modern Preaching".

734 "Music at Weddings."

735 "On Planning a Morning Service of Worship."

736 "The Parables of Modern Preaching."

737 "Puritan Religion II—Richard Baxter."

738 "Scriptural Resonances in Hymnody."

739 "Service Book and Hymnal 1958 (Lutheran Hymnal)."

740 "Singing Plainsong Psalms To-Day."

741 "That Abominable Word, 'Mission'."

742 "These Cloistered Academics" (An address probably given at Oxford, 1957).

743 "Thomas Goodwin on Regeneration" (A pamphlet).

744 "Towards a Christian Judgment" (A chapter for a book, 1966?).

745 "The Wholeness of University Life" (An address probably given at Oxford).

IV. Original Compositions

denotes hymn tune not written by Erik Routley

KEYBOARD

M1 *25 Festive Hymns for Organ and Choir; descants & varied accompaniments to well-known hymn tunes.* Dedicated to Joan Lippincott, 1982.
Augsburg 11–9475 organ/conductor score; 11–9474 choral score.

M2 *Festival Praise: a hymn service.* Full score with brass parts entitled: *Companion to Festival Praise*, 1979.
Hinshaw HMB 120 full score; HMB 119 singer's part.

M3 *Hunsdon House*, op. 2; for two pianos, 1940.

M4 *Organ Preludes*, op. 1: LOVE UNKNOWN*.—TALLIS I*.—AIREDALE*.—LAWES 32*, 1938/9.

M5 *Organ Preludes*, op. 10: Laetatus.—De Profundis. Composed at Oxford, 1957.

M6 *Postlude in Eb*, op. 8; for organ. Composed at Wednesbury, 1945.

M7 *Sonata for Two Pianos in A Minor*, op. 37. Composed for William & Louise Cheadle; first performance 4 August 1982.

M8 *Variations on a Waltz by Brahms*, op. 3; for piano, 1941.

M9 *Wrestling Jacob*, op. 9; for organ. Composed at Oxford, dedicated to Eric Thiman, 1950.

STRINGS

M10 *Sonatina in A Minor*, op. 4; for violin & piano, 1943.

M11 *String Trio in G*, op. 5. Composed at Wednesbury, 1943.

VOCAL

M12 *Songs*, op. 6: King David.—June. Composed at Dartford, 1947.

M13 *Songs*, op. 7: The inn.—The rolling English road. Composed at Dartford, 1948.

M14 *A Wedding Song*, op. 30; medium voice & kbd., based on the English folk tune "O waly waly", 1979.
Hinshaw HMV 110.
See also No 581 & H18.

CHORAL

M15 *Beginnings and Endings*, op. 38; SATB. Composed for John Kemp, Sr., 1982.

M16 *By Gracious Powers*, op. 17; melody by Joseph Gelineau, SATB & kbd. Composed for the choir of Princeton Theological Seminary, 1975.
Hinshaw HMC 165, 1976.

M17 *Christ in Glory*, op. 16; SATB & org. Composed for Raymond Hall & the choir of St James's, Newcastle, 5 September 1972.
Worldwide Mus. Pub., 1980.

M18 *Come, O Thou Traveller Unknown*, op. 34; WOODBURY, SATB & org. Dedicated to Carlton Young, 1981.
Agapé ER 1970.

M19 *Come Redeemer*; based on Franz Schubert's "Birthday Hymn," D.763, SATB & org., 1976.
Hinshaw HMC 166.

M20 *Draw Nigh to Thy Jerusalem*, op. 28; LODER, SATB & org., opt. brass quartet. Composed at Evanston, IL, 1979.
Flammer A-5909, 1980.

M21 *The Golden Carol*; melody by Ralph Vaughan Williams. U. & org.
Oxford Univ. Pr. U 102, 1963.

M22 *Good News for All*, op. 36; ORCHARD ROAD, for choir of 4 equal voices & org., opt. brass quintet & timpani. Composed in 1982 for Helen Kemp for the Children's Festival Service, Westminster Choir College, 9 May 1983.
Hinshaw HMC 645; instr. parts available separately.

M23 *Hymns as Simple Anthems*, op. 33: My faith looks up to Thee, OLIVET*.—Lord, teach us how to pray, WIGTON*.—Lift up your heads, TALLIS VII* (opt. brass & cong.).—Eternal Father thou has said, ILLSLEY*.—Hear what God the Lord hath spoken, AIREDALE* (revision of op. 1 no. 3).—O for a closer walk, STRACATHRO*; SATB & org.
Agapé ER1917, ER1918, ER1922, ER1919, ER1921, ER1923; 1981.

M24 *Light and Salt*, op. 18; SATB & org. Composed for Princeton Theological Seminary, 1975.
G.I.A. G-2300, 1980.

M25 *Lord of All*, op. 35; SATB & org. Commissioned by the First Presbyterian Church, Meadville, PA.
Anglo American Music Pub. Co., NY, 1982.

M26 *Master Speak*, op. 27; SA & org.
G.I.A. G-2276, 1979.

M27 *A Nature Hymn for Artists*, op. 24; MONTREAT, SATB &/or cong. & org. Commissioned by the Conference on Worship & Music of the Presbyterian Association of Musicians, Montreat, NC, 1977.

Hinshaw HMC 308, 1978.

M28 *Praise*, op. 20; SHERIDAN, U or SATB & org., opt. cong. Commissioned by the Westminster Presbyterian Church, Lincoln, NE, dedicated to Gordon & Helen Betenbaugh, 1976.
Hinshaw HMC 192. [see also H17 for the original text and T70 for the melody.]

M29 *Sing We Triumphant Hymns of Praise*, op. 21; SATB, org. & brass quartet. Composed for Westminster Choir College Commencement, dedicated to the graduating class of 1977.
Hinshaw HMC 275.

M30 *The Strain Upraise*, op. 13; AUGUSTINE, STB, cong. & org. Composed for Augustine-Bristo Church, Edinburgh, 1965.

M31 *This Joyful Eastertide*, op. 19; VREUCHTEN*, SATB & org. Composed for Princeton Theological Seminary, 1975.
G.I.A. G-2301.

M32 *Three Canticles*, op. 12: Of the incarnation.—Of penitence.—Of divine love. SATB, cong. & org., 1969.
Novello MW 24.

M33 *Two Canticles*, op. 23: O ruler of the universe.—Prayer of Manasseh; U or 2 pt. &/or cong. & org. Commissioned by the Episcopal Church, 1978.
Hinshaw HMC 240, HMC 241.

M34 *Two Canticles of Isaiah*, op. 31: The first song of Isaiah (12:2–6), U, cong. & org.—The second song of Isaiah (55:6–11), SATB, cong. & org. Composed 1980.
Hinshaw HMC 682, HMC 684, 1983.

M35 *Two Carols*, op. 32: Remember, trad. English.—From heaven high, VOM HIMMEL HOCH* (opt. instrs.). SATB & org. Composed 1979.
G.I.A. G-2317, G-2349, 1981.

M36 *Two Carols Arranged*, op. 15: King Jesus hath a garden.—Tomorrow shall be my dancing day, trad., SATB. Composed for St James's, Newcastle, 1970.
G.I.A. G-2318, 1980.

M37 *Two for Pentecost*, op. 22: Canticle for Pentecost—. Carol for Pentecost; SATB & org., 1978.
Hinshaw HMC 267.

M38 *Two Hymns by Alexander*, op. 29: Risen with Christ.—When morning gilds; COTSWOLD* & LANCING* by Alexander Brent Smith, SATB & org. Composed 1979.
Flammer A-5934, A-5958, 1980.

M39 *Ye Sons and Daughters*, op. 25; O FILII ET FILIAE*, SATB & org. Composed 1979.
G.I.A. G-2280.

M40 *Your Voice, O God*, op. 26; CARTIGNY, SATB & org., 1980. G.I.A. G-2275.

V. Original Hymns, etc.

denotes a translation or paraphrase of an original from another language.

A. Texts

Text   *Associated Hymn Tune*

1966

H1 "All who love and serve our city"   BIRABUS

1970

H2 "New songs of celebration render"*   RENDEZ
    From "Entonnons un nouveau cantique", Psalm 98,,   À VOUS
    paraphrased by Roger Chapal

H3 "There in God's garden stands the tree of wisdom"*   DIVA SERVATRIX
    Based on the Hungarian "Paradicsomnak te szép élö fàja or Hungarian melody
    Kiràly Imre von Pécselyi"

1972

H4 "Christ is risen, Death is vanquished"*   Tanzanian melody
    A Swahili Easter song, "Bwana yesu Kafufuka",
    Joas Kijugo

H5 "Go in peace, and God be with you"*   Traditional Israeli
    Israeli blessing, translated via the German   melody
    "Gehe ein in deinen Frieden", Helmut König

H6 "God is love, God is love"*   Indian melody
    From Hindustani: "Main Prima hun"

H7 "Good Spirit of God, guide of your children"*   GOOD SPIRIT
    From "Espirit, toi que guides
    tous les hommes"
    Didier Rimaud

H8 "Happy is he who walks in God's wise way"*   SRI LAMPANG
    From Thai: Psalm 1

H9 "Our Jesus is Saviour, Lord and friend*   KH'NGA/EASTER SONG
    From "Notre Dieu Savauveur est Jésus", Abel Nkuinji

H10 "Praise God! Peace to all men!"* [later published as "Glory   Berthier melody
    to God" (1983)]
    From "Gloire à Dieu", Jacques Berthier

272

H11	"Praise to you, Jesus Christ"* From "Gloire à toi, Jésus Christ", Dominique Ombrie	Dominique Ombrie melody
H12	"Seeking water, seeking shelter"*' From "Comme cerf un Altéré brame", Psalms 42 & 43, paraphrased by Roger Chapal	GENEVA 42
H13	"We have one Lord"* From "Un seul Seigneur", Lucien Deiss	Deiss melody

1973

H14	"Father, with all your gospel's power"* From "Erhalt uns, Herr, bei deinem Wort", Martin Luther	ERHALT UNS, HERR
H15	" 'Light and salt' you called your friends"* From Japanese hymn by John Jyigiokk Tin	SU-KONG-PAN

1974

H16	"Praise the Father in his holy place"* Based on Psalm 150	TAMIL

1976

H17	"In praise of God meet duty and delight" For the occasion of writing, see M28 and T70	SHERIDAN
H18	"Surprised by joy no song can tell" Wedding Song, see No. 582 and M14	ER suggested MELCOMBE, later associated with O WALY WALY

1977

H19	"The earth is the Lord's and its fulness' Written for Trinity Presbyterian Church, Atlanta, GA [see T76]	NEW HOPE

1978

H20	"God, omnipotent, eternal"	RHUDDLAN

1980

H21	"Glady to God's holy temple" Written for the First Presbyterian Church, Allentown, PA	MICHAEL

1982

H22	"God speaks and all things come to be" [see H 27] Based on Psalm 119	ES SIND DOCH SELIG ALLE
H23	"O mighty God! Creator and Redeemer" Based on Psalm 83, Mk 4:35, John 16:14	O STORE GUD

H24	"Christ, gladdening light of holy glory"*	Greek Orthodox melody
	Greek "Phōs Hilarōn"	
H25	"Christ, the Church's Lord"	PADUCAH
	Written for a hymn competition arranged by a church in Paducah, KY [see T93]	
H26	"God shows the way to heaven"*	Thai melody
	From a Thai hymn by Prachan Chantima	
H27	"God is love: God is light"*	French melody
	From "Dieu est amour", Dominique Ombrie	
H28	"Grant this to me Lord: Let me live"	———
	Paraphrase of Psalm 119. Line 19 became line 1 of H22	
H29	"High on the mountain Moses prayed"	WHITEHALL
	Based on Ex. 33 and 2 Cor. 12	
H30	"If I today have grieved my Saviour's heart"*	SI FUI MOTIVO
	From "Si fui motivo", C. M. Battersby, after the trans. by Sara M. de Hall	
H31	"Keep in mind that Jesus Christ is now risen"*	Deiss melody
	From "Souviens-tui de Jésus Christ", Lucien Deiss	
H32	"What is someone had recognized us"*	Sven Erik Bäck melody
	From Finnish "Tank om nägen Känt igen", after the prose trans. by Margot Toplis	
H33	"When the wind caresses the waves of the sea"*	Japanese melody
	From an anonymous Japanese song	
H34	"Where am I? Lost am I!"*	ONDE ESTOU
	From the Portuguese "Onde estou?", G. Junior	

NOTE. Many of these unpublished texts were written in the period between 1970–1972 when Erik Routley was working on *Cantate Domino* (1974).

B. Hymnals in which the Texts Appear

1967

Dunblane Praises II (UK)   *Associated Hymn Tune*
   Scottish Churches' House, Dunblane, Perthshire, Scotland.
    4 "All who love and serve your city"   BIRABUS

1969

Hymns and Songs (UK)
   The Methodist Publishing House, London
    3 "All who love and serve your city"   a) BIRABUS
                                                        b) CITIZENS

New Songs for the Church, Book I (UK)
   Galliard, Great Yarmouth, Norfolk, England
   Edited by Reginald Barrett-Ayres and Erik Routley.
    21 "All who love and serve your city"   BIRABUS

1970

Sing (USA)
  Fortress Press, Philadelphia PA
  122 "All who love and serve your city"   CHARLESTOWN

1971

New Life (UK)
  Galliard, Great Yarmouth, Norfolk, England
  66 "All who love and serve your city"   LAUS DEO

The Hymnbook of the Anglican Church of Canada and The United Church of Canada
  (CAN), Toronto, Canada
  168 "All who love and serve your city"   DOMINIAN-
                                                             CHALMERS

More Hymns and Spiritual Songs (USA)
  The standing Commission on Church Music of the Episcopal Church.
  Walton Music Corporation, New York
  H-1 "All who love and serve your city"   LYON FIFTY-NINE

1972

Songs for the Seventies (UK)
  Galliard, Great Yarmouth, Norfolk, England and the St Andrews Press,
  Edinburgh, Scotland, and Galaxy Music Corporation, New York
  38 "All who love and serve your city"   BIRABUS

The Worship Book (USA), United Presbyterian Church,
  Westminster Press, Philadelphia, PA
  293 "All who love and serve your city"   CHARLESTOWN

St James Church, Newcastle-upon-Tyne (UK)
  Printed privately by St James Church, Erik Routley, editor
  6 "All who love and serve your city"   BIRABUS

1974

Cantate Domino: an ecumenical hymn book, published on behalf of the World Council of
  Churches, Bärenreiter Verlag; Kassel, etc.; full music ed: Oxford University Press 1980 [UK]
  Erik Routley, general editor
  4 "Seeking water, seeking shelter"*   AINSI QUE LA BICHE REE
  6 "New songs of celebration render"*   RENDEZ À DIEU
  7 "Happy is he who walks in God's wise way"*   SRI LAMPANG
  40 "All who love and serve your city"   LYON/BIRABUS
  70 "God is love"   Indian Christian Lyric
  86 "Our Jesus is Savior, Lord and friend"*   KH'NGA
  87 "Christ is risen, death is vanquished"*   Tanzanian melody
  98 "The cloud of chaos parts"*   French melody
  105 "Good Spirit of God, guide your children"*   Belgian melody

275

122	"Father, with all your Gospel's power protect us"*	ERHALT UNS, HERR
130	"Light and salt you called your friends"*	SU-KONG-PAN
131	"There in God's garden stands the tree of wisdom"*	Hungarian melody
138	"Called to keep the unity"*	Deiss melody
181	"For all your wonders"*	Berthier melody
201	"Go in peace, and God be with you"*	Israeli melody

Praise for Today (UK)
Psalms and Hymns Trust, London, England
| 3 | "All who love and serve your city" | BLESSING |

1975

New Church Praise (UK)
The United Reformed Church in England and Wales
Saint Andrew Press, Edinburgh, Scotland
1	"All who love and serve your city"	a) BIRABUS
		b) CHARLESTOWN
66	"New songs of celebration render"*	RENDEZ À DIEU

Westminster Praise (USA)
Hinshaw Music, Inc., Chapel Hill, NC
Edited and compiled by Erik Routley
27	"Father, with all your Gospel's power protect us"*	ERHALT UNS, HERR
30	"There in God's garden stands the tree of wisdom"*	DIVA SERVATRIX
35	"Happy are they who walk in God's wise way"*	SRI LAMPANG
56	"All who love and serve your city"	CHARLESTOWN

1977

Ecumenical Praise (USA)
Agapé (Hope Publishing Company), Carol Stream, IL
8	"Praise the Father in his holy place"*	TAMIL
9	"New songs of celebration render"*	RENDEZ À DIEU
54	"All who love and serve your city"	BIRABUS
55	"All who love and serve your city"	CHARLESTOWN
82	"Good spirit of God, guide us your children"*	GOOD SPIRIT
97	"Our Jesus is Savior, Lord and friend"*	KH'NGA/EASTER SONG

The Australian Hymn Book (1977)/*With One Voice* (1979)
Collins Liturgical Publications, Sydney, Australia, and London, England
| 562 | "All who love and serve your city" | a) BIRABUS |
| | | b) MARCHING |

The Worship Book
Privately printed for the United Reformed Church, Somerville, NJ
| 4 | "All who love and serve your city" | CHARLESTOWN |

Lutheran Book of Worship (USA)
    Inter-Lutheran Commission on Worship.
    Published by Augsburg Publishing House, Minneapolis, MN
436   "All who love and serve your city"   BIRABUS

One World Songs (UK)
    Methodist Publishing House, London, England
29   "All who love and serve your city"   ALTON

Sixteen Hymns for Today for use as simple anthems (UK)
    RSCM, Croydon, England
16   "New songs of celebration render"*   RENDEZ À DIEU

Hymns III (USA)
    The Standing Commission on Church Music of the Episcopal Church.
    The Church Hymnal Corporation, New York
220   "New songs of celebration render"   RENDEZ À DIEU

Partners in Praise (UK)
    Galliard, Great Yarmouth, Norfolk, England
159   "All who love and serve your city"   CITY

Catholic Book of Worship II (CAN)
    Gordon V. Thompson, Ltd., Toronto and Ottawa, Canada
659   "New songs of celebration render"   RENDEZ À DIEU

More Hymns for Today (UK)
    William Clowes and Sons, Ltd., London, England
    A second supplement to *Hymns Ancient and Modern Revised*
165   "New songs of celebration render"*   RENDEZ À DIEU
181   "There in God's garden stands the tree of wisdom"*   DIVA SERVATRIX

Songs of Thanks and Praise (USA)
    Hinshaw Music, Chapel Hill, NC
6   "Father with all your Gospel's power"*   ERHALT UNS, HERR
17   "God omnipotent, eternal"   RHUDDLAN

Songs of Worship (UK)
    Scripture Union, London, England
76   "The earth is the Lord's and its fullness"   NEW HOPE

1981

Celebration Hymnal, Volume 2 (UK)
Mayhew, McCrimmon, Great Awakening, Essex, England
484   "For all your wonders, O Lord God"   Berthier melody

Seaside Hymns and Songs (USA)
Privately printed for First Methodist Church
  Clearwater, Florida
    2   "All who love and serve your city"   BIRABUS

1982

Hymns for Today's Church (UK)
  Hodder and Stoughton, London
343   "New songs of celebration render"   RENDEZ À DIEU

Supplement to the Book of Hymns (USA)
  The United Methodist Publishing House, Nashville, TN
857   "All who love and serve your city"   CHARLESTOWN

1983

Hymns for Humanity (USA)
  Monumental United Methodist Church, Portsmouth, Virginia
  Deborah Carr, editor
  32   "All who love and serve your city"   CHARLESTOWN

Hymns and Psalms. A Methodist and Ecumenical Hymn Book
  London: Methodist Publishing House, 1983
  23   "God speaks and all things come to be"   ES SIND DOCH SELIG
                                                   ALLE
  491   "New songs of celebration render"*   RENDEZ À DIEU

Hymns from the Four Winds (USA)
  Abingdon Press, Nashville, TN
  A collection of Asian–American hymns
  74   "'Light and salt' you called your friends"*   SU-KONG-PAN

1984

The Summit Choirbook (USA)
  Dominican Nuns of Summit, NJ
  72   "There in God's garden stands the tree of wisdom"   DIVA SERVATRIX

Hymnal Supplement (USA)
  Agapé, Carol Stream, IL
  41   "New songs of celebration render"*   RENDEZ À DIEU
  84   "All who love and serve your city"   BIRABUS

Hymnal 1982 [but not published until 1985] (USA)
The Standing Commission on Church Music of the Episcopal Church
  The Church Hymnal Corporation
  New York, New York

20	"All who love and serve your city"	a) BIRABUS
		b) CHARLESTOWN
334	"New songs of celebration render"	RENDEZ À DIEU

Rejoice in the Lord (USA)
  Reformed Church in America, Eerdman's Press, Grand Rapids, MI

82	"Happy are they who walk in God's wise way	SRI LAMPANG
119	"New songs of celebration render"*	RENDEZ À DIEU
307	"There in God's garden stands the tree of wisdom"*	DIVA SERVATRIX
466	"O mighty God"	O STORE GUD
485	"All who love and serve your city"	CHARLESTOWN
500	"Gladly to God's holy temple"	MICHAEL
519	"Surprised by joy"	MELCOMBE

VI. Original Tunes for Hymns, Carols, etc.

A. Tunes

Tune		Date of Composition	Original Hymn Text
T1	FONTHILL	1930	"Now that the daylight fills the skies"
	[unpublished? See T24]		6th century Latin tr. J. M. Neale
T2	IFFLEY	1936	"Awake, O Lord, as in the time of old"
			Henry Twells
T3	HEADINGTON	1937	"Beyond, beyond that boundless sea"
			Josiah Conder
T4	FARNINGHAM	1937	"There's a wideness in God's mercy"
			F. W. Faber
T5	LULLINGTON		"There is a land of pure delight"
			Isaac Watts
T6	MAGDALEN GROVE	1937	"Lord, for the things we see"
			John Greenleaf Whittier
T7	GLORIA	1937	"Glory, glory to God in the highest"
			W. Tidd Matson
T8	ALFRISTON	1938	"My soul awake! Thy must forsake"
			Jane Elizabeth Livrock
T9	WILMINGTON	1938	"Nearer, my God, to thee"
			Sarah Flower Adams
T10	JUDGMENT	1939	"The Lord will come and not be slow"
			John Milton
T11	NATURE	1939	"Hark, my soul, how everything"
			John Austin
T12	KEMSING	1939	"Oh, the bitter shame and sorrow"
			Theodore Monod
T13	HORTON KIRBY	1938/9	"Ye fair green hills of Galilee"
			E. R. Condor
T14	MARPLE BRIDGE	1940	"To thee, our God, we fly"
			W. Walsham Flow
T15	MILL BROW	1941	"Art thou weary, art thou languid"
			J. M. Neale
T16	CHALFONT PARK	1943	"Eternal light! Eternal light!"
			Thomas Binney
T17	KINGSTANDING	1940?	"O valiant hearts, who to your glory
		revised 1977	come"
			J. S. Arkwright

T18	CLIFF TOWN	1943	"Not only for the goodly fruit trees tall" Ella S. Armitage
T19	PILGRIM'S WAY	1942	"My faith it is an oaken staff" Thomas T. Lynch
T20	SUTTON COURTENAY	1943	"Come, let us anew" Charles Wesley
T21	ABINGDON	1944	"And can it be, that I should gain" Charles Wesley
T22	IMBERHORNE	1946	"Father of mercy, lover of all children" Francis John Moore
T23	WYCH CROSS	1947	"Lord Jesus, in the days of old" J. Ashcroft Noble
T24	FONTHILL [cp T1]	1947	"Wide as his vast dominion lies" Isaac Watts
T25	BARTLET	1948	"What can I offer Jesus" S. D. Karanuratne
T26	MACRENNAL	1948	"Be thou with me" S. D. Karanuratne
T27	SELBIE	1948	"God of mercy, God of truth" S. D. Karanuratne
T28	SION'S DAUGHTERS revised	1938 1977	"Sion's daughters, sons of Jerusalem" Adam of St Victor tr. Gabriel Gillette
T29	SAINTHILL	1949	"Life eternal, life victorious" Albert Bayly
T30	TYES CROSS	1949	"What doth the Lord require" Albert Bayly
T31	COLEMAN'S HATCH	1949	"High and lifted up" Albert Bayly
T32	GRAVETYE	1949	"She was a city proudly strong" Albert Bayly
T33	PANTYCELYN	1950	"Guide me, O thou great Jehovah" William Williams tr. Peter Williams
T34	CHURCH HANBOROUGH	1952	"O where is he that trod the sea?" T. T. Lynch
T35	VARNDEAN	1953	"Jesus lives, and Jesus leads" Edwin Paxton Flood
T36	MEKLSHAM	1957	"Lord God, whose fingers formed from clay" Christopher Driver
T37	CLARITAS	1959	"Love divine, all loves excelling" Charles Wesley
T38	WHITSUN CAROL	1960	"On the Day of Pentecost" T. C. H. Clare

T39	AUGUSTINE	1960	"Let all the world in every corner sing" George Herbert
T40	CARCANT	1961	"Blessed are the poor in spirit" Norman Elliott
T41	CASTLETON	1961	"All ye who are to mirth inclined" Anon
T42	GRACEMOUNT	1962	"Jesus, thou joy of loving hearts" Ray Palmer
T43	CRAIGMILLER	1962	a) "Great God of love and laughter" Violet Mary Caird b) "O God of earth and altar" G. K. Chesterton
T44	GIFFORD	1963	"By the cross of Jesus standing" Horatius Bonar
T45	ST BLANE	1963	"Lord, look upon our working days" Ian M. Fraser
T46	WOOLWICH	1963	"We met you, Lord, one evening in the way" Christopher Driver
T47	ELGIN PLACE	1964	"Fill thou my life, O Lord my God" Horatius Bonar
T48	THE HAYES	1966	"For the bread that we have eaten" Brian Wren
T49	GREEN LAKE	1968	a) "Creation is Lord, we give you thanks" W. deWitt Hyde b) "The Church of Christ in every age" Fred Pratt Green
T50	SHARPTHORNE	1968	"What does the Lord require" Albert Bayly
T51	STAWARD PEEL	1968	"When Jesus walked by Galilee" Fred Pratt Green
T52	PERKINS	1969	"Eternal God, whose power upholds" Henry Hallan Tweedy
T53	WOODBURY	1969	"Come, O thou traveller unknown" Charles Wesley
T54	MAIDEN WAY	1970	"Beyond the mist of doubt" Donald Hughes
T55	CORBRIDGE	1970	"God, who spoke in the beginning" Fred Kaan
T56	WANSBECK	1970	"Lord, as we rise to leave this shell of worship" Fred Kaan
T57	KILLINGWORTH	1970	"Sing we of the modern city" Fred Kaan

T58	DURHAM	1972	"We meet you, O Christ, in many a guise" Fred Kaan
T59	ZACCHAEUS	1971	"Zaccheus is an excise-man" Fred Pratt Green
T60	CARTIGNY	1972	"Your voice, my God, calls me by name" Fred Pratt Green
T61	VINDOLANDA	1973	"You, living Christ, our eyes behold" Bishop E. R. Morgan
T62	MO RANCH	1973	"Come, Christians, join to sing" G. E. Bateman
T63	LAMBLEY	1973	"Forgive us, Lord, the selfishness" Stephan Orchard
T64	MAPLE GROVE	1974	"Nature with open volume stands" Isaac Watts
T65	LAUDERDALE	1975	"Breathe on me, breath of God" Edwin Hatch
T66	KILNS	1975	"Now that night is creeping" C. S. Lewis
T67	ALTHORP	1975	"Thank you, Lord, for water, soil and air" Brian Wren
T68	DAYTON	1975	"A stable lamp is lighted" Richard Wilbur
T69	PASSAIC	1976	a) "Let there be light, O Lord of hosts" W. Merrill Vories b) "Jesus shall reign, where 'er the sun" Isaac Watts
T70	SHERIDAN	1976	"In praise of God meet duty and delight" Erik Routley
T71	HOPEWELL	1976	"God, creator of all things" Sister Jane Patricia
T72	JARROW	1976	"Sing we triumphant hymns of praise" St Bede of Jarrow tr. B. Webb and J. M. Neale
T73	MONTREAT	1977	"Almighty Father of all things that be" E. E. Dugmore
T74	ROUND VALLEY	1977	"Master, speak, thy servant heareth" Frances Ridley Havergal
T75	NESHANIC	1977	"Our Father we have wandered" Kevin Nichols
T76	NEW HOPE	1977	"The earth is the Lord's, and its fulness" Erik Routley

T77	BOOTHBAY HARBOR	1978	"God of grace and God of glory" Harry Emerson Fosdick
T78	LONSDALE	1979	"Thank you, God, for water, soil and air" Brian Wren
T79	STONYBROOK	1978	"Our Father, the all-giving" Ruth Pitter
T80	EDGERTON	1978	"Son of the Lord most high" G. W. Briggs
T81	HOPE PARK	1979	"Ye who the name of Jesus bear" Scottish paraphrases
T82	BEDEN'S BROOK	1979	"Shepherd divine, our wants relieve" Charles Wesley
T83	LODER	1979	"Draw nigh to thy Jerusalem, O Lord" Jeremy Taylor
T84	EVANSTONE NEW	1979	"Jesus, my Lord, how rich thy grace" Philip Doddridge
T85	HERONTOWN	1979	"The day of resurrection" J. M. Neale
T86	SPRINGDALE	1980	"O dearest Lord, thy sacred head"
T87	RECTORY MEADOW	1980	"O Prince of peace" Timothy Dudley-Smith
T88	JULIAN	1980	"Rejoice in God's saints" Fred Pratt Green
T89	FOUNTAIN	1980	"A child was born of God" Albert Bayly
T90	OATLANDS	1981	"O Christ, who sinless art alone" A. W. Witherspoon
T91	KANSFIELD	1982	"Joy and gladness" George W. Bethune
T92	LITTON	1982	"Go forth for God" J. R. Peacey
T93	PADUCAH	1982	"Christ, the Church's Lord, you know us" Erik Routley
T94	MASSANETTA (Orchard Row)	1982	"We have a gospel to proclaim" Edward J. Burns
T95	KENTON	1968	"I would choose to be a doorkeeper"
T96	BRIGHTEST AND BEST		"Brightest and best of the sons of the morning" R. Heber
T97	FEATHERSTONE	1969	[No text]
T98	LAC DU FLAMBEAU	1981	[No text]

CANTICLES

Canticles, op. 11

T99	1969	Te Deum
T100	1969	Offertory canticle
T101	1969	Prayer canticle
T102	1969	Easter canticle
T103	1969	Aaronic blessing
T104	1969	Whitsun canticle
T105	1975	Acclamation
T106	1975	Gloria in excelsis
T107	1975	Sanctus and Benedictus
T108	n.d.	Agnus Dei
T109	n.d.	Sursum corda

See also Nos.: M32, M33, M34, M37

CAROLS, BALLADS, ETC.

Date of Composition		*Associated text*
T110	1961	"The cedar of Lebanon" R. F. Littledale
T111	1961	"Now the green blade riseth" J. M. C. Crum
T112	1961	"Song of Mary" Mollie Caird
T113	1963	"Where is he? the wise men asking" James Fraser
T114	1969	"Working days" Ian M. Fraser
T115	1970	"I sing of a maiden, op. 14" Composed for St James's, Newcastle
T116	1972	"Water in the snow" Brian Wren
T117	1980	"You were a child of mine" Brian Wren
T118	n.d.	"It was not in the springtime" Anne Scott
T119	n.d.	"Rejoice O people" Albert F. Bayly
T120	n.d.	"Welcome, Yule"
T121	n.d.	"Who is this Babe?" F. B. Merryweather

B. Hymnals in which Erik Routley Tunes, Harmonisations, etc., appear

1951

Congregational Praise (UK)
  Independent Press, London.

11	FONTHILL (1947)	"Wide as his vast dominion lies"
40	CLIFF TOWN	"Not only for the goodly fruit trees"
41	DANIEL (harm.)	"To God who makes all lovely things"
72	VENI IMMANUEL (harm.)	"O come, O come, Immanuel"
89	IRBY (harm.)	"Once in royal David's city"
146	HERMANN (harm.)	"Our Lord is risen from the dead"
149	VULPIUS (harm.)	"Good Christian men rejoice and sing"
(677)		"O Lord of life, where'er they be"
151	HOLY WELL (harm.)	"To God, with heart and cheerful voice"
210 (1)	O GOD OF LOVE (harm.)	"Spirit divine, attend our prayers"
254 (2)	AU FORT DE . . . (harm.)	"The Church's one foundation"
306 (1)	ST AGNES (harm.)	"Here, O my Lord, I see thee face to face"
(375)		"He loved me, and gave himself for me"
335	DEUS TUORUM MILITUM (harm.)	"Eternal Father, thou hast said"
(499)		"Arm of the Lord, awake, awake!"
(587)		"O Jesus, Lord of heavenly grace"
366 (2)	MILL BROW	"Art thou weary"
382	WELLS (harm.)	"From the deeps of griefs and fear"
(477—2)		"Rock of Ages, cleft for me"
389	NEUMARK (harm.)	"If thou but suffer God to guide thee"
432	SLANE (harm.)	"Be thou my vision"
(534)		"Lord of all hopefulness"
472	ABINGDON	"And can it be"
480 (1)	WILMINGTON	"Nearer my God to thee"
505 (2)	VIGILATE (harm.)	"Christian, seek not yet repose"
535	STOWEY (harm.)	"When a knight won his spurs"
564	ANNUE CHRISTE (harm.)	"Almighty Father, who for us thy Son didst give"
628	WYCH CROSS	"Lord Jesus, in the days of old"
639	SUTTON COURTENAY	"Come let us anew"
682	IMBERHORNE	"Father of mercy"
721	OLWEN (harm.)	"All poor men and humble"
845 (A)	PSALM XCVII (chant)	"The Lord reigneth, let the earth rejoice"

1957

Christian Praise (UK)
  The Tyndale Press, London, England

198	WELLS (harm.)	"Sinners Jesus will receive"
235 (1)	ABINGDON	"And can it be"
243	WYCH CROSS	"Thee will I love"
316	WELLS (harm.)	"Father, Son and Holy Ghost"
317	SLANE (harm.)	"Be thou my vision"
387	OLWEN (harm.)	"All poor men and humble"

1958

Sunday School Praise (UK)
 National Sunday School Union, London, England
379   MILL BROW   "I am trusting thee"
478   CLIFF TOWN   "Who is my neighbor"

1960

Church Hymnal (Ireland)
 General Synod of the Church of Ireland, A.P.C.K., Dublin, Ireland
151   HERMAN (harm.)   "Redeemer! Now thy work is done"
526 (1) VIGILATE (harm.)   "Christians, seek not yet repose"
592 (2) WILMINGTON   "Nearer, my God to thee"

1961

University Carol Book (UK)
 H. Freeman, Brighton, England
164   CASTLETON   "All ye who are to mirth inclined"
177   "The cedar of Lebanon"
186   GRAIN OF WHEAT   "Now the green blade riseth"

1962

Baptist Hymn Book (UK)
 Psalms and Hymns Trust, London, England
 84   DONNE SECOURS (harm.)   "O joyful hope, in weary hearts awaking"
230   ABINGDON   "Creator spirit, by whose aid"
650   WYCH CROSS   "O Lord of life whose power sustains"
712 (2) SUTTON COURTENAY   "Come, let us anew"

New Songs (Supplement) (UK)
 Privately printed for the Congregational Church, Redhill, Surrey
915   VARNDEAN   "Jesus lives and leads"
920   PANTYCELYN   "Guide me, O thou great Jehovah"

1963

The Treasury of Easter Music (UK)
 Blandford Press, London
 42   VULPIUS (harm.)   "Good Christian men rejoice and sing"

1964

Hymns for Church and School (UK)
 Novello and Company, London, England
237   AUGUSTINE   "Let all the world in every corner sing"
301   SLANE (harm.)   "Lord of all creation, to thee be all praise"

Hymns for the Celebration of Life (USA)
  Beacon Press, Boston, MA

83	CLIFF TOWN	"Not only for the goodly fruit trees tall"
174	CLIFF TOWN	"Why is my neighbor?"

1965

Anglican Hymn Book (UK)
  Church Society, London, England

60 (2)	WYCH CROSS	"O God of ages"
94	OLWEN (harm.)	"All poor men and humble"
168	CLIFF TOWN	"Draw nigh to thy Jerusalem, O Lord"
201	HERMAN (harm.)	"God is ascended up on high"
264	VARNDEAN	"Jesus lives and Jesus leads"
375 (2)	CLIFF TOWN	"Come ye yourselves apart"
406 (2)	MILL BROW	"Holy father in thy mercy"
467 (2)	MILL BROW	"Art thou weary"
478	WELLS (harm.)	"Sinners Jesus will receive"
523	NEUMARK (harm.)	"If thou but suffer God to guide thee"
558	ABINGDON	"Leader of faithful souls"
571	SLANE (harm.)	"Be thou my vision"
572	SLANE (harm.)	"Christ be my leader"
573	VIGILATE (harm.)	"Christians seek not yet repose"
627	WELLS (harm.)	"Jesus, Master, whose I am"
628	WELLS (harm.)	"Father, Son and Holy Ghost"

Dunblane Praises I (UK)
  Scottish Churches' House, Dunblane, Perthshire, Scotland

1	ST BLANE	"Lord, look upon our working days"
9	Contemporary Folk Carol	"Where is he? The wise men asking"
10	EDDLESTON	"Fill thou my life"
11	CLARITAS	"Love divine"
12	GIFFORD	"By the cross of Jesus standing"

The Hymnal (Australia)
  Aylesbury Press, NSW, Australia

148	CLIFF TOWN	"Draw nigh to thy Jerusalem"
305	CLIFF TOWN	"Come ye yourselves apart"
766	SUTTON COURTENAY	"Come, let us anew"

1968

Faith, Folk and Nativity (UK)
  Galliard, Great Yarmouth, Norfolk, England

21	Contemporary Folk Carol	"Where is he? The wise men asking"

288

Faith, Folk and Festivity (UK)
   Galliard, Great Yarmouth, Norfolk, England
   26   ST BLANE   "Lord, look upon our working days"

Hymns and Songs (UK)
   The Methodist Publishing House, London
   87   ST BLANE   "Lord, look upon our working days"
   98   SEAWARD PEEL   "When Jesus walked by Galilee"
   100   TE DEUM   "You we praise as God"

New Songs for the Church, Vol. I (UK)
   Galliard, Ltd., Great Yarmouth, Norfolk, England
   13   Contemporary Folk Carol   "Where is he? The wise men asking"
   20   ST BLANE   "Lord, look upon our working days"
   27   Aaronic Blessings   "The Lord bless you"

New Songs for the Church, Vol. II (UK)
   Galliard Ltd., Great Yarmouth, Norfolk, England
   33   TE DEUM   "You we praise as God"
   36   Offertory Canticle   "Blessed art thou, O Lord"
   39   Prayer Canticle   "Ask and it will be given you"
   42   Easter Canticle   "Christ our Pascal Lamb has been sacrificed"
   43   Whitsun Canticle   "I will pray the Father"

100 Hymns for Today (UK). *Supplement to Hymns Ancient and Modern Revised.*
   William Clowes & Sons, London, England
   99   SHARPTHORNE   "What does the Lord require"

Sing (USA)
   Fortress Press, Philadelphia, Pennsylvania
   27   ST BLANE   "Lord, look upon our working days"

Te Decet Laus (USA)
   "A hymnal for the musician", ed. by Oliver S. Beltz, Loma Linda, CA
   136   ABINGDON   "And can it be"

Eternal Light (USA)
   Carl Fischer, Inc., New York, NY
   1   CHALFONT PARK   "Eternal light"
   2   HORTON KIRBY   "Ye fair green hills of Galilee"
   3   IFFLEY   "Draw nigh to thy Jerusalem"
   4   PILGRIM'S WAY   "My faith it is an oaken shaft"
   5   CHURCH HANBOROUGH   "O where is he that trod the sea?"

6	CLARITAS	"Love divine, all loves excelling"
7	CRAIGMILLAR	"The voice of God is calling"
8	GRACEMOUNT	"Jesus thou joy of loving hearts"
9	ELGIN PLACE	"Fill thou my life"
10	THE HAYES	"For the bread that we have eaten"
11	CARCANT	"Blessed are the poor in spirit"
12	GREEN LAKE	"Creation's Lord, we give you thanks"
13	PERKINS	"Eternal God, whose power upholds"
14	WOODBURY	"Come, O thou traveller"
15	MAIDEN WAY	"Beyond the mist and doubt"

The Hymn Book of the Anglican Church of Canada and the United Church of Canada (CAN)
Toronto, Canada

220	WYCH CROSS	"O God in heaven"
334	VARNDEAN	"Jesus, shepherd of our souls"
251	CLIFF TOWN	"O Christ who came to share"
254	WILMINGTON	"Nearer, my God, to thee"
417	OLWEN (harm.)	"All poor men and humble"

More Hymns and Spiritual Songs (USA)
The Standing Commission on Church Music of the Episcopal Church. Walton Music
Corporation, New York

| H-37 | SHARPTHORNE | "What does the Lord require" |

1972

The Book of Praise (CAN)
The Presbyterian Church of Canada, Don Mills, Ontario

140	OLWEN (harm.)	"All poor men and humble"
198	VULPIUS (harm.)	"Good Christian men, rejoice"
203	WYCH CROSS	"They set out on their home-ward road"
316	VULPIUS (harm.)	"Christ is the King, O friends rejoice"
356	ABINGDON	"Victim divine, thy grace we claim"
362	SLANE (harm.)	"Lord of all power, I give you my will"
458	SLANE (harm.)	"Be thou my vision"
576	SUTTON COURTENAY	"Come let us anew"

New Orbit (UK)
Galliard, Great Yarmouth, Norfolk, England

| 79 | WATER IN THE SNOW | "Water in the snow" |

Pilgrim Praise [Hymns by Fred Kaan] (UK)
Galliard, Great Yarmouth, Norfolk, England

| 1 | CORBRIDGE | "God who spoke in the beginning" |
| 16 | WYCH CROSS | "They set out on their homeward road" |

Praise the Lord (UK)
 Geoffrey Chapman Publishers, London, England
 54 CLIFF TOWN "Lift up your hearts"
 201 GRAIN OF WHEAT "Now the green blade riseth"

Songs for the Seventies (UK)
 Galliard, Great Yarmouth, Norfolk, England
 24 WANSBECK "Lord, as we rise to leave this shell of worship"
 43 ST BLANE "Lord, look upon our working days"

1973

The Church Hymnary (UK)
 (3rd edition) Oxford University Press, London, England
 185 OLWEN (harm.) "All poor men and humble"
 361 (1) AUGUSTINE "Let all the world in every corner sing"
 428 SLANE (harm.) "Lord of all hopefulness"
 589 DANIEL (harm.) "Forth in the peace of Christ we go"
 689 (1) WILMINGTON "Nearer my God to thee"
 691 DANIEL (harm.) "Dear Master, in whose life I see"

The Covenant Hymnal (USA)
 Covenant Press, Chicago, IL
 457 VARNDEAN "Jesus lives, and Jesus leads"

Genesis Songbook (USA)
 Hope Publishing Company (Agapé), Carol Stream, Illinois
 9 WOODBURY "Come O thou traveller unknown"

St James Church Newcastle-upon-Tyne (UK)
 Published privately by the church
 Edited by Erik Routley
 8 STAWARD PEEL "When Jesus walked by Galilee"
 20 Easter Canticle "Christ our Paschal lamb has been sacrificed"
 21 TE DEUM "You we praise as God"
 22 Whitsun Canticle "I will pray the father"
 25 AUGUSTINE "Let all the world in every corner sing"

1974

Hymns for Celebration (UK)
 RSCM, Croydon, England
 Edited by Erik Routley and John Wilson
 14 CLIFF TOWN "Lord of all good"
 23 VINDOLANDA "You, living Christ, our eyes behold"

The Hymnal of the United Church of Christ (USA)
 United Church Press, Philadelphia, PA
 60 SHARPTHORNE "What does the Lord require"

Hymnbook for use at Merchant Taylor's School (UK)
    Printed by Oxford University Press
    97   SLANE (harm.)   "Lord of all hopefulness"

Praise for Today (UK)
    Psalms and Hymns Trust, London, England
    2   ER WECKT MICH ALLE MORGEN   "All of you share my gladness
                (harm.)
    51   GOODWILL (harm.)   "Lord Christ, the Father's mighty Son"
    94   SHARPTHORNE   "What does the Lord require"

                                    1975

Baptist Hymnal (USA)
    Southern Baptist Convention
    Convention Press, Nashville, TN
    38   VARNDEAN   "Jesus lives and Jesus leads"

New Church Praise (UK)
    The United Reform Church in England and Wales, the Saint Andrew Press, Edinburgh,
    Scotland
    7   MAIDEN WAY   "Beyond the mist of doubt"
    21   TE DEUM   "Extol the Lord your God"
    24 (1) THE HAYES   "For the bread that we have eaten"
    33   CORBRIDGE   "God who spoke in the beginning"
    53   WANSBECK   "Lord, as we rise to leave this shell"
    56   ABINGDON   "Lord Christ, we praise your sacrifice"
    57   ABINGDON   "Lord Christ, your love has called us here"
    94   GREEN LAKE   "The Church of Christ in every age"
    110   Gloria in excelsis   "Glory to God in the highest"
    111   Sanctus and benedictus   "Holy, holy, holy"
    112   Acclamations   "Christ has died"

Psalmer Och Visor (Sweden)
    Statens Offentliga Utredningar, Stockholm, Sweden
    747   ST BLANE   "Lord, look upon our working days" [translated
                                                into Swedish]
Worship II: A Hymnal for Roman Catholic Parishes (USA)
    GIA Publications, Chicago, IL
    169   SLANE (harm.)   "Lord of all hopefulness"
    304   SHARPTHORNE   "What does the Lord require"

                                    1976

Westminster Praise (USA)
    Hinshaw Music, Inc., Chapel Hill, NC
    Edited by Erik Routley
    5   AUGUSTINE   "Let all the world in every corner sing"

20	DAYTON	"A stable lamp is lighted"
25	WONDROUS LOVE (harm.)	"What wondrous love is this"
26	KINGSTANDING	"Give me, O Christ, the strength"
41	VINDOLANDA	"You living Christ, our eyes behold"

1977

Ecumenical Praise (USA)
Agapé (Hope Publishing Company), Carol Stream, IL

18	TE DEUM	"You we praise as God"
30	WOODBURY	"Come, O thou traveller unknown"
38	MAPLE GROVE	"Nature with open volume stands"
64	MAIDEN WAY	"Beyond the mist and doubt"
78	ALTHORP	"Thank you, Lord, for water, soil and air"
80	CORBRIDGE	"God, who spoke in the beginning"
87	WANSBECK	"Lord, as we rise to leave this shell of worship"
110	Prayer Canticle	"Ask and it will be given you"
112	DURHAM 72	"We meet you, O Christ, in many a guise"

The Worship Book (USA)
Privately printed for the United Reformed Church, Somerville, NJ

| 20 | Whitsun Canticle | "I will pray the Father" |

The Australian Hymn Book (1977)/*With One Voice* (1979)
Collins Liturgical Publications, Sydney, Australia, and London, England

179	RINKART (harm.)	"Christ is the world's true light"
557	SLANE (harm.)	"Lord of creation, to you be all praise"
560	ST BLANE	"Lord, look upon our working days"
568	SHARPTHORNE	"What does the Lord require"

1978

Frankfurter Lieder (Germany)
Beratungstelle für Gestaltung, Frankfurt/Main, West Germany

| 45 | CORBRIDGE | "God who spoke in the beginning" [translated into German] |

Sixteen Hymns of Today for use as simple anthems (UK)
RSCM, England

| 3 | A prayer canticle | "Ask and it will be given you" |
| 10 | Whitsun Carol | "On the day of Pentecost" |

1979

Cantate Domino (USA)
Episcopal Diocese of Chicago. GA Publications, Chicago, IL

| 875 | CLIFF TOWN | "Lord of all good" |
| 890 | VINDOLANDA | "You, living Christ, our eyes behold" |

Festival Praise: A Hymn Service, (USA)
  Hinshaw Music, Inc., Chapel Hill, North Carolina
  Erik Routley, editor
10	MONTREAT	"Almighty Father of all things that be"
12	LAND OF REST (harm.)	"O Jesus, King most wonderful"
13	BOOTHBAY HARBOR	"God of Grace and God of Glory"
15	CONSOLATION (harm.)	"My shepherd will supply my need"

Hymns III (USA)
  The Standing Commission on Church Music of the Episcopal Church.
  The Church Hymnal Corporation, New York, NY
H-221	MONTROSE (harm.)	"O all ye works of God"
	(H-239)	"The Lord will come and not be slow"
H-244	SHARPTHORNE	"What does the Lord require"

Partners in Praise (UK)
  Stainer and Bell, London, England
122	Whitsun Canticle	"I will pray the father"

1980

Cantate Domino: an ecumenical hymn book.
  Published on behalf of the World Council of Churches; full music ed.: Oxford University
  Press (UK)
7	SRI LAMPANG (arr.)	"Happy is he who walks in God's wise way"
45	CORBRIDGE	"God who spoke in the beginning"
107	CARTIGNY	"Your voice, my God, calls me by name"
120	PARATA CUM TE POSCERUNT (harm.)	
123	SLANE (harm)	"Be thou my vision"
139b	GOODWILL (harm.)	"Lord Christ, the Father's mighty Son

Catholic Book of Worship II (CAN)
  Gordon V. Thompson, Ltd., Toronto, Ontario, Canada
504	ST MARY'S (harm.)	"Christ is alive!"

Laudamus (USA)
  Yale Divinity School, New Haven, Connecticut
2	DAYTON	"A stable lamp is lighted"
90	AUGUSTINE	"Let all the world in every corner sing"
154	SHARPTHORNE	"What does the Lord require"

Mainly Hymns (UK)
  John Paul the Preacher Press, Leeds, England
  Hymn tunes set to Brian Wren texts.

3	ABINGDON	"Lord God your love has called us here" (dedicated to Erik Routley)
7	WATER IN THE SNOW	"Water in the Snow"
12	JOSEPH'S CAROL	"You were a child of mine"
23 (i)	THE HAYES	"For the bread that we have eaten"
27	MAKHASANE (harm.)	"I'll try my love, to love you"
36	THE EAST IS RED	"Christ crucified is now alive"

The Marriage Service with Music (UK)
  RSCM, Croydon, England

13	SLANE (harm.)	"Lord of all hopefulness"

More Hymns for Today (UK)
  A second supplement to *Hymns Ancient and Modern Revised*
  William Clowes & Sons, Ltd., London, England

154	ABINGDON	"Lord Christ, we praise"
155	CLIFF TOWN	"Lord God, we give you thanks for all your saints"
165	RENDEZ À DIEU (harm.)	"New songs of celebration render"*
171	Whitsun Carol	"On the day of Pentecost"

Songs of Thanks and Praise (USA)
  Hinshaw, Chapel Hill, NC

18	MONTROSE (harm.)	"Break forth, O living light of God"
50	ST PATRICK (harm.)	"I bind unto myself this day"
68	CORBRIDGE	"God who spoke in the beginning"

Songs of Worship (UK)
  Scripture Union, London, England

53	MO RANCH	"Come, Christians, join to sing"
67	WANSBECK	"Lord, as we rise to leave this shell of worship"
73	SLANE (harm.)	"Jesus, we've prayed and we've read from your word"
76	NEW HOPE	"The earth is the Lord's"
97	SLANE (harm.)	"Lord of all hopefulness"

1981

Broadcast Praise (UK)
  A supplement to the *BBC Hymn Book*
  Oxford University Press, London, England

15	CHALFONT PARK	"Eternal light! Eternal light!"
98	SHARPTHORNE	"What does the Lord require"

Celebration Hymnal, Vol. 2 (UK)
  Mayhew-McCrimmon, Great Wakering, Essex, England
  499   CORBRIDGE   "God who spoke in the beginning"
  540   [mel. by N. Hodson] (harm.)   "It's a long hard journey"

ICEL Resource Collection of Hymns & Service Music for the Liturgy (USA)
  GIA Publications, Chicago, IL
  255   NESHANIC   "Our father, we have wandered"

Hymns of the Saints (USA)
  Herald Publishing House, Independence, MO
  139   WILMINGTON   "Nearer my God to thee"
  185   SLANE (harm.)   "Lord of all hopefulness"
  367   CARPENTER (harm.)   "O God from whom mankind derives its name"
  73   CRAIGMILLAR   "Where restless crowds are thronging"
  494   CARPENTER (harm.)   "Again, dear Savior, to thy name we raise"

                                    1982
Hymns for a Day (UK)
  St Andrew Press, Edinburgh
  5   SHARPTHORNE   "What does the Lord require"
  38   CLIFF TOWN   "Filled with the Spirit's power"

Hymns for Today's Church (UK)
  Hodder and Stoughton, London
  89   RECTORY MEADOW   "O Prince of peace"
  100   REUMARK (harm.)   "Wise men, they came to look for wisdom"
  132   ABINGDON   "Lord Christ, we praise your sacrifice"

Supplement to The Book of Hymns (USA)
  The Methodist Publishing House, Nashville, TN
  958   ALTHORP   "Thank you Lord for water, soil, and air"

                                    1983
Faith Looking Forward (USA)
  Agapé (Hope Publishing Company), Carol Stream, IL & Oxford University Press, Oxford
  (UK)
  Hymn tunes to texts by Brian Wren
  6   ABINGDON   "Lord God, your love has called us here"
  7   ALTHORP   "Thank you, God, for water, soil and air"
  10   WATER IN THE SNOW   "Water in the snow"
  14   Joseph's Carol   "You were a child of mine"
  30   MAKHASANENE (harm.)   "I'll try my love, to love you"
  39   THE EAST IS RED (harm.)   "Christ crucified now is alive"

Hymns and Psalms: A Methodist and Ecumenical Hymn Book (UK)
   London: Methodist Publishing House, 1983

10 (ii)	AUGUSTINE	"Let all the world"
292	Whitsun Canticle	"I will pray the Father"
369	WYCH CROSS	"O God in heaven, whose loving plan"
378	SLANE (harm.)	"Be thou my vision"
414	SHARPTHORNE	"What does the Lord require?"
451 (i)	WILMINGTON	"Nearer, my God, to thee"
458 (i)	CHALFONT PARK	"Eternal Light! Eternal Light"
500	ABINGDON	"Lord God, your love has called us here"
532	ABINGDON	"Lord Christ, we praise your sacrifice"
545	Prayer Cantible	"Ask, and it will be given you"
552 (i)	SLANE (harm.)	"Lord of all hopefulness"
699 (i)	SLANE (harm.)	"Lord of creation, to you be all praise"
797	CLIFF TOWN	"Lord of all good, our gifts we bring to thee"
819	ABINGDON	"Leader of faithful souls and guide"

Hymns for Humanity (USA)
   Monumental United Methodist Church, Portsmouth, Virginia
   Edited by Deborah Carr. Dedicated to Erik Routley

34	Prayer canticle	"We do not know how to pray"
40	DURHAM	"We meet you, O Christ, in many a guise"
43	WANSBECK	"Lord, as we rise to leave this shell"

Jesus Christ—The Light of the World (Switzerland)
   World Council of Churches. Geneva, Switzerland

| 48 | ABINGDON | "Lord God, your love has called us here" |

Renew (USA)
   St Mary of the Lake Seminary, Mundelein, IL

| 24 | SHARPTHORNE | "What does the Lord require" |

1984

Hymnal Supplement
   Agapé, Carol Stream, IL

17	CORBRIDGE	"God who spoke in the beginning"
70	LITTON	"Go forth for God"
73	ALTHORP	"Thankyou, God, for water, soil and air"
117	PATHWAYS (harm.)	"Divided our pathways"

Hymns for Praise and Worship (USA)
   Evangel Press, Nappanee, IN

| 508 | CARCANT | "Blessed are the poor in spirit" |

The Summit Choirbook (USA)
Dominican Nuns of Summit, NJ
Foreword by Erik Routley

3	LAUDERDALE	"O Child of promise, come"
112 (1)	GRAIN OF WHEAT	"Now the green blade riseth"
118	CASTLETON	"Our Lord is risen from the dead"
172	Whitsun Carol	"Day is breaking, dawn is bright"
246	WYCH CROSS	"O Lord, to Whom the spirits live"
340	CASTLETON	"All ye who long toward Christ to fly"
364	WILMINGTON	"More love to Thee, O Christ"
446	VINDOLANDA	"You, living Christ, our eyes beyold"
449	ABINGDON	"Give me, O Lord, the grace to see"
455	CLARITAS	"Love divine, all loves excelling"
492 (2)	TREE OF LIFE (harm.)	"The Tree of Life my sould hath seen"
498	CASTLETON	"All ye that are to mirth inclined"
522 (1)	SPETISBURY (harm.)	"O worship the King all glorious above"

1985

Hymnal 1982 (USA)
The Standing Commission on Church Music the Episcopal Church.
The Hymnal Corporation, New York

101	WOODBURY		"Come, O thou traveller"
165	LITTON		"Go forth for God"
281 (1)	AUGUSTINE		"Let all the world in every corner sing"
334	RENDEZ À DIEU (harm.)		"New songs of celebration render"
		(65)	"Bread of the world in mercy broken"
		(141)	"Father, we thank thee who hast planted"

Rejoice in the Lord (USA)
Reformed Church in America, Eerdman's Press, Grand Rapids, MI

11	AUGUSTINE		"Let all the world in every corner sing"
22	LONSDALE		"Thank you, God, for water, soil and air"
30	MAIDEN WAY		"Beyond the mist and doubt"
41	CHALFONT PARK		"Eternal light! Eternal light"
46	WOODBURY		"Come, O thou traveller unknown"
68	SLANE (harm.)		"Lord of creation"
82	SRI LAMPANG (harm.)		"Happy are they who walk in God's wise way"
176	SHARPTHORNE		"What does the Lord require"
237	KANSFIELD		"Joy and gladness"
245	BEDENS BROOK		"Shepherd divine our wants relieve"
260	CARCANT		"Blessed are the poor in spirit"
301	SPRINGDALE		"O dearest Lord, thy sacred head"
333	ST PATRICK (harm.)		"A hymn of glory let us sing"
		(478)	"I bind unto myself today"
374	Whitsun Carol		"On the day of Pentecost"

390	PANTYÇELYN	"Thanks to God, whose word was spoken"
466	O STORE GUD (harm.)	"O mighty God"
472	KINGSTANDING	"Give me O Christ the strength"
503	ABINGDON	"Lord God, your love has called us here"

NOTE. SLANE, SRI LAMPANG, ST PATRICK and O STORE GUD are copyrighted harmonizations: Erik Routley contributed a further 128 to this collection.

Undated

Hymns for the Homeless [after 1975]
Shelter—National Campaign for the Homeless, London

| 3 | ABINGDON | "Lord, were you in our town today?" |

St Paul's Parish Hymnal (USA)
Privately printed for St Paul's Parish, San Pablo, CA

| 31 | SHARPTHORNE | "What does the Lord require" |

Festival Service Book (UK)
RSCM, Croydon, England

| 67 | SHARPTHORNE | "What does the Lord require" |

Leader's Hymnal (USA)
Bible Study Fellowship, San Antonio, TX

| 19 | SLANE (harm.) | "Be thou my vision, O Lord of my heart" |
| 43 (a) | NEUMARK (harm.) | "If thou but suffer God to guide thee" |

VII. Recordings (Selected)

A. Audio

1951

Two lectures to th˄ Methodist Church Music Society Conference, High Leigh, Hoddesen, England, October 17, 1951.
 Lecture I—"The hymnody of Lutheran Germany"
 Lecture II—"Tendencies in English Hymnody, 1861–1950"
 Tape library of G. Edward Jones.

1965

"Commentator to the Act of Praise"
 Hymn Society Conference, Charterhouse, England, July 3, 1965. Tape Library of G. Edward Jones.
"Dorothy L. Sayers"
 British Broadcasting Company, London, England, April 28, 1965. This audio cassette is an excerpt from Erik Routley's contribution to a television broadcast.

1966

"Music Leadership in the Church"
 New Orleans Baptist Theological Seminary, New Orleans, LA, May 5–6, 1966.
 Lecture I—"Modern Anglican church music"
 Lecture II—"The rudiments of theology: the church musician and his faith; or, What's Christian about church music?"
"Music Leadership in the Church"
 Southern Baptist Theological Seminary, Louisville, KY, The Gheens Lectureship, April 12–13, 1966. Six lectures on the topic "Music Leadership in the Church." (Tapes have no titles.)
"Words, music, and the church today."
 Princeton Theological Seminary, Princeton, NJ. The Stone Lectureship, April 11–14, 1967.
 Lecture I—"Music and the new man"
 Lecture II—"Church music and alien forms"
 Lecture III—"Church music—status symbol"
 Lecture IV—"The theology of faith"
 Lecture V—"The new music"

1967

"Percy Dearmer: Hymnologist"
 Hymn Society Conference, Primrose Hill, London, July 11, 1967. Tape library of G. Edward Jones.

300

1970

"Post-1953 England and USA hymnody"
   Hymn Society Conference, Charterhouse, England, May 26, 1970. Tape library of G.
   Edward Jones.

1971

"American folk hymnody"
   Hymn Society Conference, Keswick Hall College, Norwich, England. Introduction to Harry
   Eskew's address and leading questioning at the end, July 20, 1971. Tape library of G. Edward
   Jones.
"Hymns in new shapes". Westminster Abbey, London, England, 1971.
   Erik Routley as commentator at "Come and Sing" session, May 12, 1971. Tape library of G.
   Edward Jones.

1972

"The European Psalmist"
   Hymn Society Conference in Bristol, England, July 24, 1972. Tape library of G. Edward
   Jones.
"Hymns from many nations." Westminster Abbey, London, England, 1972.
   "Come and Sing" hymn festival, May 10, 1972. Hymns taken from *Cantate Domino*. Tape
   library of G. Edward Jones.
"Hymns from Contemporary England." Westminster Abbey, London, England, 1973.
   "Come and Sing" hymn festival, May 17, 1972. Tape library of G. Edward Jones.

1973

"A survey of approaches to texts" Universa Laus conference, Wetherby, England, 1973.
   Address by Erik Routley, November 3, 1973. Tape library of G. Edward Jones.
"The Chorale Book for England: Catherine Winkworth."
   Hymn Society Conference, 1973. Address given on July 3, 1973. Tape library of G. Edward
   Jones.
"New songs of celebration." Westminster Abbey, London, 1973.
   "Come and Sing" hymn festival, May 16, 1973. Tape library of G. Edward Jones.
"New songs for a new world."
   Williams School of Church Music, Harpenden, England, 1973. Two lectures by Erik
   Routley, November 24, 1973. Tape library of G. Edward Jones.

1974

"The living voice of Isaac Watts." Westminster Abbey, London, England, 1974.
   "Come and Sing" hymn festival, May 22, 1974. Tape library of G. Edward Jones.
"Prepares for breakfast prayers the next morning."
   Hymn Society Conference, York, England, 1974. Informal remarks July 29, 1974. Tape
   library of G. Edward Jones.

1975

"Hymns of Erik Routley" London: Westminster Abbey, 1975.
   Erik Routley as commentator at "Come and Sing" session, May 14, 1975.

"Church Music: Past and future." New Brunswick, NJ: New Brunswick Theological Seminary, 1975. The first lectureship given by Erik Routley after moving to the United States, January 2, 1975. The date of the lectures were January 6–10, 1975.

    Lecture I—"Why church music"

    Lecture II—"Hymns past and present"

    Lecture III—"Modern hymnody"

    Lecture IV—"Psalms in Christian worship"

"Maturity in Christian Hymns." Kansas City, Missouri: NCR Cassettes, 1975.

"Minister and Musician: Theology, Prayer, and Praise."

    Institute on Theology, Princeton Theological Seminary, Princeton, NJ, July 1–4, 1975.

    Lecture I—"Minister and musician as artists in communication"

    Lecture II—"The livine formula"

    Lecture III—"The cross and communication: the impossibility of communication"

    Lecture IV—"Practical issues in communication"

"Music in today's church"

    Alumni day address, Princeton Theological Seminary, Princeton, NJ, February 3, 1975.

"The silence of God" (Psalm 28:1)

    Chapel service, Princeton Theological Seminary, Princeton, NJ, February 3, 1975.

1976

"About worship principles."

    Saturday Seminar, Westminster Choir College, Princeton, NJ, February 21, 1976.

1977

"Britain and America—partners in hymnody?"

    Hymn Society Conference, Salisbury, England, August 3, 1977. Tape library of G. Edward Jones.

"Church Music Institute Lectureship." Southern Baptist Theological Seminary, Louisville, KY, February 24, 1977.

    Lecture I—"Worship, maturity and music"

    Lecture II—"The wonder, reason and love content in hymnody and in our approach to church music"

    Lecture III—"The people's music—hymn tunes"

"English composers—mostly about Benjamin Britten"

    Westminster Choir College, Princeton, NJ, May 19, 1977.

1978

"Church music today: A personal view." Whittier, CA: AGO Educational Materials, 1978. Four addresses delivered at the American Guild of Organists Convention, Seattle, WA, June 27–30, 1978.

    Lecture I—"What the 20th century has not taught us"

    Lecture II—"What is happening to American worship"

    Lecture III—"The composer's work today"

    Lecture IV—"The role of the contemporary performer or director"

"Church music in biblical, theological and contemporary context." Oak Brook, IL: Bethany

Theological Seminary, 1978. A. C. Wiel and lectureship at Bethany Theological Seminary.
　　Lecture I—"Church music: Some biblical and theological insights"
　　Lecture II—"Church music: Some contemporary doubts and questions"

1979

"Church Music The dilemma of excellence." Washington, DC: Pastoral Musician, 1979. An address delivered to the National Association of Pastoral Musicians.

1980

"Christian Hymns: An introduction to their story"
　　Princeton, NJ: Prestige Publications, Inc., 1980. Six cassettes produced commercially by Prestige Publications:
　　Cassette I
　　　　Side 1—"The beginnings of hymnody"
　　　　Side 2—"Hymns and carols of the Middle Ages"
　　Cassette II
　　　　Side 1—"Reformation hymnody: The age of Martin Luther"
　　　　Side 2—"German pietistic hymnody, 1700, 1715"
　　Cassette III
　　　　Side 1—"The psalmody of Calvin's Geneva, 1539–1565"
　　　　Side 2—"The beginnings of English psalmody, 1549–1672"
　　Cassette IV
　　　　Side 1—"Isaac Watts: The liberator of English hymnody"
　　　　Side 2—"The Wesleys and the beginnings of Evangelical hymnody"
　　Cassette V
　　　　Side 1—"Some famous musicians and their contributions to hymnody: Tallis, Gibbons, Lawes, Purcell, Handel"
　　　　Side 2—"American hymnody, 1776–1900"
　　Cassette VI
　　　　Side 1—"The Romantic hymnody of England and the Oxford movement"
　　　　Side 2—"Some Victorian composers, from Dykes to Parry"
"Hymn Festival Commentary." Joint church music workshop—Indiana University and Westminster Choir College, Bloomington, IN, June 12, 1980.
"Robert Bridges—the meeting of poetry and hymnody"
　　Westminster Abbey, London, England, "Come and Sing" hymn festival, May 28, 1980. Tape library of G. Edward Jones.
"200 Years of American Hymnody"
　　Westminster Abbey, London, England, "Come and Sing" hymn festival, May 28, 1980. Tape library of G. Edward Jones.
"Worship: Talking to God, ourselves, others"
　　Thesis Theology Cassettes, *Update* 11 n 17 (August 1980).

1981

"A series of lectures on hymnody"
　　New Orleans Baptist Theological Seminary, Church Music Symposium, February 26, 1981.
　　　　Lecture I—"Hymns and the Bible"

Lecture II—"Hymns and music"
Lecture III—"The assault on hymnody: the conspiracy against it"
Lecture IV—"The relationship of the church musician and pastor"

1982

"The organ as an accompaniment instrument"
Scarritt College, Oktoberfest, Nashville, TN, October 7, 1982. This private recording was made during Erik Routley's last lecture.
"Two sermons." Massanetta Springs Bible Conference, VA, August 10–11, 1982.
Sermon I—"Sermon on Mark 2:1–12"
Sermon II—"Sermon on Matthew 16:13–17"
Recorded by WEMC-FM, Harrisonburg, VA.

B. Video

"Our new hymn book: Don't panic"
New Brunswick Theological Seminary, New Brunswick, NJ, October 6, 1982. In this video tape Erik Routley gives a lecture on the new hymnal of the Reformed Church in America, *Rejoice in the Lord* (1985).

NOTES ON CONTRIBUTORS

George B. Caird
At his untimely death, which occurred while this book was in preparation, George Caird was Dean Ireland's Professor of Exegesis of Holy Scripture, the University of Oxford. Ordained a Congregational minister, he took up academic posts in Canada before returning to England to teach at Mansfield College, Oxford, in 1959, where he later became the Principal. He was also Moderator of the United Reformed Church, 1975–1976. George Caird was a respected Biblical scholar with a world-wide reputation, and also a writer of effective hymn texts which appear in many modern hymnals. It was Erik Routley who persuaded him to write hymn texts and it was therefore fitting that he should have preached that memorable sermon at the memorial service for Erik Routley held in Westminster Abbey, 8 Feb., 1983.

Ian M. Fraser
A Scot, born in Forres, Morayshire, Ian Fraser is an ordained minister of the Church of Scotland and a member of the Iona Community for more than forty years. He has had a lifetime involvement in ecumenism and basic, practical Christianity. Ian Fraser has served as Executive Secretary on Laity and Studies at the World Council of Churches at Geneva, and for nine years was Dean and Head of the Department of Mission, Selly Oak Colleges, Birmingham. He is now Research Consultant for the Scottish Churches Council and lives near Dunblane. He was a key person in the setting up of the Dunblane Consultations on hymnody and in his own hymns, as in his prose writings, his concern is to express the Christian faith in contemporary terms. His latest book is *Reinventing Theology as the People's Work* (1980).

Raymond F. Glover
Raymond Glover is a native of Buffalo, New York, and a graduate of the University of Toronto where he studied with Healey Willan. His Masters degree is from Union Theological Seminary, New York. He has been organist and choirmaster of St Paul's Cathedral, Buffalo, Christ Church Cathedral, Hartford, Connecticut and St Paul's Church, Richmond, Virginia. He has been a member of the faculty of Berkeley Divinity School, New Haven, Connecticut and the Hartford Seminary Foundation. He was also head of the music department of St Catherine's School, Richmond. He has been a member of the Episcopal Church Standing Commission on Church Music since 1969. While chairman of the Commission's Hymn Music Committee he was editor of the Supplement II (1976) to the *Hymnal 1940* and of the hymnal supplement, *Hymns III* (1979). In January of 1981 Mr Glover was appointed the General Editor of the *Hymnal 1982*, the Episcopal Church's newly revised hymnal which is scheduled for

publication in late 1985. He writes extensively for church and music journals and is active as a workshop leader and speaker.

Frederick Pratt Green

Distinguished poet, hymnwriter and Methodist minister, Fred Pratt Green is one of the leading British hymn writers. Nearly all of his hymns have been written since his retirement —some of them at the instigation of Erik Routley. This productive period of hymnody began in 1967 with a request from the committee responsible for *Hymns and Songs*, which was published as a supplement to the British *Methodist Hymn Book* (1933) in 1969. Subsequently he published a personal collection of 26 hymns, and more recently a complete edition of all his hymn texts to date: *The Hymns and Ballads of Fred Pratt Green* (1982). In 1982 he was honoured by a Fellowship of the Hymn Society of America and a doctorate from Emory University, Atlanta. His hymns are to be found in most hymn books and collections published in the English-speaking world since 1969.

Fred Kaan

Frederick Herman Kaan is a native of Haarlem, the Netherlands. After studies in Utrecht and Bristol he was ordained into the ministry of the (then) Congregational Union in England and Wales. He is now the Moderator of the West Midlands Province of the United Reformed Church. Fred Kaan has been particularly active in ecumenical matters and for some time worked in Geneva as the Secretary of the Department of Cooperation and Witness of the new World Alliance of Reformed Churches. In recognition of this inter-church activity he has been awarded honorary doctorates from Debrecen, Hungary, and Geneva. While in his second pastorate, in Plymouth, he became actively involved in hymn writing which has resulted in the publication of *Pilgrim Praise* (1968 & 1972), *Break not the Circle* (1975), and *Songs and Hymns from Sweden* (1976 & 1983), all collections of original or translated contemporary hymns. He has been involved in the preparation of worship materials for the World Council of Churches and has served as editor or consultant for a number of important hymn books, including the WCC *Cantate Domino*. Fred Kaan's hymns have been included in virtually all larger hymnals produced in the English-speaking world in recent years.

Robin A. Leaver

Robin A. Leaver is an ordained Anglican who teaches on both sides of the Atlantic. He is Associate Professor of Church Music at Westminster Choir College, Princeton, NJ, and Lecturer at Wycliffe Hall, Oxford. He has written a number of books and many articles in the areas of theology, church music, liturgy and hymnology. His most recent publications are *Marbeck's Book of Common Praier Noted (1550)* (1982), *Music as Preaching: Bach, Passions & Music in Worship* (1982) [*J. S. Bach as Preacher: His Passions and Music in Worship* (1984) in USA], *Bachs theologische Bibliothek* (1983), *The Liturgy of the Frankfurt Exiles 1555* (1984), *Ways of Singing the Psalms* (1984), as well as editing the English edition of G. Stiller, *Johann Sebastian Bach and Liturgical Life in Leipzig* (1984). He is the first person to hold office simultaneously in three hymn societies: he is a member of the Research Committee of the Hymn Society of America, a member of the Executive Committee of The Hymn Society of Great Britain and Ireland, and Vicepresident of the Internationale Arbeitsgemeinschaft für Hymnologie.

James H. Litton

A native of Charleston, West Virginia, James Litton has served churches in Charleston, Plainsfield, New Jersey, Southport, Connecticut, the Episcopal Cathedral in Indianapolis and for 15 years was the Organist and Director of Music at Trinity Church, Princeton. At present he is the Organist and Director of Music at St Bartholomew's Church, New York City. He has been Instructor of Music at the Berkeley Divinity School, New Haven and at Butler University in Indianapolis. While in Princeton he served as Head of the Church Music Department and Assistant Professor of Organ at Westminster Choir College and was the C. F. Seabrook Director of Music at Princeton Theological Seminary. At present he is a member of the organ faculty of the Manhattan School of Music. His undergraduate and graduate degrees in organ and conducting are from Westminster Choir College, and he has done post graduate study with Allan Wicks at Canterbury Cathedral in England. He has been a member of the Episcopal Church's Standing Commission on Church Music since 1969, having served as Vice Chairman of the Commission, and as Chairman of the Service Music Committee for the *Hymnal 1982*. He was the Commission's editor of *The Book of Canticles* (1979), *Congregational Music for Eucharist* (1980) and *Gradual Psalms* (1980–82). Mr Litton is active as a church music lecturer and leader, and as a conductor and organ recitalist. He has had more than 40 articles published in church and music journals, and is editor of several collections of liturgical music, medieval carols and choral music.

Alan Luff

Alan Luff is Precentor and Sacrist of Westminster Abbey and the Secretary of The Hymn Society of Great Britain and Ireland. An ex-perienced singer and choir director, he has a particular interest in the congregational and choral aspects of worship. He is the author of a small but distinguished number of hymn texts and has arranged and written music for psalms and canticles. He has a special concern for churches where resources are limited. An Englishman who speaks Welsh fluently, Alan Luff has collected and edited Welsh traditional carols: *The St Deiniol Carol Book* (1974). He met Erik Routley at the Dunblane Music Consultation, which led to a fruitful collaboration.

Caryl Micklem

Thomas Caryl Micklem is a native of Oxford, the son of Edward Romilly Micklem, Chaplain and Tutor of Mansfield College, Oxford, and nephew of Nathaniel Micklem, Principal of Mansfield College. After studies at Mansfield College, Caryl Micklem was into the (then) Congregational, later United Reformed Church, ministry, and served several pastorates including Kensington Chapel, London. He is now the Minister of St Columba's United Reformed Church and chaplain to Reformed students at the university in Oxford. He has been chairman of the Hymnody Group of the United Reformed Church and is currently a member of the Council of the Royal School of Church Music and of the Executive Committee of The Hymn Society of Great Britain and Ireland. He has also been on the editorial boards of the journals *New Christian* and *Reform*. He edited the trilogy *Contemporary Prayers for Public Worship* (1967), *More Contemporary Prayers* (1970), and *Contemporary Prayers for Church and School* [= *As Good as Your Word* in USA] (1975). Caryl Micklem is the writer of numerous hymn tunes and texts which have been appearing in British collections since 1951.

307

Ruth Micklem

Margaret Ruth (Monro) Micklem is a native of the Scottish border country, the daughter of a country doctor and now the wife of Caryl Micklem. Before her marriage she studied at Oxford and then was Editorial Secretary for the journal *Time and Tide*. Ruth Micklem has also been the director of a public relations consultancy and a teacher for an adult literacy course. All this was in addition to her demanding roles as wife, mother and director of the ministerial home. Ruth admits to playing hymns on the piano, but only when Caryl is out.

Ray E. Robinson

Ray Robinson is Professor of Music and President of Westminster Choir College in Princeton, New Jersey, a position he has held since 1969. Prior to the Westminster appointment, Dr Robinson served as Dean of the Peabody Conservatory of Music in Baltimore, Maryland. A writer on various musical subjects, he has written for the *Baltimore Evening Sun*, where he was music critic in the mid-1960s, and for periodicals such as *The American Organist, The Choral Journal, Essex Institute Quarterly, The Hymn, Journal of Church Music, Journal of Research in Music Education, Ovation*, and *Symphony Magazine*. He is also the author of *Choral Music: A Norton Historical Anthology* (1978), *Krzysztof Penderecki: A Guide to His Works* (1983) and co-author of *The Choral Experience* (1976) and *A Study of the Penderecki St. Luke Passion* (1983). Dr Robinson is presently writing a book on choral conducting.

Russell Schulz-Widmar

A native of Chicago, Dr Russell Schulz-Widmar is a graduate of Valparaiso University and the School of Sacred Music at Union Theological Seminary in New York. His DMA is from the University of Texas at Austin. He is the Director of Music of the University United Methodist Church, Austin, Adjunct Professor of Church Music of the Episcopal Theological Seminary of the Southwest in Austin, and Lecturer in Church Music at the Austin Presbyterian Theological Seminary. Dr Schulz-Widmar was the editor of the hymnal supplement, *Songs of Thanks and Praise* (1980), and is a frequently published author and composer. At present he is Dean of the Evergreen Music Conference, Evergreen, Colorado and a member of the Advisory Board of the Hymn Society of America. He is a member of the Standing Commission on Church Music of the Episcopal Church and is chairman of the commission's Hymn Music Committee for the *Hymnal 1982*. He also served on the Hymn Text Committee for the same hymnal.

Don E. Saliers

Don Saliers is Professor of Theology and Worship at Candler School of Theology of Emory University in Atlanta. A native Ohioan, he was educated at Ohio Wesleyan University and Yale University, from which he received his MDiv and PhD degrees. He was a Fulbright Research Fellow at St John's College, Cambridge University, and immediately following his graduate studies, Dr Saliers taught at Yale Divinity School. He is an ordained United Methodist elder, having served churches in rural Ohio, the inner-city in New Haven, Connecticut, and as organist-choirmaster for University Worship at Emory University. Dr Saliers has been active in United Methodist and ecumenical circles for many years, leading conferences and workshops across the country. He has published widely and is the principal writer of *Word and*

Table (1976), *From Ashes to Fire* (1979), and *From Hope to Joy* (1984). His latest book is *Worship and Spirituality* (1984), a sequel to *The Soul in Paraphrase: Prayer and the Religious Affections* (1980).

John Wilson

Now in busy retirement, John Wilson, the Treasurer of The Hymn Society of Great Britain and Ireland, has been quietly and effectively influencing English hymnody for nearly fifty years. After many years as a music master at English public schools at Tonbridge and Charterhouse, he went on to teach keyboard harmony at the Royal College of Music, London. He was the principal editor of *Hymns for Church and School* (1964) and has been consulted both formally and informally by practically every British editor of hymn books produced over the past twenty years or so. He was actively involved in at least five major hymn collections, the latest being *Hymns and Psalms. A Methodist and Ecumenical Hymn Book* (1983). Erik Routley valued his friendship and expertise highly.

Paul W. Wohlgemuth

Paul Wohlgemuth has an extensive background in church music, including sixteen years as Head of the Music Department at Tabor College, Hillsboro, Kansas, where he graduated. Dr Wohlgemuth is now Professor of Music, Department of Fine Arts, Oral Roberts University, Tulsa, Oklahoma. He has written a number of articles and books, as well as editing hymnals, including acting as Chairman-editor of *Worship Hymnal* (1971), the official hymnal of the Mennonite Brethren Church, and currently serves on the prestigious National Standards Awards Panel of

ASCAP [American Society of Composers, Authors and Publishers]. His most recent book is *Rethinking Church Music* (revised 1981).

Brian Wren

A minister in the United Reformed Church in England, Brian Wren is currently a freelance education consultant and writer. He has an active concern for world poverty and world peace and has worked for such agencies as Christian Aid, Oxfam, Third World First, and is a member of the British Christian Campaign for Nuclear Disarmament. He is a distinguished hymn writer who recently issued a collected edition of his texts: *Faith Looking Forward. The Hymns and Songs of Brian Wren with many Tunes by Peter Cutts* (1983). He is also the writer of thoughtful prayers. One of the reasons why he has freelanced since 1983 is to allow himself more time to write in the areas of hymnody, liturgy, and theological education.

Alec Wyton

A native of London, Dr Alec Wyton was educated at The Royal Academy of Music, London, and at Oxford University. At an early age he served as sub-organist at Christ Church Cathedral, Oxford. Before coming to the United States he was organist and choirmaster of St Matthew's Church, Northampton. In 1950 he became Organist and Choirmaster at Christ Church Cathedral, St Louis, and in 1954 he began a twenty year tenure at the Cathedral of St John the Divine, New York City. He has served as Adjunct Professor at the School of Sacred Music, Union Theological Seminary, New York, and as Head of the Organ Department of Westminster Choir College, Princeton. From 1964–69 he was national president of the American Guild of Organists. In 1974 he was appointed organist and choirmaster of St James' Church in New York City. Dr Wyton's compositions have been published by most major publishers in this country. During his years at the Cathedral in New York he played or conducted premiere performances of music by composers as varied as Benjamin Britten, Roger Sessions, Ian Hamilton, Richard Felciano, Duke Ellington, William Albright and Ned Rorem. In 1974 he was appointed national coordinator for the Standing Commission on Church Music of the Episcopal Church whose work during the past several years will culminate in the *Hymnal 1982*.

Carlton R. Young

Carlton Young was eduated at the Cincinnati Conservatory-College of Music and Boston University School of Theology. He has served as director of music in parish churches as well as campus chapels. Dr Young has been choral director and director of graduate studies in church music at Perkins School of Theology; Scarritt College; and since 1978 at Candler School of Theology, Emory University, Atlanta. He is recognized for his many compositions for church choirs written in a diversity of contemporary styles, as well as for his performance and editing of traditional choral literature. His edition of Handel's *Samson* was published in 1985. Dr Young has been the editorial director of hymn publishing projects including: *The Methodist Hymnal* (1966); *Ecumenical Praise* (1977); *Supplement To The Book of Hymns* (1982); and *Hymnal Supplement* (1984). Since 1971 he has served as editorial consultant to Hope Publishing Company. He is a past-president of The Hymn Society of America, and frequent contributor to that society's quarterly, *The Hymn*, as well as other professional journals. Dr Young is an ordained minister in The United Methodist Church and since 1966 has served as director of music for that denomination's general conferences.